# PHARSALIA

**environmental
history
and the
american
south**

*pharsalia*

An Environmental Biography
of a Southern Plantation, 1780–1880

LYNN A. NELSON

The University of Georgia Press  *Athens & London*

Paperback edition, 2009
© 2007 by the University of Georgia Press
Athens, Georgia 30602
www.ugapress.org
All rights reserved
Designed by Erin Kirk New
Set in Sabon by Bookcomp, Inc.

Printed digitally in the United States of America

The Library of Congress has cataloged the
hardcover edition of this book as follows:

Nelson, Lynn A., 1967–
    Pharsalia : an environmental biography of a southern
plantation, 1780–1880 / Lynn A. Nelson.
    xviii, 295 p., [8] p. of plates : ill., maps ; 24 cm. —
(Environmental history and the American South)
    Includes bibliographical references (p. [259]–285) and index.
    ISBN-13: 978-0-8203-2627-6 (cloth : alk. paper)
    ISBN-10: 0-8203-2627-5 (cloth : alk. paper)
    1. Massey family. 2. Agricultural ecology—Virginia—
Pharsalia Plantation—History. 3. Agriculture—Virginia—
Pharsalia Plantation—History. 4. Agricultural
conservation—Virginia—Pharsalia Plantation—History.
5. Slavery—Virginia—Pharsalia Plantation—History.
6. Pharsalia Plantation (Va.)—History. I. Title. II. Series.
S451.V8 N45 2007
630.9755'49309034—dc22

                                        2006016069

Paperback ISBN-13: 978-0-8203-3416-5
        ISBN-10: 0-8203-3416-2

British Library Cataloging-in-Publication Data available

*For my parents*

# CONTENTS

# MAPS

# FOREWORD

With *Pharsalia: An Environmental Biography of a Southern Plantation, 1780–1880*, we are pleased to inaugurate a new book series, "Environmental History and the American South." It is a superb volume with which to do so, for in the humble yet daunting task of telling the environmental life story of a plantation on the margins, Lynn Nelson gives us a history that should long occupy a central place in our understanding of the environmental history of the South. More than that, *Pharsalia* is a model of fine-grained agroecological history that transcends its regional focus and presents its readers with a challenging, even counterintuitive argument about the historical relationship between agricultural sustainability and capitalist intensification. By paying careful attention to the intricate details of environmental management in a single place—an analysis made possible by the meticulous record keeping of the Massie family, who presided over the plantation they called Pharsalia—Lynn Nelson shows us how much the nature of place matters to a larger story of agricultural reform and modernization that we thought we already understood.

*Pharsalia* returns us to a cultural hearth not only of the modern conservation movement but also of environmental history. For in the early twentieth century, as one well-known and well-studied group of conservationists battled over how the West's public lands would be managed, another group pondered the environmental consequences of the nation's, and particularly the South's, attachment to expansive agriculture. At the center of this latter group was North Carolina native Hugh Hammond Bennett, who pioneered the field of soil conservation, but a number of other reform-minded agricultural economists and historians also turned their attention to the destructive legacy of southern farming. In the works of Avery Craven, Lewis Cecil Gray, and Arthur Hall, we see not only early and innovative efforts to do what we might today recognize as environmental history but also the realization that environment was a category of analysis critical to the history of the American South. And these reform-minded progressives in turn focused attention on the agricultural reformers of a century earlier, men such as John Taylor and Edmund Ruffin who had mixed fierce sectionalism with pleas to care for the region's soils in the service of a more settled agriculture. Indeed, environmental historians such as Jack Temple Kirby and Steven Stoll have recently returned our attention to these formative figures, claiming for them central roles in the American environmental tradition and providing us with a more critical picture of their accomplishments and legacies. Lynn Nelson too is writing in this tradition, but he has given us something that was notably missing from previous studies of the South's agricultural reform tradition—a careful rendering of what happened on the ground when reform ideas met local environmental realities. The result is not merely a more complicated story but an entire recasting of this reform tradition.

The problem Nelson settles on is a simple but compelling one. Why, given the obvious appeal of a settled and independent agriculture, did so few Piedmont farmers and planters heed the advice of reformers and intensify their operations during the nineteenth century? Why, almost a century after reformers had decried the extensive and destructive tobacco culture of the region and offered a sensible model for independent intensification as an alternative, were the Piedmont soils that Hugh Hammond Bennett trod upon so galled and degraded? The reformers had offered an apparent roadmap for renewal, so why had so few farmers followed their careful directions? Nelson finds some intriguing answers to these questions in William Massie's attempt to settle within the borders of Pharsalia and seek a prosperous agroecological independence. As Nelson shows in vivid detail, settled sustainability was difficult to achieve on the ground, in the midst of a pulsing agroecosystem whose constituent parts—human as well as nonhuman—were alternately responsive and intransigent, and whose boundaries were alternately confining and porous. So, reluctantly, William Massie moved in the direction of capitalist intensification, trading away the goal of complete autonomy for a set of market relations that ultimately helped him and those who worked the plantation, slave and free, to move in the direction of sustainability. Indeed, Nelson suggests that Massie's embrace of capitalist intensification, which historians have long assumed meant a departure from sustainability, was actually a reasoned though risky redefinition of agricultural sustainability after the prescriptions of "book farmers" had failed him. But Massie was lucky, and then only for a while. Most Piedmont farmers did not have the resources he did, and they thus could not escape the fundamental incapacity of generic agricultural reform prescriptions to contend with the complex ecological processes of place that made intensification without capitalization so challenging.

During the late nineteenth century, the Massie family itself faced new difficulties in reconciling the local environment, the demands of the marketplace, and their deep yearning for landed independence. They could not have all three. While their new mode of production ultimately helped them contend with the intricate challenges posed by the local environment, their cultural attachment to gentry status became the irreconcilable variable in the equation. That so much of the Virginia countryside is "worked" today by gentleman farmers who have earned their wealth elsewhere is strong testimony both to this enduring gentry ideal and the incapacity of the land itself to provide for the prosperity that so many of its residents associate with landedness.

By bringing Pharsalia back to life for us, Lynn Nelson provocatively revises one of the central narratives of southern, and for that matter North American, environmental history. In so doing, he reveals how much environmental historians have to gain by retraining their gaze on the American South, and how much southern historians will profit by taking the environment seriously as a category of analysis.

PAUL S. SUTTER
Athens, Georgia

# ACKNOWLEDGMENTS

In a slight departure from tradition, I want first to thank my family for making this work possible. My parents were both professors of history, and they raised me with a deep love of the discipline, the excitement of research, and the joys of teaching. My wife, Antoinette, has given unstinting love and support throughout this project. She and our children, Nathan and Beth, have been especially forgiving when Daddy goes to campus in the evening to work on "the Book."

Within the limited means of a public university, Middle Tennessee State has been very supportive of this project. I have taken advantage of the Walker Library's Interlibrary Loan office, as well as a Faculty Research and Creative Activity grant from the College of Graduate Studies. My chair, Thad Smith, has been consistently generous to me. My colleagues and my students have made Murfreesboro a wonderfully enriching place to work.

I have been helped along the way by many friends and intellectual mentors. At the University of Kansas, Peter Mancall and Donald Worster kindled my interest in early American environmental history. At the College of William and Mary, my dissertation director, Thad Tate, as well as Jim Whittenburg, Lorena Walsh, and Kevin Kelly, helped shape and mature my ideas. I owe an even bigger debt to friends from William and Mary's graduate program, including Ben Goldberg, Sheila Phipps, Dave Rawson, Andy Shocket, and Bob Smith, as well as other members of the W&M mafia around the country, especially Tim Silver, and honorary members Warren Hofstra, Kenneth Koons, and Robert Mitchell. They have all helped make my journey to a doctorate and the professoriat a successful one.

I have also been helped enormously by the people at the archives where I have researched Pharsalia's history, including Brent Tarter and Chris Kolbe at the Library of Virginia; Nelson Lankford and Frances Pollard at the Virginia Historical Society (who also supported this project with an Andrew Mellon Research Fellowship); and the staffs of the Research Library at Colonial Williamsburg, the Special Collections departments at the Swem Library at William and Mary, the Perkins Library at Duke University, the Alderman Library at the University of Virginia, and the State Historical Society of Wisconsin.

The historians of the Tye Valley deserve special mention. Local histories like this one rely on the long, laborious, generally unrewarded and usually unrecognized labor of love that is community and family history. The life's work of people like Beth Goodwin, Catherine Seaman, and the other members of the Nelson County Historical Society, the clerks of Amherst and Nelson Counties, as well as Lee Marmon and the late Bailey Fulton Davis have all laid the foundation on which this project rests. Perkins Flippin, Beth Goodwin, and the other members of the Massie family were also gracious in opening Pharsalia to me and my digital camera, and guiding me across the plantation and the neighborhood.

And I am most thankful to all, here and gone, who have nurtured in me both faith and hope.

# PHARSALIA

The Soils of Old Virginia

Hugh Hammond Bennett, founder of the Soil Conservation Service and one of America's leading twentieth-century conservationists, liked to tell a story about his first experience with the agricultural and environmental history of Virginia. In 1905, Bennett had just graduated from the University of North Carolina with a degree in chemistry. His boss in the Bureau of Soils sent him, along with South Carolinian W. E. McLendon, to map the soils of Louisa County, in the center of Piedmont Virginia. The Piedmont was the heart of the South, extending from the Fall Line to the mountains, stretching south and west across the old slave states, through Virginia and the Carolinas into Georgia and on into Alabama and Mississippi. The Virginia Piedmont was a country of low, rolling hills covered with a rich, dense red clay soil underneath forests of oak and hickory. The region was also the cradle of the South and the United States: First settled by planters and slaves moving west out of the Tidewater, by the time of the Revolution the Piedmont was the home of Virginia's revolutionary patriots. Presidents Washington, Jefferson, Madison, and Monroe all lived on "red land" plantations, while their mentor Patrick Henry farmed land in Louisa County itself.

By the time Bennett arrived in the Piedmont, though, that tradition was a melancholy memory, marked on the land by a few evocative place-names and run-down mansions. Louisa itself was a rural backwater—scraggly, impoverished farms and old field pine stands broke up the forests, barely connected to the outside world by muddy roads leading to poorly served branch rail lines. In addition to the normal survey work, Bennett and his partner were told to report on the relationship between the county's poverty and its agricultural soils. According to Bennett, Louisa's residents claimed their red clays were barren, and the local farmers made little investment in improving their agriculture. Few of them believed that new crops, new equipment, or new methods would lead to prosperity in the Virginia Piedmont.

Bennett was a native southerner, though, and he had been raised on the region's lost glories. While no great romantic when it came to the "Old South," Bennett never accepted that a region famous for its past prosperity and power was innately infertile. In later years, he would recall having a revelation that connected past and present as he and his partner went about their assignment. As Bennett would tell the story, he and McLendon

> were stirring through the woods down there . . . when we noticed two pieces of land, side by side but sharply different in their soil quality. The slope of both areas was the same. The underlying rock was the same. There was indisputable evidence that the two pieces had been identical in soil makeup. But the soil of one piece was mellow, loamy, and moist enough even in dry weather to dig into with our bare hands. We noticed this area was wooded, well covered with forest litter, and had never been cultivated. The other area, right beside it, was clay, hard and almost like rock in dry weather. It had been cropped a long time. We figured both areas had been the same originally and that the clay of the cultivated area could have reached the surface only through the process of rainwash—that is, the gradual removal, with every heavy rain, of a thin sheet of topsoil. It was just so much muddy water running off the land after rains.[1]

Bennett popularized the term "sheet erosion" to describe rainwater steadily, disastrously, washing topsoil from farm fields into muddy southern rivers, leaving infertile subsoils behind. In finding such a stark contrast between the Piedmont's farmed and forested land, Bennett also understood the struggles of the region's agriculture as a historic, not just a natural, problem. This realization propelled him from being a scientist from the South to being a southern historian—and a southern conservationist. Piedmont soils were a fragile resource, and their destruction had crippled the region's economy for more than a century. Louisa County was poor, Bennett decided, because of what had been done to its fields back in the

eighteenth and early nineteenth centuries and because of what had not
been done since then to repair the damage. But what had once been done,
Bennett reasoned, could now be undone, if one was ready to learn from
the mistakes of the past.

Bennett's career within the Department of Agriculture progressed steadily, as the young southerner was identified with the cause of soil conservation. His moment arrived with the Great Depression and the New Deal.
In the frenzy of government planning during the Roosevelt years, Bennett
sold the idea that soil erosion was a major obstacle to national recovery.
At his urging, Congress passed the Jones-Dempsey Soil Erosion Act in
1935, creating the Soil Conservation Service (SCS) to take control of the
federal government's erosion-control work. Most importantly, the SCS
organized soil conservation districts around the country, through which
local farmers got broad powers to regulate private land use in their communities. Bennett headed up the service until his retirement from government service in 1951, making it one of the most influential organizations
in American conservation.

Despite the SCS's national charge, the general public associated the
agency and its chief with the fight against the Dust Bowl—the plague of
windblown soil erosion that devastated the western plains during the late
1930s. Bennett often encouraged this, knowing that the reams of statistics
he could compile would never match the visual and emotional impact of
the terrifying dust storms sweeping across the drought-ridden plains. A
skilled promoter of himself and his cause, Bennett's greatest performance
came during congressional hearings for the Jones-Dempsey Bill. Hearing
that a massive dust storm was making its way east, Bennett stalled the
committee until the sky outside turned brown and dark. "This, gentlemen," exclaimed Bennett, pointing out the window, "is what I have been
talking about!" From that time on, most Americans thought of soil conservation as part of the struggle to manage the natural resources of the
trans-Mississippi West more efficiently.[2]

And yet, on many other occasions when Bennett told the story of soil
erosion and the battle to control it, he did not return to the dry winds
and dusty skies of the high plains. Instead, his personal connection with
land and people remained the southern Piedmont. He was raised on a

sand-hill farm in North Carolina, and the eroded clay soils of Louisa County, Virginia, had galvanized his thinking and forged his career. In his writings and speeches, Bennett preferred to describe erosion in terms of poor tenant farmers growing cotton and tobacco on Piedmont fields. As a child, he had seen the erosion of the region's soils and the rural poverty that he later believed was its result. In his mature years, Bennett still thought of soil conservation in terms of its impact on the southern farmers he grew up with.

In the early 1940s, Bennett coauthored a short book boasting of the SCS's good works, *This Land We Defend*. In it, he described the archetypical target of the SCS's programs, an imaginary farmer named "Fred Johnson." "Johnson" turned out to be an impoverished southern dirt farmer busily wasting the soils of his rented cotton land. "All these fields are about worn out," Bennett recorded his man drawling, "so I guess I'll have to clear me a patch over yonder on that hill this winter." No matter what Bennett might have said in Washington, his nightmare of the soil erosion crisis was not a dust storm turning the noonday sky pitch black. Instead, the son of the southern Piedmont probably had more bad dreams about "gullies . . . huge gullies too deep to plow over and forget, stretching their gnawing fingers into our fields." Bennett understood the destruction of agricultural soils as a southern problem, and returned to the South in word and deed throughout his career.[3]

### *The Roots of Southern Conservation History*

Hugh Hammond Bennett was not alone in his obsession with the South's problems or in his hope that the federal government could help his native region. During the 1930s, progressive southerners flooded into Washington, taking up positions throughout the federal agencies responding to the Great Depression. They looked to the New Deal for an answer to the South's greatest problem: the appalling rural poverty that ground down men like "Fred Johnson." After the American Revolution, the South's farm economy had fallen behind the rest of the developed world. The devastation of the Civil War widened the gap. Enormous numbers of southern farmers, black and white, slipped into tenancy, debt peonage, and abject poverty. With limited incomes, they could do little to support the development of the South's economy, infrastructure, or education system. By the early decades of the twentieth century, the poverty of southern farmers had become a national scandal. Critics painted a grim picture of a "benighted" South, populated by half-starved multitudes with rotting teeth, hookworm, and pellagra, living barefoot and half clothed in leaky, unpainted shacks. Southern progressives resented the nastiness of the stereotypes and tried to celebrate the virtues of their native region's farmers. Yet they also recognized that much of the South's farm population *was* desperately poor. Leading the inhabitants of the rural South out of this purgatory was the great cause of southern reformers.

Commentators offered many explanations for the inability of southern farmers to turn a profit. Some argued that the region's muggy climate limited the productivity of market foodstuffs like cereal grains, beef cattle, and dairy. Others blamed that climate for infecting its farmers with a variety of diseases—or for just making them lazy. Merchants condemned the region's reliance on cotton for keeping it an economic colony. Technocrats decried the lack of roads, dams, and electricity, while educators condemned the South's underfunded school systems. Progressives said slavery and Jim Crow slowed agricultural progress, while racists denounced the South's African American population's supposed lack of a work ethic. All called for some kind of "agricultural reform"—new institutions supporting new methods of farming that would save the rural South.

As the leader of the South's conservationists, Hugh Hammond Bennett fingered another culprit—soil degradation. In the first settlements along the Chesapeake Bay, Bennett would explain, southern farmers attacked a vast land with limited labor and technology. With prices for export staples like tobacco high, southerners farmed "extensively." They cleared wide swaths of mature forest, only to scratch out a few crops before nutrient exhaustion and erosion left their fields sterile. With so much "free land" close at hand, there was little incentive to conserve soils. In time, more labor and scarcer land should have encouraged more careful husbandry. Yet the erosion and exhaustion went on through the nineteenth into the twentieth century. Bennett and his followers argued that extensive farming led to destructive soil erosion, which led to declining crop yields, loss of land values, tight farm credit, and desperate rural poverty across the

South. Their solution built on previous demands for the reform of southern agriculture, but with an additional emphasis on soil conservation.

Southern agricultural reformers wanted the federal government to join the fight to educate and assist southern farmers in the practice of conservation husbandry, believing that restored soils would restore the rural South. Still loyal to the region's old ideal of independent farmers, they wanted federal conservation programs to serve southern farmers—helping them achieve prosperity while restoring their autonomy. Soil conservation, Bennett promised, would save southern farm families like "Fred Johnson's," giving them "a roof over their heads that didn't leak . . . a coat of paint for the house . . . better health for everyone . . . security, which [they] haven't known for years . . . eventual farm ownership . . . better financial standing, debts paid and credit good once more . . . a sharp rise in [their] self-respect and their standing in the community," and a profitable farm handed on to the next generation. While Bennett argued that all these blessings showed "how much conservation really [meant] to America," he was thinking of how it could revive the fortunes of southern farmers.[4]

In this way, Bennett and his southern fellow travelers created a distinct mission for agricultural conservation—one that put government regulation at the service of private property. That they took a different tack was not surprising, though. The South had a conservation tradition that owed little to pioneers in water and forest resource management like W. J. McGee and Gifford Pinchot. Indeed, southern soil conservationists were active long before Vermonter George Perkins Marsh defined erosion as an international problem. Virginia planters were describing soils as a natural resource needing careful husbandry before the Revolution. These planters also argued that the preservation and efficient use of soil was not just sound farm business but a public challenge on which the prosperity and power of the whole community depended. "Since the achievement of our independence, he is the greatest patriot who stops the most gullies," Piedmont Virginia's own Patrick Henry reportedly declared in 1771.[5] Yet the early southern conservationists were also conservatives—defenders of an old order of independent farming that united slave-owning planters with poor dirt farmers in their possession of private property and political liberty. Southern soil conservation was a means to defending the traditional landscape and society of the rural South.

Southern soil conservationists worked at the crossroads of public policy and individual autonomy, struggling to change attitudes before regulating land use. Gifford Pinchot and other Progressive conservationists wanted scientifically trained civil servants, safely insulated from politicians and the public, to manage government-owned resources on public lands for the broadest national benefit. The southerners, on the other hand, celebrated private property and the ideals of personal independence and opportunity that lay behind it. Even when handed the New Deal's liberal writ for public planning, Bennett continued to focus on outreach, education, community consultation, and local self-government. Within the conservation movement, the local farmers who ran the soil conservation districts were a far cry from the uniformed professionals of the Forest and National Park Services. Through leaders like Bennett, southern conservation made a key contribution to America's struggle to reconcile personal liberty, national prosperity, and environmental regulation. To understand modern American conservation, we must understand the environmental history of the rural South where so much of it developed.

That story was dominated by a great problem, one that troubled Hugh Hammond Bennett throughout his career. For all his successes during the 1930s and 1940s, Bennett still struggled to save the men of the rural Piedmont. Sinful extensive farmers like "Fred Johnson" were not sure they wanted to be redeemed by the gospel of soil conservation. Bennett put their indifference into "Johnson's" mouth: "I guess we just wouldn't have time," the prototypical southern dirt farmer explained with a shrug. "I'm not saying conservation wouldn't be a good thing—it might be. I don't know."[6] Southern conservationists struggled to understand and combat such attitudes. Perhaps inherited practices had hardened into unquestioned habits, they thought, or the weed of ignorance had taken root in the hard soil of poverty.

Whatever the reason, southern farmers seemed unwilling to accept that soil degradation was the problem, or that conservation might solve it. They kept plowing the same furrow as their fathers and grandfathers— typically straight up and down the Piedmont hills, much to contour-plowing advocate Bennett's annoyance—while watching their topsoil wash away. Wealthy landowners adopted some of the reform program, but most poorer farmers and tenants wound up abandoning the land to the care of the forest instead. Despite Bennett's efforts, the South's "Fred Johnson's" would not or could not take up new methods. After World War II, they slipped away to the cities, and the rural Piedmont of Bennett's childhood slipped away into memory and long stretches of second-growth pine. The crusade for soil conservation was a struggle with the powerful inertia of southern life. The problem was as much historical as it was ecological or technical—Bennett and the Soil Conservation Service were trying to conquer the past.

Bennett tried to understand the South's agricultural habits by returning to the cradle of southern farm tradition, eastern Virginia. In an era when most American historians began their stories in Massachusetts, Bennett started on the banks of the Chesapeake, "the ground first cultivated by white man in this country . . . near the birthplace of America." In his hands, though, the southern genesis of the nation began a troubled, not triumphant, narrative. Extensive farming had led to permanent ecological damage, depopulation, and poverty. In eastern Virginia, Bennett explained, "Much of the [land] is still predominantly poor because of the wide-spread erosion that began three hundred years ago. Ancient gullies are to be seen there . . . still deep enough to furnish indisputable evidence of the truth of an early observer who . . . [recalled]: ' . . . farm after farm . . . worn out, washed and gullied, so that scarcely an acre could be found in a place fit for cultivation.' " The farming established in the Tidewater was carried into the Piedmont, Bennett claimed, where the same destruction ensued, and then it spread across the rest of the South. Bennett had learned back in 1905, the eroded South began in Old Virginia.[7]

Bennett began to dig into the history of Virginia's soils with more than his hands. In the papers of Piedmont planters of the previous century, he discovered how long the confrontation between soil conservationists and environmental degradation had been going on in Virginia. As Piedmont planter James Madison put it in 1818, "The value of our red hills is probably exceeded by that of no uplands whatever," but only if they were kept "under a mode of cultivation which guards their fertility against wasting rains."[8] The problem was old, and so was the fight against it.

Bennett turned this to his rhetorical advantage, calling down the names of great Virginians who took up the cause of the soil. Extensive farming and soil loss were the ancient enemies of America, and conservation was as patriotic now as it had been then. Thomas Jefferson particularly caught Bennett's eye, and the third president's struggle to conserve the red clay at Monticello featured frequently in Bennett's talks, culminating in a 1944 pamphlet, "Thomas Jefferson: Soil Conservationist."[9] The Soil Conservation Service claimed to inherit a proud tradition.

While celebrating that legacy, though, Bennett noticed that the nostrums the service was peddling to southern farmers were almost *exactly* the same ones Jefferson and his contemporaries had touted more than a century before. The SCS was urging farmers to plant cover crops; George Washington and others had adopted the English program of sowing leguminous grasses as cover crops and soil nitrogen-builders before 1800. The SCS was pushing contour plowing to slow down rainwash erosion on steeper hillsides; Jefferson's son-in-law Thomas Mann Randolph had invented a hillside plow to contour the slopes of the Virginia Piedmont in the early nineteenth century. The SCS bureaucracy thought itself innovative for diving into experiment and extension, but Piedmont planters had founded agricultural societies to share and disseminate their ideas through meetings, publications, and fairs. If the soil conservationists of the early 1800s had failed to save places like Louisa County, what chance did the Soil Conservation Service have fighting the same battle with the same weapons? What had happened to soil conservation in nineteenth-century Virginia?[10]

Although Bennett's doubts rarely peeped through his aura of energetic confidence, he struggled with this question. Perhaps to avoid repeating earlier failures, Bennett pushed past simple filiopietism into serious research on Virginia's agricultural history. Bennett hired the historian Lois Olson to form an Erosion History Section within the Soil Conservation Service. Olson conducted a series of seminars in erosion history for SCS and Department of Agriculture workers during the late 1930s. One of her featured speakers was a researcher named Arthur Hall. Bennett's speeches and writings about Jefferson were largely based on Hall's work, particularly a 1937 pamphlet the young man wrote for the Department of Agriculture, "Early Erosion-Control Practices in Virginia." Hall made Bennett and other SCS historians aware of the fight by Jefferson, Randolph, and their neighbors to slow the erosion of the Piedmont's red clay hillsides. He also revived the reputations of Virginia's greatest farm reformers, John Taylor of Caroline and Edmund Ruffin. Hall expanded his work into a 1948 dissertation entitled "Soil Erosion and Agriculture in the Southern Piedmont: A History" that became a common citation for later government soil scientists.[11]

Hall was just one of several southern historians who rose to prominence during this period by analyzing the old struggle of Virginia farm reformers to change traditional practices. Avery Odell Craven, born in Iowa to a family of North Carolinians, began researching Virginia's agricultural history for his dissertation during the early 1920s. His 1926 volume, *Soil Exhaustion as a Factor in the Agricultural History of Virginia and Maryland, 1606–1860*, laid out the argument that extensive cultivation had let soil degradation devastate the Old Dominion. The Piedmont in particular, Craven explained, had been an enticing trap for Virginia farmers. Settlers were lured past the Fall Line by the Piedmont's hardwood forest, which farmers of that time saw as the sign of fertile land underneath. In many ways, they were not disappointed. Compared to the sandy, swampy coastal plain, Piedmont Virginia's soils were well drained, less acidic, and rich in nutrients, "well-suited . . . to the requirements of general farming," as Craven laconically put it. Yet the Piedmont also had heavy rains, and "where the lands are rolling and broken . . . as in many parts of this region, the [soil] losses [became] serious." Topsoil erosion exposed the dense red clays, which were then broken by rainwash gullies or baked into hardpan. Craven quoted Revolutionary-era planters lamenting the devastation that Bennett would rediscover in 1905. But frontier farmers had little incentive to conserve those vanishing soils, Craven claimed. The agricultural surplus they produced came "from an extravagant spending of the natural resources of the newer community. Seeming abundance of raw materials [encouraged] waste."[12]

Craven's work influenced everyone interested in southern agricultural history, particularly the Department of Agriculture's leading land-use economist, Lewis Cecil Gray. An early convert to the creed of soil conservation, Gray was the leading proponent of federal purchase of "submarginal" lands in danger from erosion and exhaustion. Gray also turned his attention to southern agricultural history, producing, in 1933, the magisterial *History of Agriculture in the Southern United States to 1860.* Like Craven, Gray argued that Virginia's colonial farming was known by its "extensive and exploitative character." Farmers had pursued a policy of "deliberate exhaustion of the soil," clearing land with abandon, cultivating carelessly, and then deserting their fields to waste the soils of the frontier—"making from one to three moves in a single generation."[13] Galvanized by Bennett and the Soil Conservation Service, scholars like Craven, Gray, and Hall filled in the details of Virginia's agricultural history, looking for answers to the problems southern conservationists had with the past.

Like Bennett, however, they saw their scholarship as a brief for the reform of southern agriculture. Craven and the others praised earlier attempts at what the new agency was promoting. Gray confidently announced that contour plowing, cover crops, and the like had all been widely adopted in Virginia, so that "by 1860 notable progress had been made in the prevention of erosion." Hall offered similar congratulations, and Craven was even more emphatic, declaring that an antebellum generation of reformers had spread a "revival" in Virginia farming, so that "by 1860 soil exhaustion had ceased to be a problem in Virginia and Maryland."[14] While these scholars laid the foundation for southern environmental history through their work on Virginia, their story of decline and renewal dodged that troubling question: If Virginia's pre–Civil War soil conservationists had applied intelligent strategies with great success, why had Louisa County's soils been in such a sorry state when Hugh Hammond Bennett arrived in 1905? Why was the SCS still so desperately needed a century later? The gap between the passion of the antebellum reformers and the indifference of so many of the farmers of Old Virginia was still reflected in the zeal of Bennett and the fatalism of the "Fred Johnsons" of the South. Converting the farmers of the twentieth-century South was a struggle. Similarly, understanding why the Old Dominion's farmers had not better conserved their soils kept troubling southern environmental historians—for decades after Hugh Hammond Bennett's death, in fact. In this book, I hope to offer some understanding of why southern conservationists from Patrick Henry to Hugh Hammond Bennett could not save the rural South.

### The Agroecological History of Virginia

Since World War Two, academic scholars have followed the southern conservation historians of the New Deal era, trying to explain the failure of agricultural reform in Virginia. The agricultural interests of the Virginia patriots and the fascination with plantation slavery keep drawing historians' attention back to the soils of the Old Dominion. The interplay between ecology, agriculture, and politics in the lives of Virginia's leaders has received plenty of attention. Scholars have also reviewed, attacked, and revised Craven, Gray, and Hall's belief in the success of Virginia farm reformers. Edmund Ruffin, the Prince George County planter who advocated raising the pH of Tidewater soils with marl and was one of the South's greatest "fire-eaters," has attracted a great deal of attention. In the wake of a landmark 1939 biography by Craven, Ruffin's career has inspired another full-length biography, several book chapters, and two volumes of selected writings since 1990. This century's first survey of antebellum American agriculture used Ruffin's career to illustrate the contradictions of antebellum southern farming.[15]

Yet for all this, we still do not have a definitive narrative of Virginia's pre–Civil War agricultural environment. Some researchers have echoed Craven's praise for elite reformers, while others have turned that argument on its head, blaming soil degradation on reformers themselves, who supposedly abandoned wiser traditional methods for unsustainable intensification. Most historians now agree that conservation husbandry was not widely adopted, but they differ on what thwarted the spread of new techniques. Slavery, climate, and simple obstinacy among tradition-minded farmers have all found their advocates, and attempts to synthesize have foundered.[16]

Part of the problem is that a fair amount of this work treats the study of Virginia farming as a sidebar to southern political and intellectual history.[17] With a few exceptions, scholars have worked from the private papers of elite reformers and the major farm periodicals. While these sources have provided insight into the world of Madison, Ruffin, and

John Taylor of Caroline, they do little to explain the choices made by ordinary planters and farmers. Elite conservationists did not explain their neighbors' actions beyond accusing them of being blind to their own best interests. This hole in the sources has left us struggling to understand the "real-world" choices made by farmers outside the circle of conservation spokesmen. The inability of the "true believers" to empathize with the rest of the agricultural class was recognized before the Civil War. Many unsympathetic nineteenth-century commentators described agricultural reform as "book farming," a set of fool's-gold nostrums that sensible men rejected. "Practical farmers" were men who made tough decisions based on experience with the land and the market.

While we should be cautious about stark dichotomies, the critics of "book farming" did have a point. Grand schemes for restoring Virginia's soils offered few concessions to local ecology, farm finances, and a host of other complications. "Practical farmers" had to confront a complex set of problems that neither reformers nor conservation historians have analyzed as a whole. We know a great deal about the plans of the early southern soil conservationists for the region's agriculture. We understand much less about the men who tried to apply those designs to the work of farming—in unique environments, in unique historical circumstances. To explain the environmental history of the southern farm, we need to take a closer look at the practical farmers of nineteenth-century Virginia.

The most promising way to understand the story of the Old Dominion's soils is agroecological history. Agroecologists study farms as ecosystems, natural communities in which human beings and other species interact with one another and the physical environment in dynamic ways. When we consider agriculture in this way, we will not mistake farming for a pastoral, harmonious coexistence of humanity and "nature." We will also see beneath the modern ideal of the industrial farm, a perfect biotic machine engineered by humans. Instead, we can see agriculture as an attempt by human beings to reorder an ecosystem's relationships to their own benefit. All plants and animals reshape their environments, but none have the technological or cultural capabilities of human beings to create dramatic transformations of the landscape. An ecosystem has a given amount of biotic productivity, set by the amount of energy entering the system, water supply, soil nutrients, and other limiting factors. Resident plants and animals divide up this productivity through a range of cooperative and competitive relationships. As a result, "natural" ecosystems are usually populated by a diverse array of species. Farmers attempt—with some success—to eliminate that diversity in favor of their chosen crops and livestock. Trees and shrubs are dug up, weeds hoed up or poisoned, pests and predators chased off or shot; all so that every spare bit of light, water, and nutrients is seized by the crops. Farming is a radical transformation of the environment.[18]

Agroecology teaches us, though, that we should not mistake this transformation for complete human mastery. For all the power farmers have to reorganize biotic communities, they still "negotiate" with crops, livestock, soils, and weather to determine the shape of agricultural ecosystems. Nor are farmers ever fully successful at keeping the "undesirables" out of their fields. Farmers organize agricultural environments and direct their productivity toward human goals, but they cannot create ecological processes out of whole cloth. By studying the ecosystems created by the cooperation and struggle between farmers and the species they live with, agroecologists confront the dynamic between human cultures, economics, and technologies, and the other inhabitants of the planet.

In placing human beings back into the ecosystem, the best agroecological studies become historical in nature as well. Agroecosystems may be managed in a "sustainable" way, but they will never be stable. Human beings organize our societies on a much wider scale than a typical farm. We are also continually re-creating these institutions as we interact and develop. The power of historical change alters the ways in which farmers try to master agricultural ecosystems. On the farm, complex groups of people interact with diverse, changing environments to create relationships that are best studied both chronologically and ecologically. We need to locate farms in specific places and specific times.[19]

Using agroecology to take southern environmental history down to ground level puts the lurid descriptions of soil degradation and the schemes of the first southern conservationists into better perspective. Consider an ubiquitous feature of early Virginia's landscape—the wood rail farm fence—in agroecological terms. For farmers, these fences embodied their ambition to control the natural environment. By drawing geometric shapes on the ground, individuals could own land as absolute personal property. On this property their fences would make them masters, not only of themselves but also of everything that occupied the land. Virginia's antebellum conservationists embraced this vision, sitting in their plantation studies mapping out property lines and fields, carefully charting the movement of crops, labor, and nutrients between different parts of an idealized machine. These men intended their fences to turn the paper plans on their desks into real landscapes they could survey from their windows.

Virginia farmers, however, never achieved their aspirations for the wood rails stacked in snaking lines around their property. Those fences could not prevent the movement of air, water, seeds, insects, or even self-willed animals. Farmers wound up moving their fences around environments they could not control as often as they transformed the environments inside those fences. Indeed, Virginia's farmers retained a fondness for the "worm fence"—rough-hewn rails stacked diagonally atop one another without fence posts—for decades after it had been abandoned elsewhere. Its most attractive feature was that it could easily be picked up and moved around the farm. Across the eighteenth and much of the nineteenth century, rotting rails stacked in haphazard fashion stretched across the state's fields. Worm fences were evidence of Virginia farmers' grudging acceptance that they had not completely divided and conquered the land that on paper they owned.

Virginia's fences could not erase the independent purpose of other living and nonliving things, yet they did transform the environment. So, thinking agroecologically, we should not ignore fences. In the first place, the fence organized the activities of the dominant animal species in Virginia's ecosystems, human beings. On either side of a Piedmont farm fence, one could see dramatically different environmental processes. Second, for every plant seed, insect, animal, or particle of matter that breached the worm fence's fragile barrier, there were those whose lives were transformed by being unable to get past that obstacle of rails. Fields of tobacco, corn, wheat, and clover pasture are deeply dissimilar things, and all far different from the forests of oak, hickory, chestnut, and pine that surrounded them in early Virginia. The divisions between these microenvironments—and their interactions across that worm fence—were the result of the role Virginia farmers played in shaping the state's rural

landscape. To get beyond the gap between perfectly planned soil conservation and the impossibly inadequate reality the planners saw around
them, we need to find the middle ground where new techniques met ecological realities. To understand Old Virginia's "practical farmers," we
need an agroecological history of the Virginia farm.

## Pharsalia Plantation and Environmental Biography

An agroecological history recognizes that a farm is an evolving set of ecological relationships bounded by geography and the power and intentions
of human beings. Given that, biography is a good narrative model. A farm
has a context in the physical environment, previous human occupation of
the land, and the surrounding human society. It has a "birth," when its
boundaries are first established, previous species are removed and new
ones introduced. It has a "life span" as the ecological relationships between humans and domesticated and wild species establish themselves
and are modified by the farmers and other factors. In time, a farm "dies"
when the ecology that defined it is, for whatever reason, broken beyond
recognition.

The biographic model is not perfect, of course. Since ecosystems consist
of relationships, they lack the discrete boundaries between life and death,
or between self and other, that the human subjects of biographies do. As
the builders of fences found, separating a farm from the outside world, or
its beginning from its end, is a bit arbitrary. Yet, as with the farm fence,
the divisions are present, and crucial. An environmental biography of a
farm can analyze the ways human beings interact with the natural world
in historical time. It gives us a chance to explain how Virginia farmers
dealt with the questions of soil degradation and conservation—a chance
to escape the past that bound Hugh Hammond Bennett to the struggles
and failures of Thomas Jefferson and Edmund Ruffin.

Virginia agroecological history faces obstacles, though. Compared with
the northern states, Virginia's land and tax records are spotty, and fewer
private papers survive. This is one reason, of course, that so many Virginia
environmental historians relied on the farm reform periodicals and the
writings of major conservationists. They are the only place that provides
a broad picture of farming in the Old Dominion before 1850. If we want

to get beneath the obsessions and biases of eager reformers, though, we need to track down one of the handful of detailed farm diaries kept by a Virginian and do a case study of a single plantation.

One of the best-documented nineteenth-century Virginia farms is Pharsalia plantation in Nelson County, owned by the Massie family. The bulk of Pharsalia's records come from its owner throughout the antebellum era, William Massie. A wealthy but unremarkable Piedmont planter, Massie kept extensive records of his various personal and business activities. These were preserved by his descendants, and later by agents of the International Harvester Company interested in his dealings with the company's forefathers, Robert and Cyrus McCormick. Residing now for the most part at the Center for American History at the University of Texas, and available on microfilm as well, William Massie's papers are one of the largest collections of plantation papers that survive from the antebellum South. They have been of particular interest to such eminent historians of southern slavery as U. B. Phillips and Eugene Genovese, who used Massie's records to support their interpretations of the South's "peculiar institution."[20]

Beyond documenting his relations with Pharsalia's slave community, though, Massie's papers offer a wealth of detail about the agricultural and environmental history of Pharsalia plantation. One outlying set of Pharsalia records, now housed at Duke University, are two volumes somewhat misleadingly named Farm Accounts. Upon closer inspection, they turn out not to be financial records, but rather a remarkably detailed diary of farming activities at Pharsalia. Like many farm diarists of the period, Massie recorded seasonal labor routines, but he was also very interested in the environment at Pharsalia. Massie recorded information on the state of every field, forest, and stream on the plantation. When combined with his business records, the Farm Accounts tell the story of the agricultural environment of antebellum Pharsalia, and the ways in which Massie, his overseers, and his slaves tried to manage the plantation's changing ecological relationships in response to volatile crop markets while sustaining the Massie family's status as gentry planters of Old Virginia.[21]

A good biography establishes context before moving on to birth. To begin an environmental biography of Pharsalia, we first need to understand the plantation's environmental setting. William Massie and his slaves created Pharsalia from lands on the western edge of the Virginia Piedmont. The plantation lay near the banks of the Tye River, at the foot of one of the largest mountains of the Virginia Blue Ridge, 4,063-foot-high Priest. The Priest is an ancient geologic formation, created during the Permian period as Africa's collision with North America forced metamorphic granites and assorted sedimentary rocks up and over the Shenandoah Valley and Allegheny Mountains. The Priest's steep and rocky slopes have long prevented arable cultivation. The mountain, now part of the George Washington National Forest, is crossed by the Appalachian Trail and became a federally designated wilderness area in 2000. Yet millions of years of erosion from the Priest, along with the weathering of its outlying ridges, created tillable soils below.[22]

Pharsalia sat in a four-square-mile triangle of comparatively level land bounded on the north by the Priest and its neighbor the Little Priest; the Tye River on the east; and a run of low ridges to the south. This neighborhood is dominated by the Cecil clay and Cecil sandy loam soils that cover much of the rest of Piedmont Virginia. Both soil types are characterized by upper horizons of organic material lying on top of a deep layer of red clay. While these soils were fertile when first cultivated, they were very vulnerable to water erosion. The Blue Ridge forces air flowing from the west up more than a thousand feet. This wind pattern creates frequent, intense rain storms on the eastern face of the Ridge. These storms give rise to recurring flash flooding that washes soil, trees, and rocks down onto the foothills and narrow floodplains below. Tye River floods regularly deposit drifts of gravel and sand over arable low grounds, and stream management is an ongoing challenge for property owners. Rainfall also attacks the foothill ridges, and when cleared for planting they erode so quickly that farming in the neighborhood is under constant threat. One of the streams crossing Pharsalia earned the name Muddy Branch before the Massies arrived, and the Pharsalia slaves had to fight to prevent mud-filled stream swamps from encroaching onto crop fields and to keep mill ponds clear of sediment. After the topsoil washed from cleared fields, the red clays were exposed. They drained poorly and quickly baked into hardpan in the hot sun, leaving bare, red patches that resisted the hardiest weeds—what Piedmont farmers called "gall'd" land.[23]

Despite these problems, the Cecil soils at the foot of the Priest did support a rich forest. Before the devastating Asian chestnut blight was introduced early in the last century, the American chestnut dominated the Blue Ridge highlands. As one climbed down the Priest's slopes in the eighteenth and nineteenth centuries, the chestnut stands were broken up by growing numbers of black, white, and red oaks. Farther down, chestnuts slowly disappeared, and hickory trees began joining the oaks. This combination would replace the chestnuts as the blight ravaged the species during the first half of the twentieth century. Isolated stream hollows, such as a small patch above the Pharsalia plantation house the Massies called "the Cove," were important microenvironments. Leaf litter from the chestnut forests on the upper slopes accumulated in deep, organically rich soils, while surrounding hillsides protected the hollows from the worst effects of cold and wind. The forests in places like the Cove were poor cousins of the famously diverse "cove forests" in the rest of Appalachia but still included a varied set of trees, including yellow poplar and sweet gum. While isolation and steep slopes made these patches difficult to farm, their fertile soils earned them a reputation as superior land. Throughout the region, these coves became the sites of small tobacco fields and orchards that needed rich earth and security from the weather.[24]

The environmental context of a farm cannot be understood without reference to its historical development. By the time William Massie's father, Maj. Thomas Massie, bought land at the foot of the Priest, the region had been occupied by human beings for thousands of years, and by European and African Americans for six decades. Like most American farms, Pharsalia was made not from a "wilderness" but from a human landscape. When Europeans first arrived in Virginia, the Pharsalia neighborhood was inhabited by the Monacan Indian nation. The Monacans practiced a subsistence system typical of the eastern woodlands, combining river bottom fields of corn, beans, and squash with hunting and gathering. Despite the problematic claim of Virginia explorer John Lederer that a large savannah cleared by Monacan forest burning lay in the area in the 1650s, the nation was declining in numbers and influence throughout the seventeenth century. After disease and war with the Virginia colonists took their toll, the bulk of the Monacans were driven from the area by the Iroquois around 1680 and migrated either north into Pennsylvania or south to the Roanoke River country. A handful of families held on, established a settlement at Bear Mountain in nearby Amherst County, and gained tribal recognition from the state of Virginia in 1989. However, the environmental impact of the Monacans at the foot of the Blue Ridge was almost certainly negligible after the late seventeenth century. The first Virginians who arrived several decades later found the area covered by a mature oak, hickory, and chestnut forest that indicated a long period of uninterrupted succession.[25]

The land that would become Pharsalia plantation was first patented by a Scottish-born parson, planter, and frontier land speculator named Robert Rose in 1738. After moving permanently to the area ten years later, Parson Rose added to his holdings in what was then Albemarle County until he owned more than forty thousand acres of largely un-cleared forest. Parson Rose's slaves built the first fences in the neighbor-hood, establishing a small quarter near the confluence of the Tye River and Hat Creek, just south of Pharsalia. In 1744, overseer John Ross and eight of Rose's slaves grew tobacco on a small farm named Bear Garden. After the Parson's death in 1751, his lands and slaves were inherited by his children, who built plantations in the area. Given the lack of records from the next generation of Roses, the state of the Pharsalia site during this pe-riod is uncertain. Since other Piedmont land speculators leased out many of their properties, and since Pharsalia consisted of some level, arable soils, it is likely that some of the land in the neighborhood was cleared and cultivated by poor, transient tenant farmers. Like others in Virginia, these mostly nameless and forgotten men and women would have fenced off small tracts, quickly felled and burned the oak, hickory and chestnut forest, and then used hoes to scratch crops of tobacco and corn from the ash-enriched soil. After a few seasons, the once-fertile fields would have been exhausted, and the tenants would have set up their fences around new patches of temporary farmland deeper in the forest.[26]

After being forsaken by these tenants, the "old fields" in the triangle of land at the foot of the Priest began a successional pattern typical of the Virginia Piedmont. During the first years after cultivation had stopped, annual weeds, particularly horse- and ragweed, crabgrass, and asters, col-onized the bare soil. After a few seasons, broomsedge and small loblolly and cedars replaced the weeds before giving way to a more mature pine forest. But more than fifty years are necessary for a Piedmont old field to

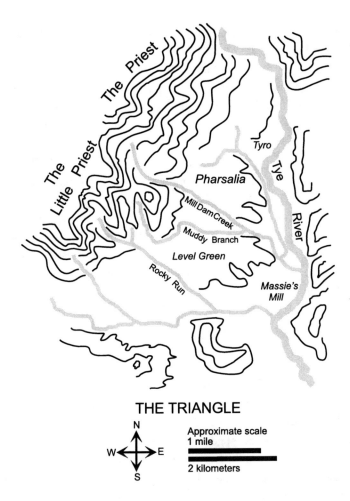

THE TRIANGLE

N

W ← → E

S

Approximate scale
1 mile

2 kilometers

support a hardwood forest and build a mature Cecil soil profile. Rarely would the farmers who settled in the region during the eighteenth century have allowed this to happen. Instead, they adopted a variety of field and crop rotation systems or abandoned their farms to migrate over the mountains to the west.[27]

The farm fences raised in the neighborhood of Pharsalia became more permanent during the lifetimes of Parson Rose's five sons. While they faced many of the financial struggles that troubled Virginia tobacco farmers during the later eighteenth century, the Roses still became substantial planters, owning dozens of slaves and building plantations to match. The homes they built and the social position they acquired demanded a more durable kind of farming—and a closer attention to their property lines. The triangle of arable ground at the foot of the Priest was bequeathed to John Rose and became part of his larger Rose Isle estate. Money problems, however, forced him in 1796 to sell 3,111 acres, including a large part of the triangle, to Frederick County, Virginia, planter Maj. Thomas Massie (1747–1834).

Major Massie soon moved his family from Frederick to the Tye Valley, settling permanently in the neighborhood by 1803. He acknowledged the triangle's topography by naming his plantation home Level Green. As his three sons, Thomas, Henry, and William, came to maturity, he began carving pieces out of the estate for them. For his youngest son, William (1795–1862), Major Massie reserved the northeastern corner of the triangle, deeding it to the young man when he married Sarah Steptoe in 1815. The slaves given to William Massie by his father and father-in-law built a substantial house at the foot of the Priest overlooking fields they planted in tobacco, corn, and wheat. Reflecting the revolutionary republican politics of his father, a Continental Army veteran, Massie named his new plantation Pharsalia, after the tragic poetic history of the Roman civil wars by Lucan. William made his home at Pharsalia until his death in the second year of the American Civil War. Throughout those years he tried to sell crops for profit, climb out of debt, and keep his family in the ranks of Virginia's rural gentry. To reach those goals, William Massie tried to turn Pharsalia into an efficient, sustainable agricultural ecosystem by following the advice of Virginia's farm reformers—introducing new crops and new techniques, and conserving soils.

In accordance with William Massie's will, Pharsalia was divided among his widow (and fourth wife), Maria, and three of his children, sons Hope and Bland and daughter Florence. As the children were absent or still minors in the years after the war, Maria Massie continued to manage the entire plantation in trust for years. Once the Massie children came of age, they and their creditors gradually split up Pharsalia. It finally passed out of the family's hands after Maria's death in 1889. Descendants of William Massie bought back the main house and some of the surrounding land in the 1930s and took up farming again. By that point, however, the estate had been divided, and the crop and livestock mix had changed dramatically. Moreover, the Massie heirs had come into money and no longer depended entirely on farming for their income. The twentieth-century estate was named Pharsalia, but it was not the agricultural ecosystem that had existed in the previous century. That Old Virginia plantation died with Maria Massie.[28]

But from the records of William Massie and his family, a detailed and enlightening environmental biography of Pharsalia plantation emerges. Inevitably, William Massie plays a central role in this story, but only as the dominant member of the dominant species in the plantation's biotic community. As Pharsalia's owner discovered when briars, wheat rust, stream swamps, and rainwash gullies invaded his fields, the fences his slaves built around Pharsalia were not impenetrable barriers. While he might have dreamed of running his plantation with the complete control an engineer has over a machine, in practice Massie and the slaves who labored in Pharsalia's fields had to struggle and compromise with the other species that shared their environment. Nor was Massie's control of Pharsalia's human population absolute. The white farmers who lived in the mountains and hollows around the plantation thwarted his attempts to control the environment beyond the plantation's fences—and sometimes even inside them. The slaves at Pharsalia worked reluctantly and frustrated Massie's attempts to reduce them from a community to an efficient labor force. Even Massie's own family had ambitions for Pharsalia that undermined his schemes. It is in that lack of control, that tension between the conservation husbandry Massie tried to adopt and the actual ecological relationships that made up Pharsalia plantation, that we can look for answers to the questions Hugh Hammond Bennett and other southern environmental historians have asked. By studying Pharsalia as a living agroecosystem to determine what obstacles to reformed agriculture Massie faced, we can infer how similar struggles might have discouraged other Virginia farmers from trying to conserve soils.

The Massie family's struggle to sustain their aristocratic status with the new agricultural techniques they were learning from Virginia's soil conservationists played out across the nineteenth century at the foot of the Priest. The ecological history of the forests, soils, and fauna of the site cannot be separated from the human history of the Massie family, their bondsmen and -women, their neighbors, and the marketplace, society, and culture in which they lived. To be fully understood, these histories need to be joined in an environmental biography.

## Intensification, Conservation, and Capitalism at Pharsalia

So what was the life story of Pharsalia plantation? What can it tell us about the struggle of southern farmers to adapt soil conservation to their traditional agriculture? What broader lessons can we learn from the specifics of this well-documented but unremarkable nineteenth-century plantation? Maj. Thomas Massie and his son William began by following the agricultural and environmental wisdom of Virginia's colonial past. American lands appealed to European colonists because of their low cost and the easy exploitation of their "resources." In a frontier area with abundant land and few people, profitable agriculture meant maximizing labor efficiency. Farmers looked for the easiest ways to steer the land's productivity toward crop growth. The result was that "extensive" cultivation lamented by the southern environmental historians of the New Deal era.

Cutting down and burning the mature forest released soil nutrients to tobacco and corn plants, richly rewarding the small amount of labor required. But the colonial planters' fixation on profiting from labor, rather than land, obstructed the forest ecosystem's means of soil renewal. While the leaves of chestnut and oak trees fell to the forest floor and decayed into organic humus, much of the biotic productivity of a commercial farm was shipped away. Inevitably, the loss of nutrients and organic material in this trade depleted soils, and yields began to decline rapidly. Rather than investing scarce labor in conserving soils, though, Virginia farmers with ample land would abandon their worn-out old fields and clear "new grounds."[29]

Reclearing second-growth forests did not provide the same fertile soils, so Virginia farmers headed into the mature forests to the west—from the Tidewater into the Piedmont during the eighteenth century, then over the mountains into Kentucky and Tennessee after the Revolution, and on to the deep South after the War of 1812. While white and black migrants stayed inside Virginia's borders, planters remained positive about expansion. But once they began disappearing over the mountains, unease grew, despite the veneer of Jeffersonian confidence in the West. Planters fretted about whether to make the move themselves, worried that they would lose family connections, control over their slaves, and their social and political standing. For Virginia as a whole, emigration meant losing population, labor, and capital to other states, crippling the Old Dominion first economically, then politically.[30] By the early nineteenth century, the Virginia gentry's comfort with extensive cultivation had ended.

For the Massies, the alternative to emigration was *intensification*.[31] Extensive farming let biotic productivity go to waste because planters lacked the labor to direct it toward crop plants. Intensifying farmers worked harder to capture more of their agroecosystem's productive energies for crop plants and domestic livestock. Increasing per acre yields meant sacrificing labor productivity, of course, but this new calculation was appealing to many of Virginia's white farmers. As James Madison put it in 1818, "Whilst there was an abundance of fresh and fertile soil, it was the interest of the cultivator to spread his labor over as great a surface as he could. Land being cheap and labor dear . . . it was profitable to draw as much as possible from the land. Labor is now comparatively cheaper and land dearer. . . . It might be profitable, therefore, now to contract the surface over which labor is spread."[32] Soil conservation was an outgrowth of the process of intensification. If land values were increasing, it made economic sense to control the agroecosystem's long-term productivity, rather than just thinking about increasing annual yields. If labor was getting cheaper, it made sense for planters to send their slaves to catch topsoil before it washed away, to collect animal manure and plow it in, and to plant legumes that supported nitrogen fixation. At a psychological level, soil conservation also meshed with the white male Virginian's desire for personal autonomy. If he could control his own resources, rather than relying on fickle markets, then the fences of the intensive farm would defend him against all manner of threats. Although they were tempted, Major Massie and his youngest son chose not to head west over the mountains. Instead, they pursued intensification and experimented with soil conservation in the hopes of achieving a rigid independence—ecological, financial, and personal.

For decades, William Massie tried to intensify Pharsalia's agriculture while making it ecologically independent. His slaves rotated crops, manured the fields, conserved the eroding soils, selected crop seed, and bred cattle and hogs. By the mid-1840s, though, all that effort had made Pharsalia neither profitable nor sustainable. Intensification through hard labor did not move quickly enough. The Massies were upper-class consumers and consequently in debt. To get the money he needed to sustain his family, Massie sold crops on a highly competitive market. As farmers around the Atlantic world adopted new technology, crop varieties, powerful fertilizers, and the like, Pharsalia lost ground. At the same time, the plantation's fences were being besieged. *Independent intensification*— the conservation of soils and the selective improvement of native crop and livestock species—raced against the pathogens, pests, and weeds that tried to colonize Pharsalia. Too often, Massie's schemes and the labor of his overseers and slaves lost that race. Invaders like stem rust and briars battled grain and tobacco in the fields—and often won. By the 1840s, the Massies were in hard financial straits—and their plantation in agroecological crisis.

Massie was able to escape this trap in the years before the Civil War by becoming a capitalist farmer. Fearful of adding to his debts or upsetting the carefully managed ecology at Pharsalia, Massie had always been conservative when investing in agricultural reform. In the late 1840s, Massie decided to be aggressive and embraced *capitalist intensification*. In this approach to intensification, the farmer brought in new crop varieties, improved livestock, high-powered fertilizers, and efficient farm equipment. These imports promised to capture more of the agroecosystem's productivity, intensifying the farm quickly and winning that race against the economic and biotic competition. The approach was capitalist, because these imports had to be purchased at high cost, so farmers saw them as investments that had to be redeemed in the form of higher yields. Since it was part of the broader program of intensification, soil conservation still played a role in capitalist agriculture. Certainly market demands could limit investment in conservation, but long-term profits would suffer. Large investments demand large returns, typically coming in over a long period of time. It made no sense for Massie to experiment with new crops and fertilizers, only to see Pharsalia's soils exhausted or washed away before he had learned how best to use them. So while Pharsalia's owner was the most entrepreneurial, the plantation's labor force maintained crop rotations and manuring schedules even more scrupulously, and fought erosion with even greater vigor. By speeding up intensification *and* conserving soils, Massie was rewarded with both high profits and a decrease in Pharsalia's agroecological difficulties.

With these successes, Pharsalia seemed financially successful and ecologically stable on the eve of the Civil War. Weaknesses remained in William Massie's system, though. Despite the success of capitalist intensification, Massie was tempted by quick profits from exploitive cultivation right down to the end. On the other hand, capitalism sacrificed the ecological and financial autonomy independent intensification promised. Tied to ecological experiment and needing constant investment, Pharsalia could not easily be broken up into inheritances. William Massie's death in 1862 initiated the breakup of the plantation, and the devastation of Virginia by the war made capital hard to come by. His widow and executrix, Maria Massie, managed Pharsalia's agroecology conservatively to protect their children's inheritance, and those children kept trying to maintain a prewar gentry lifestyle. Stagnating profits and troubling debts encouraged—or forced—the next generation of Massies to break up and sell off most of Pharsalia later in the nineteenth century.[33]

The Massie family's effort to incorporate agricultural reform into commercial farming at Pharsalia was both a success and a failure. Investing in conservation proved to be a sound business and ecological strategy. At the same time, though, that kind of farming struggled to support their dream of possessive individualism—to live independent, prosperous, and secure on their own farms. The key to the inability of southern conservationists to redeem the region's farmers lay in this contradiction. From Patrick Henry to Hugh Hammond Bennett, southern farm reformers believed that independent, small-scale agriculture could be profitable as long as soil resources were managed efficiently. But as the Massies discovered at Pharsalia, intensive, sustainable, profitable farming demanded ecologically and financially risky investments. Most southern farmers never had the capital needed to make those kinds of investments. Even the well-off Massies struggled to invest enough to keep Pharsalia profitable. Their poorer neighbors were unable or unwilling to take the chance, and so left their soils to erode. Across the South, entrepreneurial farmers were the ones who practiced conservation, but they defined it simply as a profitable investment. The "Fred Johnsons" gave up the battle, abandoning the land to nonresident capitalists, government agencies, and private timber farmers. The degradation of southern agricultural soils slowed after the Second World War, but at the price of seeing independent farming steadily lose ground. The life of Pharsalia plantation foreshadowed the fate of southern farming and the southern environment in the twentieth century.

## Property Lines and Power before Pharsalia, 1738–1796

Pharsalia plantation had two sets of "parents." The first were southerners: Maj. Thomas Massie, the wealthy Virginia planter who purchased the land from which Pharsalia was made and moved his family and his slaves to the banks of the Tye River at the turn of the century; his nineteen-year-old son William, who married Sarah Steptoe in 1815 and forced his father to carve off part of his estate to support his new family; and enslaved Afro-Virginians like Chester, Jessee, Mirah, and Rachel, and several others, who had been forced to follow Major Massie in his migrations from plantations in Essex County in the Tidewater to Frederick in the Shenandoah Valley and finally to the foot of the Priest, only to be handed over to the Major's son and set to work making the young man a plantation. The second was the southern landscape they set to work in: a Piedmont forest of chestnut, oak, and hickory on a stretch of gently sloping red-hill land at the foot of the Blue Ridge, cut by mountain spur ridges and fast-running streams. In the years after the end of the War of 1812, under the tutelage of his father, William Massie sent those slaves to create a plantation landscape, clearing crop fields and building the young man and his wife a house out of the forests and fields at the base of the Priest.

A good biography, though, cannot begin at its subject's birth. It should describe the background of the parents and the setting in which they lived. This is particularly true when telling the life story of an agricultural ecosystem. William Massie and his slaves did not start work until ninety years after white and black southerners had first settled the region. Pharsalia did not spring fully formed from an old-growth forest in the

Blue Ridge foothills. The plantation's human population, both white and black, were Virginians, and brought the colony's economy, technology, culture, and social system to that triangle of level ground beneath the Priest.

In the years between the arrival of whites along the upper reaches of the Tye River and William Massie's adulthood, settlers did three things typical of the southern frontier that created a new environment. First, the surveyor of Goochland County, under the direction of Parson Robert Rose and with the approval of the colonial governor in Williamsburg, drew the lines on the land's surface that would become the boundaries defining the area's biotic systems in the nineteenth century. Second, a handful of tenant farmers settled inside those property lines and began clearing out the trees and growing crops. Third, Parson Rose, his sons, and their slaves took over from the tenants, shaping the plants, soils, and organic processes of the Piedmont forest to support the more permanent economy and lifestyle of the colonial gentry. By the time William Massie received the property from his father, the land that made up Pharsalia was an agricultural rather than a "natural" environment. A biography of Pharsalia needs to explain how that happened.

*Lines on the Land*

Our national mythology describes the early American frontier as a wilderness where ordinary people could find perfect freedom. Supposedly, the old-growth forests of remote places like the Virginia Blue Ridge were untouched by the heavy hand of authority in the eighteenth century. This tale ignores the fact that "virgin" land had to be seized from the Indians before pioneers could enjoy its natural plenty. Just as importantly, pioneers found the forest lands they scouted already being mapped by surveyors working for governments and wealthy businessmen. Survey lines would scarcely have been visible to a traveler in the 1730s. The other species that inhabited the land would have ignored them entirely. Yet these imaginary boundaries would, in time, organize the revolutionary changes human beings would make to the ecology of the region. By the early nineteenth century, the lines that surveyors drew on paper would become the fences that divided plantation and farm, field and forest.[1]

Virginia surveyors worked on behalf of wealthy speculators in land, often engaging in the business themselves. Land speculation became a fixture of the colony's economy and political order just after the settlement of Jamestown. Struggling to attract settlers to the unprofitable colony, the Virginia Company of London instituted America's first "headright" system in 1617. This law gave fifty acres of undeveloped land to any person immigrating—or paying for someone else to immigrate—to Virginia. This seemed a good bargain to seventeenth-century entrepreneurs, and they continued to think so over the next two hundred years. The business affairs of wealthy Virginia planters were based not just on slaves and tobacco but also on tracts of uncleared forest on the western frontiers of the colony. The colonial governor's office served as a clearinghouse for these purchases, awarding large grants to prominent planters. Grantees in turn pressured local governments to support their speculations.[2]

The most important support those local governments gave to speculators in the Piedmont was the services of the county surveyor. Unlike some other colonies, Virginia was aggressive in establishing county governments on its frontiers, and the writ of county courts extended well beyond the line of settlement. County surveyor was the most important appointment made on the Piedmont frontier. Before anyone could claim the forests as private property, the county surveyor had to record an entry for the land, then plot and record the boundaries of the tract. Surveyors knew the best unclaimed land and might work quickly for privileged clients. This made the job a patronage plum, and surveyors typically worked on behalf of political benefactors in the local and provincial gentry. By the time the western Piedmont was being settled, the position of surveyor had become important enough that members of the lower ranks of the aristocracy rushed west to claim the position in order to advance their own speculations. When the county surveyors were done, the forests of the Piedmont had been legally acquired by upper-class land speculators. Small tobacco farmers who moved west up the river valleys from the Tidewater had to negotiate with this alliance of businessmen and public officials to gain access to the land. While some chafed at the unseen lines running through the forest, most accepted their existence. By accepting that, farmers would gradually turn them into an ecological reality as well.[3]

The land from which Pharsalia would be created was first surveyed in 1744 by the surveyor of Goochland County, William Mayo, and his assistant, Peter Jefferson. Jefferson, who in all likelihood did the actual fieldwork, used a survey system first codified in sixteenth-century England. The surveyor went into the field with a tripod-mounted compass to calculate angles at corner points and then measured lines between them using chains marked off into 16½-foot-long "rods," or "poles." When the angles and distances that bounded the tract had been recorded as its "metes and bounds," the surveyor could return home, calculate the tract's area in acres, and draw up a plat, a legal document defining the geographic extent of personal property rights. This system was far from perfect. Surveyors were chosen more for local knowledge and political connections than for professional training. Ambitious land speculators looking to acquire property wanted their surveys done posthaste, often at the expense of accuracy. The geometry of speedily taken surveys rarely added up; plats overlapped one another; and many had to be redone in later decades to help resolve endless rounds of lawsuits. However, the colonial survey system was effective in establishing the boundaries of properties that would become the borders of agricultural environments.

Land surveys in the early South were clearly instruments of elite power. Indeed, the English survey system had first been codified, and the profession of surveyor created, in order to help members of the aristocracy assert their legal authority over lands they were seizing, either from the dispossessed Roman Catholic Church in England or from peasants whose traditional holdings they hoped to enclose. Virginia surveyors performed a similar function on the Piedmont frontier. Their surveys gave members of the colony's elite (often themselves) an instrument to take control of the resources of the oak and hickory forest away from Native Americans and poor white settlers. In the case of the land at the foot of the Priest, the elite in question was Robert Rose. Rose, an Anglican parson of Scottish descent, came to Virginia with several other members of his family during the 1710s. He soon became a protégé of Lt. Gov. Alexander Spotswood and maintained excellent connections among the colony's aristocracy throughout his life. In 1746, he used these links to obtain a call to pastor Saint Anne's Parish in the newly formed Albemarle County. This move reflected Parson Rose's growing interest in speculating in lands in the western Piedmont, which began when he patented 1,300 acres in Orange County in the mid-1730s. Rose acquired the level triangle at the foot of the Priest in 1744, as part of a huge grant of 23,700 acres along the Tye and Piney Rivers surveyed by Peter Jefferson. In the last years of his life, Parson Rose would add other tracts of undeveloped land in the neighborhood, becoming its largest landowner.[4]

A typical land speculator, Robert Rose shared the ambitions and strategies of his peers. The plans of the Virginia gentry for their western lands lay in between quick resale and comprehensive development. On the one hand, speculators expected to profit by selling most of their properties to men of lesser means who would build farms from their purchases. But the owners of large tracts of mature oak and hickory forest had greater ambitions too. Most speculators did not want to quickly resell unimproved plots for small profits. Instead, they leased out pieces of their property to tenants. This got them a short-term income, while the improvements made by poor men promised to increase property values. Many speculators also saw the fertile soils under Piedmont forests as a place to expand or renew their own estates. In fact, the best arable land in speculative tracts on the southern frontier was later turned into tobacco plantations by upper-class speculators (and their slaves). Many gentry-class speculators moved out to these new plantations and built houses and slave cabins. They then established mills and stores to encourage and profit from local development and asserted themselves as community leaders to get roads, churches, and towns built. All of this increased the value of any unsold lands that remained, enriching the speculator even more down the road.[5]

Parson Rose abandoned a comfortable living in the Tidewater's Essex County when he accepted the Saint Anne's post in 1746. His investment in Tye Valley lands two years earlier doubtless precipitated the move. He established a farm and built a house he called Bear Garden, just down the Tye River from the triangle. Parson Rose encouraged local development by building a mill on nearby Hat Creek. He also helped develop regional transportation, being generally credited as the inventor of the double-dugout canoe used for much of the next century to transport large hogsheads of tobacco down the shallow rivers of the Piedmont. The thousands of acres he patented provided an inheritance his children turned into some of the largest plantations in the region. They also provided tracts to

sell to latecomers to the area like Nathaniel Hill, Zachariah Taliaferro—
and Maj. Thomas Massie. Rose was not alone in combining speculation,
planting, and local economic development. The leading man of the midcentury Tye River region was Dr. William Cabell, who combined the careers of Albemarle (and later Amherst) County surveyor, land speculator,
store and mill owner, planter, and politician to great profit to himself and
the gentry clan he founded.[6]

While the Virginia system of survey and speculation did help the colony's elite impose their control over the Piedmont, it also made concessions to the region's frontier conditions. The early southern frontier was
unlike that of New England or Pennsylvania, where a powerful colonial
government dictated more orderly settlement plans. Desperate for settlers
and influence in Williamsburg, Piedmont county courts made little effort
to direct the land acquisitions of wealthy speculators. If a man had the
connections and money to get a survey made, he could patent just about
any piece of available land he wanted. Surveys twisted and turned across
the landscape, enclosing valuable bottomlands, mill sites, and arable land
while excluding less desirable environments.[7] As a result, oddly shaped
pieces of property were scattered across the countryside; much land was
unclaimed; and later planners got endless headaches trying to build roads
around people's farms.

With little government oversight, Piedmont speculators were free to try
to match their commercial ambitions with the natural landscape. Speculators expected their grants to become farmland, of course, so they sought
potentially arable land. Deeper soils, rich in organic content (usually assumed to be under mature hardwood forests), level and loamy, were seen
as the surest bets for future plantations and farms. Farms also needed
accessible water, wood, and pasture, in addition to crop fields. Speculators therefore asked surveyors to enclose flood-prone stream bottoms,
springs, hillside timber tracts, and less fertile uplands. Farmers also had
to be able to ship their crops off the farm. Proximity to potential roads
and settlements thus played a role in siting land grants. Finally, planters
wanted commercial profits from their speculations. To meet this ambition, potential town sites, mill seats, and the like were carefully noted by
surveyors and included in the lines they ran through the Piedmont forests.
From the outset, then, a tension was established between the local envi-

ronment and the invading settlers. Speculators made some concessions to the land they found but still envisioned a radical transformation of the environment within their property lines.

Robert Rose's 23,700-acre tract along the Tye River shared many of these characteristics. The lines drawn by Peter Jefferson played a fundamental role in shaping the neighborhood's future ecological relationships. The exact boundaries of the Rose tract can no longer be precisely located, either on U.S. Geological Survey maps or the landscape around Pharsalia. Trees and stone pointers used by Jefferson as corner markers have long since disappeared; the original property lines have been erased by repeated subsequent sales; and the survey was less than perfectly accurate to begin with. Eighteenth-century surveyors measured their lines with lengths of chain over the hills and down the valleys of a three-dimensional landscape. Their metes and bounds cannot be projected onto a flat map like the U.S. Geological Survey's quadrangle maps currently available. Most frustratingly, though, a small corner of a page in Patent Book 22 is missing, leaving out a couple of the lines of the grant.[8]

Yet while we cannot site the tract with perfect accuracy, we can make rough estimates of where the lines ran. More interestingly, we can also guess intelligently at the biotic communities present when the survey was made. Eighteenth-century surveyors typically used trees to mark the corners of the complicated tracts they laid out. We can therefore use the tree species mentioned in the 1744 survey to describe the larger forest ecosystem out of which Pharsalia would be created.[9] Those imaginary surveying lines reveal more about the eighteenth-century environment than the modern landscape. The tract laid out for Parson Rose enclosed most of the upper reaches of the Tye and Piney Rivers. If we imagine ourselves following the thirty-six-year-old surveyor Peter Jefferson, we can walk through the environment he found at the base of the Blue Ridge in the 1740s.[10]

Jefferson began his survey near the confluence of the two rivers in the middle of the Tye Valley. He saw around him a rich and probably dense river-bottom forest, consisting of a variety of hickories and oaks, as well as the occasional poplar. From there, he began running lines northward along the hills on the east bank of the Tye, enclosing the river's small floodplain. The valley would have closed in around him as he marched deeper into the heavily forested hills. As the steep hillsides began crowd-ing the rich soils of the floodplain, Jefferson took a few side trips into the coves from which smaller streams fed the river. In particular, he ran lines up into the hollow around Cub Creek, enclosing the gentler slopes at the foot of Three Ridges Mountain. Oak-hickory forest still predominated but would have been thinner as he moved upstream. Jefferson also stayed on the floor of the hollow. He would have seen stands of enormous chest-nut trees on the upper reaches of the ridges to either side of him. These would have held little interest for a planter like Parson Rose.

As Jefferson returned down the Cub Creek hollow and headed up the Tye again, the Blue Ridge mountains closed in. He could have heard a faint roar from the boulder falls the Tye tumbled over a couple miles upstream. Jefferson and his assistants turned away and ran lines across the Tye above Castle Creek. They then headed back south and west, skirting the steeper slopes of the Priest and Little Priest mountains. To Jefferson's right, the mountains rose up like a chestnut-covered wall, climbing nearly three thousand feet in less than two miles. Away to his left, though, he could see the triangle of arable ground sloping down toward the Tye River and away toward the Piney to the west.

Parson Rose was interested in arable land that could be incorporated into plantations or sold to tobacco farmers. The triangle was covered with the prized hardwood forest over rich clay and loam soils, and Jefferson ran his lines carefully around its edges. He stayed beneath the range of the chestnut trees that dominated the upper slopes of the Little Priest and the Priest. But pioneers believed that oak trees above meant fertile soils below. This drew Jefferson part of the way up the lower slopes of the two mountains. As he measured lines along the spurs of the Priest and Little Priest, Jefferson found trees typical of the lower slopes of the Blue Ridge peaks. Oak forests dominated the headwaters of Rocky Run, the knob at the foot of the Little Priest that the Massies would later call Ned's Hill, and the large Cove tucked in between the Little Priest and its larger neighbor. When deeded to the Massies by John Rose, the inclusion of these forests would tempt Major Thomas and William to send their slave axmen up the slopes in search of fertile soils for tobacco. As a result, Pharsalia would wind up with serious erosion problems during the early nineteenth century.

As the soils grew thinner and rockier, and the temperatures lower, a few other trees found a niche before giving way to the chestnuts farther above. From a poplar on the Tye River floodplain, the surveyors headed up the Cove, finding a maple tree above the oaks. After returning to the oaks on the more level part of the tract, Jefferson again ran lines up the hillside, marking a corner on a chestnut oak growing on a low bluff of the Little Priest. He then headed back down the ridge to a white oak on the banks of the Piney River. After crossing the Piney River at the foot of another "Catholic" hill, the Friar, Jefferson and his assistants turned east again. They recrossed the river and measured lines through the oak forest along the southern edge of the triangle. The surveyors worked their way along the base of a low ridge that stretched from the Piney to the Tye just below the modern village of Massie's Mill. They then headed south again, closing the survey around the bottomlands below the confluence.

When they reached the Tye River they once again found themselves in bottom forest. Two poplars, a beech, and a gum tree joined a handful of white, red, and black oaks in serving as corner markers in the survey. They also seem to have found a stretch of old field. Jefferson would have stepped out of the dense, mature oak forest along the river banks into a dry, sunlit stretch. Broomsedge and other pioneer grasses would have covered the clearing, with a few scrub cedars beginning to colonize the area. Jefferson skirted the edge of the field, searching for two markers along the bottom that might survive for several decades. Not seeing any mature trees, he chose a white oak "sapling" and two red oak "bushes," joined at the root.

While it seems unlikely that a Monacan crop field would have lasted since the seventeenth century, certainly Peter Jefferson and his assistants were not the *very* first white men to move through the area. Squatters could have hacked out a plot to grow corn for a year or two as they raced west ahead of gentlemen surveyors and sheriffs. Any clearing was tempting to a planter speculator, though. It could offer an immediate farm to rent, forage for his plantation cattle, or even a space to plant a little tobacco without the effort of clearing the dense bottomland forest. Parson Rose's first plantation, Bear Garden, as well as the settlement of Roseland, were sited farther down the Tye River near its confluence with the Piney. But Jefferson took the time to run some rather complex lines around the ridges and coves at the edge of the river above Massie's Mill to include the old field.[11]

At the end of a couple of days' work, Peter Jefferson could then stand along the banks of the Tye and look back up the valley. It would have been beautiful, but also forbidding. Much of the country was mountainous, and most of it was covered in a mature hardwood forest of half-century and older oak trees. But Jefferson would already have seen in his mind's eye an agricultural landscape defined by the survey lines he had just run. He had encircled the level, fertile soils in the neighborhood and was prepared to turn them over to Parson Rose for sale, clearing, and planting. The modern environment of the neighborhood, characterized today by thickly wooded ridges and mountains above cleared fields on the flats and river bottoms, was set in motion by Peter Jefferson. Some of his survey lines probably still survive as stark ecological boundaries on the landscape.

Peter Jefferson was the archetypical Piedmont land surveyor. He got his position as a neighbor and friend of the well-connected surveyor William Mayo. He used his status to begin speculating in lands—and to marry into that most powerful of Virginia's gentry families, the Randolphs. When Albemarle County was formed out of western Goochland, Jefferson was appointed its assistant surveyor, as well as a justice of the peace and lieutenant colonel of the county militia. He later advanced to county surveyor and member of the House of Burgesses. Peter Jefferson surveyed much of western Virginia for the crown and for speculators, and patented tens of thousands of acres for himself. These lands, including a mountain just south and east of the Albemarle County seat, was the basis of the fortune he handed on to his son, Thomas. Thomas Jefferson retained his father's passion for bringing order to the land, but wound up rejecting the system his father had been part of. Forty years after Peter Jefferson surveyed the triangle for Robert Rose, his son helped push the first U.S. Land Act through Congress. That law established the famous square-grid survey system, under which federal surveyors plotted out the western frontier in regular townships, sections, and quarter sections. Thomas Jefferson's motivations in abandoning the Virginia model were complex. He hoped that federal surveyors would be less partial to the elite and that the simple, rational square grid would get land on the market quickly and cheaply. Peter

Jefferson's son also hoped that federal control would ensure rapid settlement while tying westerners to the national state. Either way, Thomas Jefferson understood the Virginia plan of survey and speculation as giving members of the colony's elite power over the west but leaving them on their own to confront the challenges of turning the forests into farms.

In 1744, the land inside Peter Jefferson's survey of the triangle remained an unsettled frontier. Parson Rose lacked the capital and labor to immediately transform the ecology of the land he now owned, and he may even have struggled to enforce his claim of ownership. The squatter's old field Peter Jefferson found warned of a long and difficult task turning property lines into a visible landscape. In the earliest years of white settlement in the Tye River region, wild game and feral livestock continued to wander across the invisible grant lines. Timber poachers and the occasional squatter faced little threat from the preoccupied authorities. Yet the legal and cultural importance of Jefferson's lines would soon play a role in creating distinct ecosystems on either side of the borders. On the one hand, Jefferson's survey was a concession to the unruly nature of settlement on the southern frontier. On the other, it brought the influence of the early South's ruling elite to the foot of the Priest. The people who would actually work that land, both settlers and slaves, would wind up bound by Peter Jefferson's lines and subject to the ambitions and schemes of Parson Robert Rose for the Piedmont frontier.

## Commons and Property

Colonial surveyors and land speculators made a crucial division in nature at the beginning of the settlement process. Land grants split the Piedmont landscape into two categories: private property and unclaimed commons. Parson Rose brought in tenants and slaves to clear and farm portions of the 23,700-acre tract that now belonged to him. However, Peter Jefferson's survey left soils, plants, and animals outside the Parson's property lines under a unique, separate system of "management." Unclaimed lands were treated as commons in the early South, their resources freely available to any white man who might take them. Timber, fish, and game; valuable wild plants such as ginseng; forest grazing; and a variety of other "products" were all gathered by frontiersmen. Even though the mid-eighteenth-century Tye Valley was only populated by a handful of settlers, the open access they had to the landscape outside the patent lines created real changes.

Parson Rose's land in the triangle was nearly surrounded by such commons. While the river bottomlands farther down the Tye to the south had been patented by the speculator John Carter, the surrounding mountains went unclaimed. Most visible of these, of course, were the Priest and its companion to the west, the Little Priest. Erosion from the two peaks' crystalline rocks created the rich soils now in the Parson's possession—the triangle below. That weathering also left their slopes very steep and their own soils extremely thin. Bedrock rested just beneath a few inches of decaying leaf litter. Only hardy plants like the American chestnut could survive the winds, cold, and difficult terrain. Successful speculations had to be made with arable land, and Jefferson carefully excluded the steepest slopes from his patent. Useless for row crops, the mountains would remain unclaimed into the 1790s.

Similar, if slightly less extreme, conditions existed on the southern edge of the triangle, where a broken ridge covered with oak and hickory rose five hundred feet above the level. Like the steeper mountains on the north side, the thin, stony soils under this forest would have been much more daunting to clear and farm than the more level stretch between them. The ridge and mountain ecosystems remained productive, though, and tempting resources were available. Chestnuts grew a hundred feet high on protected slopes; deer and bear foraged the mast beneath; and fish moved up the swift-running Tye River. And when the forest burned, wild grasses leapt upon the thin soils, producing bald meadows that provided rich pasture.

White settlers subjected these commons to the most extensive kind of exploitation as they arrived in the region. With no personal incentive to preserve the resources on land they did not own, frontier settlers quickly snapped up what they could get from the slopes of the Blue Ridge. Game animals were soon hunted out or else driven from the mountain forest by half-feral pigs and cattle that migrated along with settlement. By the early nineteenth century, probate inventories in the neighborhood of the 1744 Rose patent were largely free of the hunting "guns" once common among Virginia farmers. Nor do the few surviving store ledgers from the period indicate a continued market for powder and shot.[12] Timber-cutting on unclaimed land is much more difficult to quantify. The circumstantial evidence, however, suggests rapid exploitation across the Piedmont frontier. Frontier landowners frequently restricted timber cutting by their tenants. They complained ceaselessly about the damage done by forest fires and timber poachers who strayed across their grant lines looking for uncut trees.[13] Both the poor and the rich harvested unclaimed trees, limited only by distance from their claims and the small number of axmen at work.

Foraging livestock and their owners transformed the landscape even further. Lacking the labor to support themselves solely from crops, or to clear and plant cultivated pastures, frontier settlements needed to use forest mast to feed meat animals. The Virginia government supported them by mandating that farmers fence in their crops, rather than their livestock. Completely enclosing large frontier land grants like Parson Rose's 23,700 acres was prohibitively expensive. This left the cattle and hogs to wander freely between claimed and unclaimed land, grazing in the forests, mountain balds, and abandoned old fields.[14] Borrowing from the game management techniques of the South's native peoples, eighteenth-century backwoods farmers set unclaimed forests on fire every spring. This sped the process of land-clearing and improved the grazing for their animals. Undergrowth burned off by these fires added potassium and phosphorus-rich ashes to the underlying soil. These nutrients gave a brief burst of productivity while opening a path to the young shoots admired by foraging animals. But recurring fires also prevented the slow buildup of organic material that characterized uninterrupted Piedmont forest succession.[15] The eating habits of the livestock reinforced this reduction of the forest understory. Hogs, in particular, grubbed for the roots of hardwood tree seedlings and gobbled acorns. The appearance of hogs challenged the dominant position held by the various oak species in the frontier forest. In addition, frontiersmen set fires with little regard for unowned timber and soil resources. Left to burn out of control, they could destroy mature hardwood forests and restart the process of forest succession under new circumstances. Large patches of the Piedmont forest reverted from chestnut, oak, and maple to loblolly pine stands.[16]

The hunters, squatters, and small farmers who roamed the Blue Ridge mountains also hoped to make money from unclaimed land. Some made small clearings in the cove forests to grow tobacco for the market. Others rounded up their free-ranging livestock and sold them to drovers heading for markets in the eastern part of the colony. Frontier settlers could also turn a profit from the fruits of the forest. A small cove off Hat Creek across the Tye from the triangle earned the name Ginseng Hollow, presumably because there pioneers found the root that could secure credit from Piedmont storekeepers. With the "free" resources of common land all around them, families to support, and money to make, small groups of frontier settlers could have an ecological impact that extended beyond the tiny clearings they made for crop fields across the Piedmont landscape.[17]

At the same time, survey lines were creating ecological changes inside the property of the Piedmont speculators. The pioneers who farmed unclaimed land or squatted on unsettled grants were the model extensive farmers. Low in number, lacking in capital and technology, and shut out of political power, backwoodsmen just modified the oak-hickory and chestnut forests around them. With minimal management, they plucked out what they could and moved on when resources ran out or when creditors and sheriffs caught up with them. The wealthy men who were engrossing the best lands in the Piedmont, on the other hand, wanted to intensify the agroecology of their properties. Land grants were cheap on the Piedmont frontier, but not free. Robert Rose paid £118.10s for his 23,700-acre patent, a small price for the land but a sizable sum for a Scotch parson and small slaveholder. That investment immediately limited the Parson's willingness to see its plants and soils denuded for firewood or a quick corn and tobacco crop. Besides, Rose wanted a substantial return on his investment. His hope for profits forced the Parson to think about intensification not just for the next crop season but for years beyond. Commodities in unclaimed commons like Ginseng Hollow were just the fruits of the forest. Commodities on grant lands like the triangle surveyed by Peter Jefferson became renewable resources. But the western Piedmont remained a frontier, and most speculators did not have enough labor to transform hardwood forest into plantations quickly. Instead, they approached intensification slowly, as they were able to assemble the labor and capital they needed.

Piedmont speculators began this transformation by enforcing the legal boundaries represented by their property lines. Frontier landowners fought for positions on the courts of frontier counties like Goochland and its offshoots, Albemarle and Amherst. They then used their authority to pursue and punish trespassers, poachers, and squatters. The process of shutting the general public off their lands was a painfully slow one, though. Settlers continued to set fires, run livestock through the woods, pillage timber, and pull down fences when they thought they could get away with it. Nonetheless, these first efforts at enforcing patent lines turned them into real environmental boundaries. Property and commons were set on different ecological paths.[18]

Having limited poor settlers' uncontrolled access to their lands, speculators moved to tie down this transient frontier population. Generous leases of the fertile land on speculative tracts enticed poorer settlers to become tenant farmers—and to accept some orders from their landlords. The rents paid by backcountry tenants seldom provided landlords with large incomes. Yet speculators like Rose could expect their leaseholders to clear the forest, build fences, and plant crops—the first steps in establishing durable farms. The dealings Piedmont speculators had with tenant farmers revealed their long-term goal of building intensive, sustainable, and profitable agroecosystems.[19]

The Roses almost certainly pursued this strategy with the lands in the triangle, given their commitment to establishing themselves as neighborhood gentry. Before Parson Robert Rose died in 1751, he had built a mill and established his own farm at Bear Garden along the Tye River just south of the triangle. His estate was then passed down to his sons, who continued using slaves to plant tobacco on the land.[20] The Roses' search for stable wealth and status would have led them to start intensifying the ecology of the rest of their father's estate. The arable soils bounded by the two Priests, the low hills to the south, and the Tye River would not have been left idle. Tenant farmers, and, in time, some of the slaves owned by the Roses, would have moved in to clear and farm tracts of land in the triangle, giving the Roses a bit of income and raising the value of the property.

Few of the Rose family's papers survive, so we cannot know for certain their relationship with the tenants who likely farmed their land. The records of the Cabells, the region's other great speculator family, do contain a number of rental agreements, and a handful of leases were recorded in the Amherst County record books. These sources may suggest the terms offered by other families, such as the Roses. The Cabells seem to have wanted intensification rather than a quick income. They demanded that their tenants make significant improvements to the lands they leased by building fences, houses, barns, and other outbuildings. In 1779, Col. William Cabell (son of Dr. William Cabell, the Albemarle and Amherst County surveyor) required a tenant farmer named Young Landrum to build a fence "10 rails and a rider high," an ambitious barrier, on Cabell land. Other leases demanded that tenants plant apple and peach saplings to start orchards. Ideally, a tenant farmer could be handed a dense stand of hardwood, and two or three years later he would give back a transformed environment. The trees would have given way to cleared fields; the land would have been fenced; and much of the infrastructure of a working farm would be in place.

The control landowners had over the labor of tenant farmers was quite limited, though. Tenant occupation of the private property on the Piedmont frontier was just a small, first step on the road to intensification. On an open frontier, tenant farmers were surrounded by the resources of the unclaimed commons; other landlords were desperate for labor; and speculators were ready to sell them property at low prices. They had too many options to be worked very hard or managed very closely by their landlords. Thus they brought into their rented farms the attitudes and techniques of extensive agriculture.

Tenant farmers on the Rose lands would have begun by clearing a few tracts from the oak forests in the manner typical of the southern frontier. They would head out in late winter and cut off a wide strip of bark around the base of the oaks and hickories on the more level ground in the triangle. This technique, known as "girdling," killed the trees by preventing the sap from rising in the spring. With the leaf cover gone, farmers could plant a crop under the dying trees or else go ahead and cut them down. If they chose the latter, standard practice was to pile the wood into large stacks on the tract and burn it. Then they would spread the ashes of these bonfires over the surface of the small field and mix them into the topsoil. By the 1780s and 1790s, some of the more ambitious of the tenants might have used small, wooden "scratch" plows. These scraped open the upper layer of the soil and mixed the ashes with a bit of the reddish brown soils beneath the upper soil horizons. Most, however, would have continued the older practice of using hoes to gather ashes and surface soil into small hills in which they would plant corn and tobacco.

This kind of slash-and-burn farming was extensive farming at its best— an ingenious way to stretch limited labor while generating good crop yields. Tenants on the Rose tract would have created new, highly fertile microenvironments in the upper reaches of the soil. Crop hills of topsoil and ashes would have gathered together the most accessible nutrients of the oak-hickory forest ecosystem. Mature forests store a great deal of organic material in both the bodies of large trees and in the slowly decaying soil matter on the forest floor. This storehouse of plant nutrients could be directed toward crop growth with minimal labor through girdling, burning, and hoeing. Removing the tree cover let light energy directly down to the soil. The incineration of felled hardwood trees released and concentrated several important elements into the ashes—particularly phosphorus, potassium, and calcium oxide. When combined by hoe with the semidecayed leaf litter and topsoil, the crop hills provided a remarkably nutrient-rich and structurally friendly environment for crop growth. This was particularly helpful given the demanding nature of corn and tobacco. Crop yields from tracts tenants cleared in the triangle would have been quite high in the first two or three seasons.[21]

Yet, as frontier landlords were clearly aware, tenant farmers had little incentive to extend the life of their fields much beyond that. The profitable commercial farms Piedmont speculators hoped to develop needed a soil that was open and well drained, as well as rich in nutrients and organic matter—a laborious thing to create. Working with little more than family members, tenant farmers lacked the means to turn the ground under just-cleared forests into sustainable crop fields. Among landlords, tenants were infamous for "wasting" those environmental resources they were able to gain clear access to. Without close supervision, pioneering tenant farmers handed back to proprietors an agricultural soil that offered little hope for future productivity.

Girdling, felling, and burning trees was easy enough. Removing stumps from the ground was much harder work—and a task that many frontier tenants avoided entirely. The tree roots choking the earth made plowing next to impossible, accounting for the fondness frontier farmers had for hoes throughout the eighteenth century. Without plowing, the nutrients of the deeper soil horizons were not cycled into the crop root zone. Crop plants quickly appropriated the nutrients available in the upper layers of the topsoil, exhausting the land. And since hoes only disturbed two or three inches of topsoil and ashes, the compaction natural to soils under mature forests remained. This made it difficult for plant roots (and associated bacteria) to get enough oxygen, water, or space to grow. Worse, hoe-cultivated topsoils had little defense against southern thunderstorms, leaving them open to destructive erosion. Eroded fields, particularly the red clays of Piedmont neighborhoods like much of the Rose tract, could turn into those hard-baked, useless "gall'd" lands after just a few seasons.[22]

Some researchers have questioned how much erosion damage frontier farming did to the soil. Sediment cores taken in the Chesapeake Bay at the mouth of the Potomac River suggest that the worst river-bottom deposition of eroded farm soils occurred after the American Revolution. A couple of prominent historians have suggested that this spike was the result of ambitious agricultural reformers replacing hoes with plows. Plows, they allege, tore up the compact lower layers of the soil, which then dissolved in the Piedmont rains and headed downstream. There are problems with this argument, though. Compacted soils could not absorb as much water, leaving rain to wash over the land and carry off soils—sheet erosion. Farm writers of the period were universal in crediting deeper plowing with creating runoff channels that limited the damage. Furthermore, whether held by tree roots or not, compacted clay soils were undercut by gullies if left without a protecting topsoil cover—a worse result for farmers than simple sheet erosion. A more likely explanation for the post-Revolutionary erosion crisis was the surge of settlers that left the Tidewater for the Piedmont in the late eighteenth century. Farmers simply cleared a lot more land during the 1780s and 1790s. They also pushed up the steeper slopes of the red hills of the western Piedmont, which were much more susceptible to gravity-driven erosion.

Nor should sedimentation rates blind us to the problems that even limited erosion could have on a hoe-cultivated field. If farmers were unable or unwilling to plow, the loss of just a small amount of topsoil could leave a field nearly barren. Even on the gently sloping fields that lay between ridge and ravine in the triangle, gravity (and a compacted soil beneath and around the crop hills) would have increased runoff carrying topsoil into Boutwell's and Mill Dam Creeks, Muddy Branch, and Rocky Run down toward the bottoms along the Tye. The exposed clays left behind would have been exhausting or impossible to hoe. The soil would also have been uninviting to any plant except the most adventurous of ragweeds and mulleins. The white oak sapling and red oak bushes that Peter Jefferson found in the old field along the Tye bottom would have been much less likely to grow on abandoned fields on the Cecil clays of the bench above. Tenant farmers on the Rose lands wanted to work just hard enough to destroy the hardwood forest of the Piedmont foothills but not enough to replace the oak and chestnut forests with a stable agricultural ecosystem.[23]

Surrounded by mature forest waiting to be cleared, most tenant farmers were uninterested in working to make farm soils sustainable. Deep plowing would have increased water retention, slowed topsoil erosion, and dug some useful nutrients up from the deeper layers of the soils in the triangle. It would also have required buying plows and breeding and caring for draft animals, on top of all the heavy labor involved in pulling stumps. Digging livestock manure back into the soil would have recycled much of the local environment's available nutrients. To collect this organic material, though, farmers would have been compelled to pen their animals, collect their droppings, and haul this fertilizer out to the fields. Few had the labor to attempt all this, nor were they willing to try on another man's property they expected to abandon in another year or two. Likewise, cover crops such as clover needed labor and investment and only gave a long-term return. Struggling tenant farmers lacked the time and resources to undertake such efforts.

The efforts frontier tenants did make to get a few more crops out of a clearing did more harm than good to the land's value. Rather than maintaining topsoils and nutrient levels, the Rose tenants might have tried to extend the life of the triangle's soils by creating a kind of reverse ecological succession in their small fields. In the most commonly understood form of succession—commonly called "facilitative succession" by ecologists—the aggressive weeds that invade a disturbed environment alter its ecology, thus enabling larger, longer-lived plants to survive. These larger plants in turn support a wide variety of micro- and macroorganisms, making the ecological community more diverse and stable as time passed. On the Piedmont frontier, facilitative succession began as pioneer weeds died, rotted, and built up the organic content of the topsoil. In crop fields, of course, this process could not occur. While erosion attacked the exposed topsoil already present, farmers took seeds, leaves, and stalks from the fields rather than adding them back to the soil. Instead of increasing as the local environment matured, nutrient content and soil structure regressed under cultivation. Rather than conserving soils, though, Virginia farmers found a way to adapt their different crops to this year-by-year decline. One man recalled the farming practices of the Tye River frontier this way:

> The old [system of cultivation] consisted . . . in clearing land, however steep, and cultivating it in tobacco, planted in hills. . . . Year after year, the land is cultivated in tobacco, until the crop fails so much as to threaten loss to the planter. Then the ground is put in corn. . . . Wheat follows corn, and corn wheat, until the land is nearly exhausted. Then perhaps a year of what is called *rest* is given, which consists in turning in the stock of the farm to eat up every vestige of vegetation that appears during the season. In advanced stages of decline, rye and oats are substituted for wheat, and when numerous galls and gullies are formed, and broomstraw covers the residue of the field, it is abandoned as worn out.[24]

In this sense, farmers turned the process of succession on its head. Facilitative succession built soils through the decay of organic matter. In a Piedmont farm field, each crop plant drained the soil's nutrients to the point only another, less demanding plant could be profitably grown.[25] The productive life of pioneer clearings was extended by this method, as was their scarce labor. The landowner, however, was left with little to show for having leased his frontier property. After this carefully managed reverse succession had exhausted the soil, farmers abandoned the clearing. In the idiom of the time, it became an "old field." Weeds and scrub like broomsedge soon invaded, resuming the slow accumulation of organic matter and nutrients in the soil. But the soil had been so reduced by erosion and exhaustion that the process took a painfully long time. Years could pass before the red clay was fertile enough just to support pioneer ragweed, mulleins, and thistles.[26] A little low-quality grazing could be had in these clearings, but Piedmont speculators wanted to see their lands planted in tobacco and corn. Those two crops are both very demanding of soil nutrients, particularly nitrogen and potassium. Tobacco is also very "quality sensitive." In less fertile soils, the leaves acquire a yellow tint and a bitter flavor that makes them unmarketable. Back in the 1730s, the colonial government had established a tobacco inspection system that forcibly confiscated and burned all but the best leaf. Under these circumstances, even the initially rich ash and topsoil hills lost the fertility to grow the crop within three seasons at the most.[27]

With the dangers of extensive cultivation in mind, few Piedmont speculators rented land to tenants for more than a year or two at a time. Many rental agreements also were careful to dictate what lands could be cleared and what might be planted there. In a lease for another tract of his undeveloped land, Col. William Cabell protected some of his more valuable creek-bottom soils. Cabell's terms only allowed the tenant "to clear a hill side above the branch . . . above his house."[28] The Roses probably made similar efforts with the triangle, hoping to maintain its soils and land values. Like the Cabells, the Parson's sons probably did not want an income from long-term landlord-tenant relationships. Tenant farmers cleared and only briefly cultivated land that was later incorporated into the Rose plantations. In fact, the process continued well into the nineteenth century on the uncleared lands in the Blue Ridge. Throughout their careers, Thomas and William Massie often used tenant farmers to open new lands on their mountain properties before sending their overseers and slaves in to complete the desired agroecosystem under their own direction. Within the boundaries set by planter-speculators, tenant farmers could contribute to the process of intensification, creating productive farm environments. Long-term care of soils, however, had to be done by landowners committed to staying put and making money. That understood, it is possible to make some educated surmises about the development of the environment in the area that became Pharsalia while the Roses were leasing out bits of it.[29]

Under the axes and hoes of tenant farmers, and under the watchful management of planter-speculators, the barely intensified ecology of private property began to split from that of the surrounding unclaimed commons at the foot of Blue Ridge. During the last quarter of the eighteenth century, the forests of the Priest and Little Priest above the triangle (large stretches of which were not patented until 1795 by the Philadelphia speculator Wilson Cary Nicholas[30]) remained a mixed chestnut and oak forest, a rocky and wooded commons only periodically disturbed by fires, summer grazing, hunting, and occasional timbering. The Rose family lands in the flat triangle below, in contrast, became a patchwork landscape of uncleared forest, crop fields in varying stages of reverse succession, and a few abandoned old fields. Robert Rose's son John, who inherited the triangle out of the 1744 grant, and the slaves he brought to the banks of the Tye River, grew crops on the alluvial soils there for half a century before selling out. Seeing the land as a long-term producer of wealth, the Roses created new ecological relationships they hoped would continue to return a profit on their speculations.

The invasion of surveyors, axmen, plow teams, and livestock would have had far-reaching effects on the hardwood forest in the triangle. Cleared lands, obviously, would have seen their ecologies completely transformed, from the flora and fauna down to the physical structure of the soil. Yet even the remaining stands of oak and associated trees would have been altered by becoming commercial property. As roads and clearings carved the forest into small patches, the ecology of a mature forest would have been reconstructed. The cool, moist atmosphere of the deep woods would have been warmed up and dried out by the proximity of sun-baked dirt and grasses a few yards away. This would have increased the possibility and impact of wildfires, slowing forest regeneration and further isolating the hardwood stands. And while the white-tailed deer that supported Indian and colonial hunters would have loved the new growth that would have shot up at the margins of field and forest, other plant and animal species that needed the protection of the forest interior would have lost habitat. And even the deer would soon have found the triangle inhospitable, as cattle and hogs owned by the Roses and their tenants dominated the forage. Settlers' animals also made up for any efforts settlers might have made at fire suppression. Devouring plants and tree saplings in the old fields and at the forest border, grazing livestock thwarted the customary forest succession of the region. While hardwood trees grew in increasingly isolated stands, the fields around them were only allowed to support grasses, scrub, and pine.[31]

The farmers Parson Rose and his sons rented to did not turn the triangle into plantation country. But dividing the local environment into commons and property was the crucial first step in creating the agricultural landscape of Pharsalia. As long as the mountainsides and hollows of the Blue Ridge around and above the Tye remained unclaimed, the oak-chestnut forest ecosystem could survive. The flatter lands below were a different story. Immediately identified by Robert Rose and Peter Jefferson as arable land, the triangle acquired a value that depended on its ability to provide a long-term supply of soil nutrients to growing crops. Hoping to turn that into profits, the Roses rented the land to tenants who attacked the oak-hickory forest and created new agroecological relationships. When the Roses took back the land in the hopes of continuing the agricultural traditions of Tidewater planters, they found a new, unstable ecology. The triangle had become a landscape that mixed all the various stages of temperate oak forest succession with diverse crop fields and grazing animals.

### The Gentry's Landscape

The Rose family took the next step in the intensification of the agricultural environment of the triangle around Pharsalia. Two years before he settled along the Tye River, Parson Rose had sent overseer John Ross and eight slaves to clear and farm the land that would become Bear Garden. After his death, his five sons—John, Henry, Hugh, Patrick, and Charles—followed in their father's path. They purchased more slaves, who built for them plantations they named Rose Isle, Geddes, Firmont, and Bellevette, alongside Bear Garden. By the time of the American Revolution, the Roses ranked right behind the Cabells as the most prosperous planters in Amherst County. The Roses, like other land speculators in the western Piedmont, used frontier lands as a tool to establish themselves as members of the gentry. The business life and culture of Virginia's rural elite was crucial in moving the South's agriculture past slash-and-burn into a more intensive agroecology. The status of the aristocrat was tied to his standing in his own county. In order to be a member of the gentry, men had to own plantations and slaves, display their aristocratic status with extravagant consumer spending—particularly on a showpiece home and grounds—and be recognized by their neighbors as business and political leaders. Yet they acquired the necessary income by selling tobacco, a crop that was exacting in its soil and cultivation requirements and fickle in its prices. Extensive agriculture and land speculation conspired to keep wealthy families mobile. But their aristocratic pretensions counteracted this, encouraging many members of the gentry to establish more permanent residence.[32]

Tobacco was the key to wealth in Virginia, but it was not the only business the Piedmont elite engaged in. Planters also built their fortunes by selling land, building gristmills, opening stores, loaning money, and practicing professions like law and medicine. The outfit of the aristocrat also included more than just slaves and money. Planters wanted the power and reputation of community leaders, so they aggressively pursued positions as justices of the peace, land surveyors, county court judges, vestrymen of Anglican church parishes, and officers in local militia companies. The biggest men among a county's elite achieved even higher social rank by standing for election to the House of Burgesses. Planters needed to earn the trust and deference of their neighbors to build business and political connections in a growing market economy and a semidemocratic political system. Holding power within (and providing favors to) the county community for long periods of time was the surest way to keep the social status conferred by public office. Planters (and their children) who chased profits by moving to fertile soils on frontier land grants were forced to rebuild their hard-won local reputations.[33]

Furthermore, displaying aristocratic status in the eighteenth century came to have an environmental component that rewarded stability over mobility. Like the other upper classes in North America during the eighteenth and early nineteenth centuries, Virginia planters looked to the ancient nobility of England for their model of aristocracy. The English elite, of course, had long used lavish country estates to flaunt their status. During the eighteenth century, those rural showplaces grew incredibly extravagant as the wealthiest members of the nobility built flamboyant houses and surrounded them with meticulously designed and maintained gardens and grounds. Within their limited means, the colonial gentry began trying to imitate these displays. Beginning in the late seventeenth century, leading planters built sizable brick homes on their Tidewater plantations. In subsequent decades, they expanded these houses and surrounded them with outbuildings, gardens, and grounds.[34]

Despite the Tye Valley's remote location, by the end of the eighteenth century, substantial plantation homes were strewn about the region. Although few planters had the money to build the brick mansions popular along the riverbanks of the lower Tidewater, the two-story wood frame houses many Tye Valley planters did erect during the eighteenth century were notable structures. Though the Roses' homes were quite respectable, the Parson's children were not the most ambitious aristocratic builders in the region. Members of the Cabell family carved a series of plantations out of the land along the north bank of the James River patented by the family's progenitor, Dr. William Cabell. On the low ridge above their fertile floodplain fields, the descendants of Dr. Cabell built a string of impressive federal-style brick homes, including Soldier's Joy, Montezuma, Union Hill, Liberty Hall, Bon Aire, and Edgewood. A testament to the commitment to the neighborhood and to the gentry status those homes symbolized, most of them survive today and are still owned by family members.[35]

These plantation homes and the grounds around them became islands of intensive ecological management in a sea of agricultural adaptations to the forest ecosystems of the early South. Large plantation homes, of course, were expensive to build, and the lawns and gardens also demanded considerable investment of labor and money. Gardens, both ornamental and vegetable, required soils to be built up with manures, pond mud, and mulch. Overseers and slaves, and increasingly the black and white women of the plantation, spent years carefully cultivating fruits and vegetables, flowers, and other plants that came to identify the plantation home to many family members. Grounds had to be designed, cleared, planted (often in imported trees and grasses), and then maintained with constant toil.[36]

The big house landscape was as intensive as managed ecosystems got in the early South. This kind of effort would hardly have been a good investment if planters expected to keep migrating. Acquiring status was a long-term process, and mansions and grounds had to stand for decades and across generations. Out in the crop fields, ecological resources like topsoil and manure were often wasted because they did not repay the labor needed to save them for agricultural production. But many ambitious gentry planters were willing to spend the effort to bring these resources to the big house and invest them in making the management of the grounds sustainable.

Gentry status, therefore, and particularly the intensive agroecology of the gentry home place, encouraged planters to stay put. Three developments in the Piedmont landscape symbolized their desire for geographic stability. First, planters laid out a family graveyard on the grounds of nearly every plantation house, in the expectation that they, and many of their descendants, would live and die there. To make sure this happened, large numbers of eighteenth-century planters took a second step: following the example of the English nobility they entailed their plantations. An entail legally required that the plantation be maintained intact so that irresponsible heirs could not sell the land off in small pieces. Such sales would eventually sacrifice the tie between their status and the substantial investment that had gone into turning a slave quarter in the forest into a suitable home for an aristocrat. While Thomas Jefferson took the lead in abolishing entail in post-Revolutionary Virginia, the wish to maintain a permanent link between family and land remained a powerful force among the state's gentry. Virginians railed against westward migration, lamenting the abandonment of "the cherished scenes of our childhood and the hallowed tombs of our ancestors."[37] Today a Massie family graveyard lies just behind the main house at Pharsalia, intermittently maintained by descendants who reacquired the plantation during the 1930s.[38]

The third symbol of the intensification the gentry hoped to impose on the Piedmont was the most important, and the most problematic: plantation slavery. Slavery was a more aggressive response by intensifiers to the frontier demographics of the colonial South. Unable to control enough white labor to develop their lands, planters purchased enslaved Africans. Government support of slavery enforced planters' ability to work Africans harder, manage them more closely, and give them less support. Owning slaves offered planters much more practical control of what people did with their property. At the same time, slaves gave their owners higher labor returns than pioneer tenants. Slavery reflected a push by Virginia farmers toward intensification and stability, and rewarded it. Indeed, Parson Rose's founding of a slave quarter along the Tye in the 1740s was typical of the Virginia gentry. Planters of that period sent slaves under the supervision of overseers to develop land grants up the colony's rivers, or the sons of the Old Dominion gentry took their inheritances of slaves into the Piedmont to establish themselves as independent planters. A fair proportion of John Rose's land at the foot of the Priest was probably cleared by the family's slaves during the second half of the eighteenth century.

But as a frontier institution, slavery also placed limits on intensification. Slaves were expensive, especially when compared with the cheap land that surrounded agricultural clearings in the Piedmont. The economic advantages slavery had over tenancy were not great enough to make very much intensification profitable. Slave owners had to make their investment in human beings pay, and extensive farming in a frontier forest generated a quick return. Initially, there was little apparent difference in the farming methods of tenants and plantation slaves. Enslaved field hands made an early appearance in the Piedmont, establishing "quarters" for their speculator owners by girdling and burning trees, and hoeing up hills of corn and tobacco. Indeed, on the Rose and Massie lands, quarters existed alongside tenant farms for decades, creating some of the same problems for agricultural sustainability. Forcing slaves to clear and burn new ground fields at these remote frontier quarters helped supplement dwindling incomes from collapsing attempts at long fallowing in the Tidewater. One planter put the equation simply: "What do the bulk of the people get here, that they cannot have for one-fifth of the labor in the western country?"[39] While perhaps a bit overstated, his calculation applied to both slave and free labor on the Piedmont frontier.

Making slavery turn a profit also encouraged tobacco cultivation. It was a sensitive and demanding crop, which reinforced extensive farming methods in the fields around the main house and grounds. In order to grow marketable tobacco leaf, planters had to provide the "sot weed" with an extremely fertile soil environment. In a region with extensive hardwood forests, the easiest way to produce such nutrient-rich soils were the old slash-and-burn tactics. This created "new grounds," which supported good tobacco, but only for two or three years. Building a highly fertile, sustainable soil through intensive amelioration took a lot more work than merely cutting down mature timber. So tobacco farmers kept shifting cultivation from one clearing in the hardwood forest to the next— even as they tried to settle down and enjoy the fruits of their migration to the frontier. As long as the frontier remained open, slave-owning tobacco farmers were tempted by the fertility of fresh land to leave their houses. The survival of extensive agriculture on the eighteenth-century Piedmont frontier can be seen in the farm records of the period—planters calculated their crop yields not to the acre, but to the hand.[40]

The effort and investment that went into building and maintaining the plantation home was not easily reconciled with the short-term exploitation of the mature forest ecosystems around them. The English aristocracy paid for their rural palaces with a farming system stabilized through centuries of experimentation in labor-intensive soil renewal. By the mid-eighteenth century, standard agricultural practice on English country estates included complex crop rotations, intensive manuring, and the cultivation of legumes. In contrast, the colonial crop progressions that used reverse succession rarely lasted more than seven or eight years before the land had to be abandoned. Even when planters had enough land to consider long fallowing, surrounding their carefully tended home places with hundreds of acres of old fields covered with scraggly grasses, woody shrubs, and young pines hardly provided a suitable backdrop for a lawn and garden.[41] And when, as usual, long fallowing could not be sustained, the ecological and financial pressure to abandon the gentry home place mounted. One Nelson County planter described the contradiction: "Men . . . have settled on lands here in the forest state, have built good houses, and made other expensive improvements, and yet have pursued such a system of culture, as rapidly impoverished their fields, and inevitably doomed them to sterility, before, in the course of nature their own lives might be expected to [be] terminated. To move in old age to a distant land . . . is an arduous task; to remain at home . . . is little less perplexing."[42]

Members of the Revolutionary-era gentry attempted to reconcile Virginia's traditional agriculture with the aristocratic home place through a halting and incomplete intensification of their farming—really an awkward series of agroecological and financial compromises. Planters took the lead in introducing plows after the Revolution. Plowing made more soil nutrients available to crop plants and helped make the looseness necessary in an agricultural soil a more permanent feature of the fields. At the same time, even the small plows planters began using in these years were useless in fields choked with stumps and tree roots. The effort needed to dig out these last reminders of the hardwood forest created another incentive to find ways to maintain the soil beyond the short life span of a crop progression.[43]

In response, farmers and planters short of land began to adopt crop rotations in the last two decades of the eighteenth century. Crop rotations attempted to stabilize intensification by turning the steady decline of soil nutrient levels in crop progressions into a managed cycle of depletion and renewal. Steps in the sequence of crops were introduced that restored certain key soil nutrients and structure undermined by cropping. The most basic of these steps was simply short-term fallow. Farmers plowed the remains of harvested plants back into the soil of crop fields. They then allowed the field weeds and wild grasses to colonize the clearings. These plants checked the advance of soil erosion and added more nutrients and biotic material to the topsoil when they themselves were plowed under after a season or two.

Cultivators also began pasturing livestock in these fallow fields or even penning them in permanent barns and carting their wastes from there out to the fields. Animal manure added a spike of valuable nutrients that might otherwise have been dropped in the woods by free-ranging cattle and hogs and not become available to crop plants for decades. During the eighteenth century, many English cultivators had begun experimenting with fallow cover crops like various species of clover or turnips—legumes that aided the growth of soil bacteria that "fixed" nitrogen from the soil and air into molecules that other crop plants could take up. A few more cosmopolitan planters adopted this idea in the last years of the eighteenth century, and the practice slowly spread.

The most common crop rotation plan used in post-Revolutionary Virginia was a simple three-field system. Planters put each parcel of their

cleared land onto a three-year cycle: rotating each field's use between tobacco, corn, and then simple wild grass fallow with livestock forage. In
the decades after the Revolution, slave and family labor was still typically
much too valuable to spend on the complex and ambitious schemes being
used in England. Advocates of importing such intensive methods into the
South faced a difficult struggle—often on their own plantations. As the
testimony of these agricultural reformers reveals, however, the three-field
system only succeeded in somewhat prolonging the life of cleared land. It
did not stabilize farm environments for the generations wishfully implied
by the gentry family's graveyard.[44]

Most planters were unwilling to invest the extra labor needed to grow
cover crops or import manures and other fertilizers. One season of fallow
out of three could not keep soil environments to the standards required
by crops like tobacco and corn, however. The three-field system was particularly vulnerable to soil erosion. Crop progressions accounted for the
topsoil and organic matter washed from hoe-cultivated fields by moving
onto less demanding crops and abandoning the land to forest succession
after a few years. A single year covered by indifferent wild grasses and
trampled by cattle and hogs, in contrast, barely slowed the decline of
the soil's ability to support crop plants. At the same time, most farmers adopting the three-field system shifted from hoe- to plow-cultivation.
Permanent fields encouraged farmers to pull tree stumps out of the soil.
They then used small, "scratch" plows to break up the soil, mixing topsoil
with the upper layer of clay. With the soil now aerated, farmers planted
both tobacco and corn in rows, rather than the customary small hills.
The plows slowed soil exhaustion a bit by turning the nutrients of the
clay horizon into the topsoil. The plows being used in the region were
too small to get more than a few inches down into the ground, and were
helpless against galls and gullies. The extra fertility did not last much
longer than the traditional new grounds.

The decline in regular land abandonment that accompanied the three-
field system also helped accelerate serious soil erosion. The era of the
three-field system was the most devastating period of soil erosion in Piedmont Virginia's history, judging from Chesapeake Bay sediment cores and
farmers' recollections of gullied fields and galled lands on the red clays.[45]
The decline in the soil environment of individual fields was slower with

the three-field system than with the crop progression. Plowing and allowing the soil time off from tobacco helped somewhat. But the long-term deterioration was still unmistakable. Soil nutrient levels and soil structure took a quick drop in a crop progression system. In the simple rotations of early national Virginia they spun slowly down the drain.

Gentry planters were also able to prolong the lives of their plantations through various financial expedients. Slaves could be profitably sold to work the fertile lands across the Appalachians. Many hard-pressed planters preferred breaking up black families and communities to investing expensive slave labor in intensifying their agricultural practices. Slaves, mansions, and land also provided a security for consumer credit, and Revolutionary-era planters became notorious for indebtedness.[46]

The need for more imported clothes, dishes, carriages, wines, books, furniture, and the like to maintain the bearing of an aristocrat never ended. One critic of the planter lifestyle railed against its demands: "The great majority . . . of our farmers and planters . . . are . . . slaves to the fashionable and ostentatious prodigality of the time. . . . The entire income is consumed in supporting a style of living . . . which each . . . feels a silly family pride in attempting to maintain."[47] As one more sympathetic planter in the Tye River region put it, "The farmer *must* have money."[48] As a result, the inability of Virginia's farmers to create sustainable intensive farms growing profitable crops led to bankruptcy for many. Others accepted the contradiction of permanent gentry home places and impermanent agriculture and abandoned the former. Planters by the thousands left Virginia during this period for the cheap, mature hardwood forests of Kentucky, Tennessee, and the rest of the Deep South, dragging their slaves with them. There the planters could at least rebuild their financial status by directing their slaves to burn the forests to create new soils.[49]

We cannot tell precisely what John Rose and his slaves were doing with the triangle lands during this era. But almost certainly, John and his siblings were practicing some form of extensive tobacco farming, and they were clearly struggling by the 1790s. After challenging the Cabells as the leading planters of Amherst County, Parson Rose's sons began selling or losing their lands. The farms they left behind probably embodied the assessment a later writer made of the neighborhood's landscape: "Scarcely any other [part of Virginia] presents to the eye of the traveller, a more wasted appearance. The old fields exhibit numerous galls and gullies, whilst decayed fences show, in many cases, the ground is abandoned, because, in the language of the country, it is *worn out.*"[50] Most of the grandchildren of Parson Rose chose to migrate from the area, and Rose Isle plantation was sold to help pay off John Rose's debts in 1811. Most importantly for this study, in 1796 he sold 3,111 acres of the land patented by his father in the triangle of valuable flatlands below the Priest to Frederick County, Virginia, planter Maj. Thomas Massie.[51]

In spite of the Roses' struggles, Major Massie saw in the lands along the Tye River a place to balance permanent agriculture and an aristocratic home place. The triangle was still part of the well-known Red-Land District, "a continuous vein of land commencing in Orange, and running parallel to the eastern base of the Blue Ridge, through the counties of Albemarle, Nelson, and Amherst,"[52] characterized by its fertile red clay soils. Early in the nineteenth century, one traveler described the region's prosperity: "There is no part of Virginia which presents to the eye of a stranger such a combination of beauty, fertility, and peculiar qualities, as the range of 'red land.' . . . From an elevated position, the observer has within view a wide sweep of hill and valley, alike covered with rich crops of clover and corn, or fields now studded thickly with wheat shocks, showing an abundant harvest."[53] While the Rose children floundered on for a few years with their family's older farms near the confluence of the Piney and Tye Rivers, Thomas Massie purchased a large chunk of the periodically farmed triangle of land at the foot of the Priest and Little Priest. While the western portion of the triangle had been earlier acquired from the Roses by the planter Nathaniel Hill, much of the gently sloping, highly fertile soils that stretched along Rocky Run and Muddy Branch down to the Tye passed into the Major's hands.

Just as with Peter Jefferson's survey back in 1744, the metes and bounds of Major Massie's purchase entered in the Amherst County deed books give clues about the late eighteenth-century landscape of the triangle. The property the Major acquired at the close of the eighteenth century contained just the kind of patchwork landscape that shifting cultivation created in the oak forest at the foot of the Blue Ridge. If one had found a spot on the slopes of the Little Priest in 1795, a ragged but clearly agricultural landscape would have spread out below. Surviving stands of oak forest would have dotted the view, interspersed with a handful of crop fields planted in corn and tobacco, and old fields full of crabgrass, broomsedge, and scrub cedar, stretching south more than a mile to the oak forest on the low ridge below.

Tenant cultivators, or perhaps a few of the Rose family slaves, had apparently been hard at work on the western border of the tract in the years before the sale. The property lines on the northern boundary of the new estate (along the foot of the mountains above) were still marked by several mature Spanish oaks and hickories. Yet the big trees had apparently been cleared down the slope, as small piles of stones known to surveyors as "pointers" were needed to mark the Major's western line with Nathaniel Hill. Farther down the creeks toward the Tye, where the land grew uneven again and had probably not been farmed, a few sets of pointers were still used, but mature gum, dogwood, chestnut, and hickory were still standing when the purchase was surveyed.

Major Massie was apparently encouraged enough by the view to make additional purchases in the neighborhood before moving his family in 1802 to the plantation home his slaves built on the property.[54] Although the Tye Valley was less populated and developed than the rest of eastern Virginia, planters and small farmers had been migrating there in sizable numbers since the Revolution. Major Massie saw a chance to establish himself as a social and economic leader of a developing community from his new plantation home. But the cost of property in a settled area was greater than for undeveloped land farther west. Back in 1744 Parson Rose had paid just over one hundred pounds for twenty thousand acres of old growth timber on the Piedmont frontier. Even accounting for inflation, the more than three thousand pounds Major Massie had to hand over for a fraction of the estate a half century later was a substantial increase.

While the mountainsides above were covered with old growth forest, a half century of settlement had left little virgin hardwood forest Massie's slaves could clear for tobacco. The cleared tracts and grassy old fields he acquired reduced the work of clearing for grain and pasture, but the long-term supply of fertile new grounds was limited. While his successes planting in Frederick County might have encouraged the Major to think he could do better with the lands in the triangle than the Roses, his long-term prospects were challenging. He was still buying into that old set of problems created by the contradiction between the gentry home place and the tobacco farming that paid for it. By the time he handed a portion of the property over to his son William two decades later, he was still struggling to reconcile the work his slaves did in and around his plantation house with what they did in the fields surrounding it.

# Independence and the Birth of Pharsalia,
## 1796–1830

In creating Pharsalia, the Massies intensified the agricultural ecology of the triangle much more than the man they had bought out, John Rose. Their farming sprang, however, from the same gentry culture that had produced Parson Robert Rose and his descendants. The southern gentleman's status began with mastery of his plantation, where his chattels produced wealth that he could translate into rank and prestige. His greatest fear, then, was losing that control and becoming a servant to other masters—political tyrants, volatile markets, rapacious creditors, or even a capricious Nature. As the promise of the Revolution faded into the uncertainty of the young republic, the Massies established their Tye Valley plantations—Level Green for Maj. Thomas Massie in the late 1790s, and Pharsalia for his youngest son, William, in 1815. The gentry were beset by threats to their independence in these years and sought stubbornly to reassert traditional principles of plantation autonomy. Like many other planters and farmers of this era, the Massies turned to the program offered by the South's agricultural conservationists. These men promised that English methods of soil maintenance would intensify southern agriculture by making more efficient use of what planters already possessed. Yet as young William Massie would discover as he and his slaves developed Pharsalia after 1815, the resources he owned were no longer quite enough to build an autonomous, prosperous plantation. Paper schemes met practical realities, ecological and economic, in the triangle. Pharsalia emerged as a more complex, and less successful, agricultural environment than the Massies had hoped.

*The Massies and the Search for Independence*

Thomas Massie's post-Revolutionary migration to the Tye Valley was a microcosm of the experience of the Revolutionary-era gentry and reflected his own growing obsession with political and personal home rule. He was born in 1747, the son of prominent New Kent County planter William Massie and his wife, Martha Macon Massie. After studying at the College of William and Mary like so many of his social peers, he took up his father's occupation and became a prosperous and respected Tidewater tobacco planter. As a junior member of the plantation gentry, the young Thomas Massie inherited their vision of absolute independence. At its core, a white man's "independence" was the complete freedom and authority he wanted to have on his own land and within his own family. To achieve this, he had to control all the necessities of life. Although perfect self-sufficiency was never attainable, it remained a standard against which white men judged their lives. In a famous letter to England, eighteenth-century planter William Byrd II encapsulated the gentry's ideal: "I have a large Family of my own, and my Doors are open to Every Body, yet I have no Bills to pay, and a half-a-Crown will rest undisturbed in my Pocket for many Moons together. Like one of the Patriarchs, I have my Flocks and my Herds, my Bond-men and Bond-women, and every Soart of trade amongst my own Servants, so that I live in a kind of Independence on every one but Providence."[1]

Thomas Massie took up his own search for independence in the last, dangerous years before the American Revolution. William Byrd II's self-satisfied dream of patriarchal independence had become an anxious obsession as ominous threats gathered around tobacco planters. The tobacco market was always a troublesome one and grew more so in the 1760s and 1770s. Rural commerce was taken over by the local factors of Scots mercantile companies. These men offered good prices for tobacco and large stocks of consumer goods. Yet they charged hefty interest rates and extended their power throughout the economy. Planters of all ranks fell into debt to these new creditors and raged against their growing dependence upon them. In response, Virginians undertook a series of Non-Importation Agreements, in the hopes of ending the empire's favoritism toward British merchants. The government in London offered few concessions, though, and planters began to dream of making America self-sufficient in consumer goods. The Revolution itself was a culmination of this reaction against dependence on the international marketplace. It merely focused on political independence from the British government as the path to personal independence from British economic interests.[2]

Thomas Massie committed himself completely to this movement. He joined the Continental Army in 1776 and rose to the rank of captain in the Sixth Virginia regiment before taking part in the army's campaigns in New York and New Jersey in the late 1770s. Massie had a brief brush with military history in 1778 when he carried orders from Gen. George Washington to Gen. Charles Lee in the runup to the Battle of Monmouth Court House. Lee's failure to carry out the orders Massie delivered led to the general's controversial dismissal. A consolidation of the state's army regiments made Thomas Massie's promotion to major superfluous. Carrying his title into private life, he retired in 1779. In 1780–81, he returned briefly to active duty as an aide to Gen. Thomas Nelson in the defense against Benedict Arnold's marauding in the Tidewater.[3]

The American Revolution proved something of a disappointment to independence-obsessed planters like Thomas Massie. Prices for tobacco fell during the 1780s and 1790s. New markets were slow to open, but the old commercial privileges of the British Empire were taken back immediately. And for all the Revolutionary rhetoric about spartan virtue, the gentry did not give up extravagant consumption. British merchants eagerly returned to Virginia once the peace treaty had been signed, demanding repayment of old balances and offering new credit. The debts and the dependence began to pile up again, and the new national government was unable or unwilling to offer southern planters a stronger negotiating position. Major Massie's American patriotism had cost him personally, as well. The pillaging of the Tidewater by Arnold's British forces apparently intruded on his New Kent County plantations, although details are lacking in his surviving correspondence. Shortly after Yorktown, Massie moved his young wife, Sarah Cocke, and his slaves from New Kent to Frederick County in the Shenandoah Valley. Massie apparently hoped the move to an interior location would protect him during future wars, and this fixation with safety from marauding British troops remained with him throughout his life. When the War of 1812 brought the British military back to the Chesapeake, the Major, by then resettled in Nelson County, purchased a tract of land and built a log house high in the Blue Ridge above his plantation. The farm, which he named Montebello, was intended as a place of retreat in case British troops reached the interior of Virginia as they had in late 1780.

Major Massie doubtless also hoped to repair the battering the Revolution had given his finances. In Frederick County he took up grist milling and wheat farming, joining a host of other planters who tried to end what they saw as a dependence on tobacco. The flour market was lucrative during these years, but volatile. Planters who abandoned tobacco also gave up the security of eastern Virginia's near monopoly over the market and began competing with grain farmers throughout the Atlantic world. Massie family tradition also held that another motivation for the Major's relocation to the Shenandoah Valley had been his worry that his family's entanglement in the competitive and expensive gentry culture would drive him even deeper into debt. Yet he soon found that the many Tidewater planter families who had settled in Frederick were recreating the Tidewater's society. This whirl of endless entertainment, high fashion, drinking, and gambling demanded heavy spending from its participants.[4] Buffeted by unfriendly markets and the ongoing demands of gentry life, Thomas Massie struggled like so many others to secure his independence.

But the ideal remained as potent as ever. The leaders of post-Revolutionary Virginia demanded a return to rural independence, a reapplication of old principles. More than half a century after Byrd, Thomas Jefferson was still idealizing the independence farming life supposedly offered. In *Notes on the State of Virginia*, Jefferson called dependence "the mark set on those, who not looking up to heaven, to their own soil and industry, as does the husbandman, for their subsistence, depend for it on the casualties and caprice of customers." "Dependence," the author of the Declaration of Independence warned, "begets subservience and venality, suffocates the germ of virtue, and prepares fit tools for the designs of ambition."[5] Yet the plantation gentry remained a struggling, colonial aristocracy. They wanted abundance along with their virtue, which meant they had to import expensive consumer goods from Britain, driving them into debt. To get the money to pay those debts they had to deal with powerful interests in the international crop market. For men who supported ostentatious consumerism by forcing slaves to grow farm produce, the market and debt were unavoidable. The "casualties and caprices" of the international trade in staple crops proved difficult to control.

As a result, the half century between 1790 and 1840 was a period of decline for Virginia's planter elite. The manifestations of this crisis were numerous. Under the burden of uncertain crop prices and heavy spending, planter debts multiplied. Thousands were driven into bankruptcy. Bankruptcy proved to be the ultimate, degrading loss of personal independence to the Old Dominion's gentry. It was a fate full of "humiliation and mortification," as one bankrupt planter in the Tye Valley put it.[6] For those who wished to escape insolvency, a popular choice was to migrate to the western frontier. Thousands of planters and farmers abandoned fields, houses, gardens, and family graves in a rush across the mountains. In the mid-nineteenth century, politician William Ballard Preston recalled, "Year after year we beheld the anxious struggling crowd, pressing forward through sunshine and through storm, over mountains and valleys, in long continuous crowds of carriages and waggons, rich and poor, young and old, white and black, master and slave, hastening with impetuous ardor and zeal to this fancied El Dorado and Elysium of the West, till we seemed, as we beheld the stream, to be left desolate and alone, amid the depopulated and abandoned scenes of our youth."[7] This migration drained Virginia of labor, capital, and simple population, which in turn left the oldest part of the South politically powerless and economically depressed.[8]

Maj. Thomas Massie felt the pull himself. Over his family's objections, he abandoned Frederick for the upper Tye River Valley, a remote corner of the less-crowded Amherst County, during the 1790s. Buying the main tract in the triangle from John Rose in 1796, Massie moved his family to Level Green plantation in 1803. He quickly resumed his new career as a grain farmer and miller along the banks of the Tye. A big fish in a small pond, he established himself as the backwoods neighborhood's leading businessman. By 1806, his slaves and hired workmen had built a large mill along the Tye, as well as a warehouse in the James River shipping settlement of New Market to store his flour and other crops.[9] He thought he had found what he wanted, a "rural retirement in an obscure situation . . . in the corner of a small county."[10] What one of the family's correspondents called "your solitary mountain" seemed to be a place where Maj. Thomas Massie could be the master of his own domain.[11]

While he remained a Virginia patriot, the lure of securing independence with cheap land and easy profits kept tempting the Major to further migration. Such undeveloped corners were increasingly hard to find within early nineteenth-century Virginia. Massie used land grant claims derived from his Revolutionary War service to acquire large tracts in Logan County, Kentucky, and later near Chillicothe, Ohio.[12] The situation was worse for Major Massie's sons, who inherited both his class status and his love of independence. As they began to seek lives beyond their father's house, the Major's sons also felt the pull of prospects for personal independence on the frontier. These desires clashed with the Major's wish to keep his family together. His eldest son, Dr. Thomas Massie, relocated to Chillicothe to practice medicine after completing his education. He was only persuaded to return to Nelson County when his father offered to let him manage Level Green and then gave him a new plantation from the Tye Valley lands. The middle son, Henry, left the Tye Valley, first for Ohio and then for a plantation in Allegheny County in the mountains. Major Massie also worried about the possibility of his youngest son, William, leaving his side. To head that off, the Major deeded William the land that became Pharsalia when the young man was only nineteen. He did so, however, in return for a debt of six thousand pounds to ensure he stayed put.[13] In later years William Massie would fight the same battles with his own offspring, trying to protect his family from the temptations of the west.

But family loyalty and local patriotism continued to suffer in comparison with independence in the worldview of the Massies. William Massie went to great lengths to keep his own son Thomas James in the neighborhood of Pharsalia. Yet in the end the father confessed that his highest goal for his eldest son was just to see him "*independent*—yes sweetly independent."[14] The dangers of debt and bankruptcy, political and commercial impotence closed in on the Massies' domain despite the victories of the Revolution and their migration to the Tye Valley. Like the rest of their state's gentry, the Massies kept looking for ways to protect their precious autonomy.

## Independence and the Plantation

Confronted on all sides by these powerful threats, many Virginians turned back to the land, the foundation of the planter's idealized independence. Defenders of the old order insisted that their state's broader economic and political failures must somehow stem from a loss of mastery at home. Rather than adapting to a capricious world, planters needed to barricade themselves on their farms. Once they reasserted control of themselves and their property, personal and political independence in the wider world would follow. Ironically, this very conservative impulse pushed many farmers to rethink their traditionally extensive agriculture. Piedmont Virginia, once the seat of revolution, was rapidly declining at the time. American victories over the southern Indian nations during the War of 1812 had opened the Deep South to settlement. Extensive farming drove farmers in search of fresh land, and eroded, exhausted fields could not compete with property that was both cheaper and more productive. While tobacco prices were tolerable for the moment, cotton was booming, and people were flooding out of Virginia to the southwestern frontier. Nor were things going to get better in the near future. The depression that followed the Panic of 1819 would devastate the state's agricultural sector, depopulate eastern Virginia, and end the Old Dominion's ascendancy in the Republic. Stung by the sight of abandoned fields, covered with gullies and weeds, anxious planters called for farmers to take a longer view when trying to intensify their state's agricultural environment—to stop "wasting" its productivity and thereby ensure sustainable gains in farm production. Gathering under the banners of "agricultural reform," "improvement," and "high farming," these men preached that the decline of the state could be stopped if planters would conserve the ecological wealth they already possessed. As one hopeful reformer put it, "the spirit of [agricultural] improvement is becoming general . . . through the state; and the time, I trust, is not far distant when Virginia, redeemed, regenerated, and disenthralled, shall reoccupy her proud position in the front ranks of this grand confederacy." [15]

Scrambling to catch this dream, a group of Charlottesville planters formed the Albemarle Agricultural Society in 1818. They hoped that a society dedicated to the study and promotion of new farming methods would galvanize the planters of their region to embrace intensification. The distress of Virginia's agricultural sector brought an enthusiastic response: Members of the plantation gentry up and down the eastern face of the Blue Ridge joined the society and began trying out the methods its members were pushing. While the Massies' homes along the upper reaches of the Tye were too remote for them to attend public meetings and fairs in Charlottesville, several other prominent Tye Valley planters, such as Thomas Stanhope McClelland, Robert Rives, and some of the Cabells, did join the society. William Massie, and likely his father as well, made up for their isolation by subscribing to the farm periodicals that appeared in the region and often republished the work of the Albemarle reformers. The *American Farmer* out of Baltimore and Virginia's own *Farmer's Register* and *Southern Planter* all found their way to William Massie's desk at Pharsalia.[16]

To add prestige to the society's start-up, its founders asked James Madison of nearby Orange County, just returned to the neighborhood after two terms in the White House, to serve as their president. Madison, who shared their outlook, accepted, delivering one of the great statements of the agricultural conservation crusade in a speech to the members. His frequently reprinted "Address to the Albemarle Agricultural Society" combined science, politics, and practical technique into a coherent program that added careful soil conservation to intensification. Madison began by theorizing that there were limits to the expansion of human agriculture and population. Only part of the earth's biotic productivity could be turned to human needs, he argued, and to push beyond them would upset the "balances of Nature," inviting a "correction" that would reduce human subsistence and population in proportion. Modern scholars, captivated by the parallels between Madison's views and those of late twentieth-century ecological science, have declared him an antebellum environmentalist. One modern historian has gone so far as to label Madison's ideas a "protean Gaia theory."[17] This interpretation, however, neglects Madison's practical conclusions. These were hardly admonitions for Piedmont farmers to stop disrupting the environment and live in harmony with nature. Instead, Madison argued that the planet's limits justified a program of determined intensification. "Motives would not be wanting to obtain for our portion of the earth its fullest share," he declared, "by improving the resources of human subsistence, according to the fair measure of its capacity." In other words, if those resources were scarce, then farmers needed to seize and exploit everything nature offered. Madison preached independence, not interdependence.[18]

Madison began his discourse on nature and agriculture with extended discussions of the balance of species, the distribution of chemical elements among them, and the distributive mechanism of the atmosphere. Yet when he got down to giving concrete advice to his neighbors, it became clear that they all understood nature in terms of the "land," by which Madison meant the soil. For a group of farmers, such close attention to a few inches of dirt spread across their fields should not be surprising. Crop plants are descended from pioneer species that exploit short-lived ecological niches in bare earth. Over time, though, species like tobacco, corn, and wheat evolved to rely on humans to improve that bare ground with tillage and fertilizer. That painstaking creation of a nutrient-rich, friable, yet bare soil is the core of agriculture. Farming revolves around clearing, plowing, fertilizing, and all the other tasks necessary to create soil environments that support crop growth. At the same time, these fragile, man-made soil environments are among the most vulnerable elements of an agricultural ecosystem. The customary farming techniques of the early South had quickly depleted the red clays of the Piedmont. Eighteenth-century planters had few chances to worry about plant diseases, groundwater depletion, overgrazing, or any of the other afflictions of agriculture. Well before they became problems, the farmers could see their stunted crops languishing in exhausted, eroded, and acidified soils. Depleted soil environments hit indebted commercial farmers particularly hard. Their search for sustainable yields could easily be thwarted by the problems with soil structure and chemistry that emerged after just a few seasons of planting. A few poor crops laboriously squeezed from depleted soils could bankrupt a farmer as fast as a depressed market. Given all this, farmers trying to understand the "nature" of their plantations turned to the study of the soil.

Soil chemistry was still in its infancy in the 1810s, and Madison did not have available the field's detailed analysis of the role of mineral nutrients in promoting plant growth. Instead, he and other men of his generation understood the role those nutrients played in the soil in the vague sense of "fertility." Madison was not quite sure how this "fertility" built up, but was quite aware that crops and erosion took it out. Without conservation, that is, preventing topsoils from washing away and replacing what was taken out by crop plants, soils quickly grew sterile and land became worthless, no matter how intensively farmed. Madison's ideal brand of intensification was Chinese farming, where "an industrious use is made of every fertilizing particle that can contribute towards replacing what has been drawn from it." Anything less was criminal waste, and it was the farmer's job "to make the thieves restore as much as possible of the stolen fertility." The Chinese peasant, however, had plenty of fertilizing particles to work with "as almost the whole of what is grown on their farms is consumed within them." Madison was unwilling, of course, to tell upper-class Virginians to abandon the commercial agriculture that took so much fertility off the farm. But for Madison, the demands of market farming made it even more important that his neighbors fight to recycle every scrap of fertility left over after the harvest had been shipped to market. Madison weighed the virtues of different cereal grains in terms of the amount of fertility contained in their marketed seeds and the stems that stayed in the barn and the field. He mulled over the proper treatment of leftover wheat straw and corn stalks, searching for the way in which all their fertility would make it back into the soil. All this work, he promised, would increase both short- and long-term biotic productivity on the farm. If Madison's address to the planters of the western Piedmont presaged anything, it was the first step toward the twentieth-century conservationist's ideal of the "maximum sustainable yield." The early southern soil conservationist was just offering a new, supposedly more visionary and effective, method of intensification.

At its root, though, Madison's vision of the relationship between nature and agriculture was also an extension of the politics of the plantation gentry. Madison called the Albemarle group a "patriotic society." His ecology of limits held a veiled rejection of the westward migration that was draining the Old Dominion. If the earth's natural bounty was finite, then the fresh soils of the West would soon run out. Madison then rejected the idea that nature was so balanced that farmers could not make more crops on the same ground. In other words, prosperity could be had right there in the southern Piedmont. If planters stayed put and intensified their farming, they could make greater profits, and secure capital and political influence for the state. This was the promise of southern agricultural conservation in a nutshell. By the early years of the nineteenth century, Virginia's leaders claimed a new front line was forming in the struggle for independence. Rather than on the battlefields of the Revolution, it was taking shape in their own crop fields. Agricultural conservation was a public crusade, Madison declared, saying that "with so many consumers of the fertility of the earth, and so little attention to the means of repairing their ravages, no one can be surprised at the impoverished face of the country; whilst everyone ought to be desirous of aiding in the work of reformation." And just as his politics glorified independence, the southern conservationist's brand of intensification aimed at the same fierce autonomy.

A profitable farm, these men insisted, monopolized its fertility—using and reusing it. Reformers argued that if they farmed efficiently and conservatively, their yields would increase and they would no longer need to keep acquiring more uncleared forest. The Massies, for instance, had spent thousands of pounds migrating across the state in hopes of escaping soil exhaustion. But as long as they kept farming extensively, plant nutrients leaked off their plantations through soil erosion, wandering livestock, competition from other plants and animals, and old field succession. Conservationists advised them to hold onto what they already had—stop erosion, collect manures, and drive off unwanted organisms. If their farms were intensive and autonomous, they would also be sustainable and profitable.[19] Hard work was needed, of course—backbreaking manual toil digging drainage ditches, collecting natural manures and plowing them into the soil, patiently breeding and caring for fatter livestock, and on and on. This was intensification as it was practiced by the Chinese peasants Madison celebrated—a hard slog squeezing every bit of productivity out of an ecosystem in the hopes of escaping the clutches of the village moneylender and regional tax collector. Of course, as long as they had slaves to do all this work for no pay, the Massies and other planters were a long way from being peons. Yet the push to escape dependence by using what you had more efficiently was similar.

Antebellum conservationists produced a flood of commentary that blamed wasteful farming for the Old Dominion's decline and promised independence through agricultural reform. One of the most distinguished of the men who saw ecological independence as the path to political independence was Caroline County planter John Taylor. John Taylor of Caroline, as he was commonly known, had a career that closely paralleled that of his contemporary Thomas Massie. Born into the Tidewater gentry, he attended William and Mary in the early 1770s and was mentored in the legal profession by his uncle, revolutionary patriot Edmund Pendleton. Like Massie, Taylor also abandoned life in the planter elite to serve in the Continental Army, rising to the rank of major before returning to his home state. After the Revolution, he forged a distinguished career as an attorney and used the profits from his trade to buy land back in Caroline, including his home plantation, Hazelwood, on the Rappahannock River. His success before the bar led him into politics, including several terms in the Virginia General Assembly and appointment to finish terms in the U.S. Senate on three separate occasions. In public life, John Taylor of Caroline was a rock-ribbed Republican, the Jeremiah of old Virginia's declining years, calling its aristocracy back to first principles. Among his books, *An Inquiry into the Principles and Policy of the Government of the United States* (1814) and *Construction Construed and Constitutions Vindicated* (1820) are together regarded as the outstanding statement of Jeffersonian principles of strict constitutional construction and states' rights. His political principles were so refined that he was often identified with the Tertium Quids, that group of strict Republicans who occasionally challenged Jefferson and Madison for subverting the cause.

John Taylor of Caroline's most fascinating work, though, drew his politics away from the abstractions of constitutional law toward the practicalities of farming. In 1813, he published *Arator: Being a Series of Agricultural Essays, Practical and Political: In Sixty-Four Numbers*, a collection of short pieces he had written for Virginia newspapers under the titular pseudonym.[20] In a series of essays titled "The Political State of Agriculture," Taylor made explicit the connection Madison had hinted at: that the state's economic and political decline began in its eroded, abandoned old fields. The failure of farmers to conserve their fertility would, he wrote, "lead to an ultimate recoil from this exhausted resource, to an exhausted country."[21] Taylor began his analysis of the crisis in good

Jeffersonian mode, listing "the political errors under which our agriculture is groaning,"[22] above all, the national government's insistence that farmers be indirectly taxed through protective tariffs to pay "bounties to manufacturing."[23] Yet he soon moved past the evils of the tariff to a detailed discussion of agricultural practices in eastern Virginia. Redemption lay on the farm, Taylor suggested to his readers, and more specifically in conserving the soil. The rest of *Arator* was taken up with a long run of articles on the various "modes of fertilizing land." This combination of political essays with discourses on manure, osage-orange fences, and pig-rearing seems odd to the modern reader. But the connection lies at the heart of the developing importance the gentry saw in the state of the agricultural environment. Just government policies could only be enforced by a prosperous, independent citizenry. That class could only be built on the foundation of ecologically independent farms.

John Taylor of Caroline's program of soil conservation was English in origin. During the eighteenth century, scientifically minded estate managers created an "agricultural revolution," improving crop yields and land values with new farm machines, crop varieties, improved livestock, and fertilizers.[24] What attracted Taylor and his southern readers the most was the way English farmers used manuring, leguminous cover crops, and complex crop rotations to hold on to and increase their soil's fertility. On progressive English estates, farmers carefully managed the ecological relationships between plants, animals, and the physical environment—and came out with more fertile soils at the end. To Taylor, English high farming was a model of agricultural independence—a perfectly controlled, self-contained system that increased fertility. By using human intelligence, technology, and labor to create closed fertility cycles, reforming southern planters believed they could become masters of nature, and thereby independent. Taylor told planters to isolate the ecology of their farms by building two connected systems that cycled fertility in farm soils: one that replaced it through crop rotations and one that did so through livestock and their manure. This double-cycle would close the ecological borders of their farms by steering the movement of fertility inside their fences. The double-cycle promised to intensify their farming—"not to impoverish, but to fertilize the soil, and make it more useful than in its natural state." If planters practiced a real "system of agriculture," their fields would yield larger harvests from richer soils, and do so for longer periods of time.[25]

For the first half of the double-cycle, Taylor drew on the complex crop rotations advocated by English reformers. The three-field system being used by most Virginia planters had only allowed fields to lie fallow one year in three—never enough to restore soil nutrients and structure completely, especially when following demanding crops like corn and tobacco. Taylor believed man-made cycles in the soil environment could be completed by bringing the ambitious five- and seven-field systems developed in England to the Old Dominion. These rotations extended each field's time out of commercial crops from one-third to more than 40 percent. Moreover, high farmers sowed the fallow fields with leguminous cover crops—varieties of clover being the most popular. Legumes, as agricultural chemists would eventually discover, aided the growth of various *Nitrobacter*, bacteria that fixed nitrogen from the air. As a result, clover could actively restore a crucial nutrient drained from the soil by other crops. Clover also produced more biomass than the scattered weeds, grasses, and briars that grew up during unmanaged fallow years. At the end of the season, farmers plowed the grass left after mowing back into the upper soil horizons as a "green manure," adding nutrients while enhancing soil aeration and drainage. After a year or two lying fallow, fields in four-, five- or seven-field crop rotations had noticeably improved soil environments. Fallow tracts in a three-field system were exhausted, eroded, and clogged with weeds.[26]

These rotations required planters to adopt England's great cereal grain, wheat, as a cash crop. In agroecological terms, wheat fit smoothly into the nutrient and biomass cycles created by crop rotations. Tobacco demanded so many soil nutrients that it thwarted rotation schemes, so new ground cultivation remained the norm—indeed, William Massie's slaves were still using this technique when planting tobacco in the late 1850s. Tobacco also called for a tremendous amount of labor—clearing and burning new grounds, building and cultivating plant beds for seedlings, transplanting those seedlings into the main fields, weeding the rows, topping the plants, then harvesting and curing them. Wheat, in contrast, was a low-maintenance crop that could be grown profitably in poorer soils.

Smooth transitions between clover fallow and wheat were therefore possible, while tobacco planters had to keep clearing forest.

*Arator*'s system of agriculture also provided a remedy for Piedmont soil erosion: deep plowing. Virginia farmers had been slow to abandon the hoe cultivation that worked so well with tobacco and corn. When they did start ordering their slaves to plow up the ground, they gave them small, one-horse "scratch" plows to do it with. Taylor told them to buy larger plows and to turn over deep furrows. This, he promised, would bring dense, solid clays to the surface while also building up ridges that would restrain sheet erosion by channeling runoff. Other aspects of the double-cycle also promised to slow down the washing of topsoils. In addition to its nitrogen-fixing qualities, clover acted as a cover crop, holding down soils that eroded when left bare or scattered with weeds during fallow years. Even better, broadcast-sown crops like wheat held down topsoils that washed away when clean-cultivated in row crops like tobacco or corn.

Planters had been aware of the conservationists' promise of renewed soil fertility for a while. A wheat farmer and grist miller like Maj. Thomas Massie saw possibilities in the depleted old fields of the triangle, while tobacco planters like the Roses looked to sell out. John Taylor of Caroline would have been critical of Massie's attempts to grow wheat in a three-field system, but he at least admitted the possibility of such an approach. In contrast, tobacco in rotation was an oxymoron—the "sot weed" was "not admissible into any good system of agriculture."[27] Major Massie was far from alone in abandoning the tobacco farms of the Tidewater for the grain economy of the interior. As wheat and rye prices climbed during the European wars of the 1790s and 1800s, many Virginia planters embraced hard grains. Once in the Tye Valley, Thomas Massie found plenty of local farmers ready to join the trend and bring wheat to his mill.[28] For all the additional fallow time and the effort put into unmarketable cover crops, English crop rotations with cereal grains promised to intensify cultivation while maintaining profits. Restoring soil nutrients and structure increased productivity and market return over the long haul.

Planting clover on fallow fields also helped high farmers create a cycle of livestock and manure. Animal husbandry in the early South had been extensive and casual. Most cattle and hogs were "free-ranging," wandering the forests and old fields before being periodically rounded up and slaughtered.[29] This cheap, labor-saving pastoralism let plant nutrients escape from the agricultural ecosystem. Free-ranging animals went feral, expending in respiration much of what they consumed outside the fences. The large, lethargic, and profitable cattle and hogs that appear at agricultural fairs today are only distant cousins to the skinny, mean-tempered, mangy animals that wandered the forests and old fields of the southern frontier. The hogs that the Pharsalia slaves slaughtered in the 1820s and 1830s rarely weighed more than a gaunt 150 pounds on average. Worse, free-range livestock scattered their manure for miles around the plantation. William Massie referred to his "sandy-hill hogs" grazing in the forests on the unplowable ridges on the south end of the triangle, their feces lost to his fields. As late as the 1830s, his slaves still drove some of Pharsalia's livestock up the Blue Ridge to graze in the forests and on the balds during the summer. A concentrated source of nutrients was lost to a soil environment that needed to replace those lost to crop harvesting.[30]

More-intensive livestock management, however, kept nutrients within the agroecosystem. John Taylor of Caroline advised planters to pen cattle and hogs inside fenced clover pastures during the growing season. During the winter, they were to be housed in sturdy barns to feed on hay and corn fodder. In both cases, of course, farmhands had to work harder to confine and care for the animals. But soil nutrients were not lost to the agroecosystem. Penned animals put their energy into flesh and fat rather than respiration. Likewise, their manure was carefully contained. The nutrients the animals consumed stayed in the pasture through their excrement. Barnyard manure could be collected and carted wherever the farm manager wanted to restore his soils.

"Manuring" then, as much as crop rotations, clover, or wheat, was John Taylor of Caroline's recipe for intensification and sustainability. "Skill and industry" applied to animal husbandry and manure management, he promised his readers, "would as suddenly but more permanently improve the face of our country as paint does that of a wrinkled hag."[31] Plowed-under animal feces provided the intensive farmer's fields with some of the high nutrient levels of colonial tobacco grounds. Mature forests were disappearing from early nineteenth-century Virginia. Intensively managed herds, on the other hand, could, in theory, provide an endless supply of manure.

Two processes that centered on capturing and maintaining soil nutrients meshed to form the double-cycle. On one side, fields in rotation were rested and restored by clover fallows before being put back into wheat. On the other, clover pasture fed the livestock that produced the manure that could be plowed back into the same fields. Such carefully managed ecological cycles promised to make farm fields more fertile by conserving and concentrating the fertility inside the fences. Individual farms could achieve an environmental self-sufficiency that would end their owners' dependence on the outside world for capital or natural resources. The double-cycle was the basis of John Taylor of Caroline's and other southern agricultural conservationists' push to achieve independence through intensive and sustainable farming.

In the pages of *Arator* it seemed simple and effective. Many loyal Virginians were facing a choice between emigration and bankruptcy. James Madison, John Taylor of Caroline, and other reformers offered a third path, one they promised led back to home plantations, family mansions, and graveyards, to prosperity and power. *Arator* became both bible and manual to planters chasing that promise. As one avid high farmer later explained, "never has any book on agriculture been received with so much enthusiastic applause, nor has any other had such widespread early effects in affecting opinion, and stimulating to exertion and improvement."[32] But when "practical" farmers tried to apply Taylor's ideas to their own fields, they found a host of problems impeding "improvement." *Arator* wound up being one of the best examples of book farming—a perfectly worked out system of theoretical agriculture that ordinary planters struggled to establish when faced with an uncooperative environment, short markets, and demanding creditors.

The first, crucial problem was described by Taylor's heir as leader of the southern high farming movement, Prince George County planter and farm periodical editor Edmund Ruffin. Shortly after the War of 1812, Ruffin had come into his family's old plantation, Coggin's Point, an exhausted Tidewater farm on the southern bank of the James River. Like so many of his peers, Ruffin became an "enthusiastic admirer of 'Arator,'" but was quickly frustrated when he tried to follow his hero's advice. He rotated crops, plowed deeply, planted clover, penned his livestock, and manured his fields. His reward, he soon realized, was a soil much worse than he had inherited. The physical environment of Coggin's Point, it turned out, was very different from Taylor's Hazelwood. On the coastal plain, deep plowing just dug through the loamy topsoil and exposed a loose, sandy lower horizon. The exposed subsoil then washed away, leaving Ruffin's fields gullied and gall'd. Worse, the double-cycle did not revive his soils. Clover would barely grow; manure seemed to do nothing; and his crops diminished just as surely as those of his neighbors who farmed more extensively. The land "would not take manure," they informed him, and soon Ruffin was again facing the fear that had driven him to embrace high farming: "the universal approved resort, in all such cases, of emigrating to the rich western wilderness."[33]

The trouble, Ruffin had to accept, was the difficulty of imposing an English agroecosystem on the South's local environments. John Taylor of Caroline had not done much to differentiate climate or soil types in his analysis. Fertility was fertility—one's fields had it or did not, and the major variable deciding that question was the way they were cultivated. But as Ruffin discovered, his agricultural mentors had "filled my head with notions which were, even if proper in England, totally unsuitable to this country." The double-cycle, its crops, animals, and the relationships between them, had all been developed across the ocean. But the physical environments of the south Atlantic were very different from those of northern Europe. In the Tidewater's warmer climate, year-round rainfall percolated through sandy soils, leaching out base compounds and leaving a low pH behind. English hard grains struggled in such acidic dirt, but the leguminous grasses suffered the worst damage. "Clover could not be made to live on land of this kind," Ruffin recalled, "[or] yielded the entire occupancy of the ground to natural weeds after one year."[34] Worse, soil acidity destroyed the nitrogen-fixing *Nitrobacter* that clung to the roots of the clover. The keystone of the double-cycle—a leguminous cover crop that provided pasture for large livestock herds—was ill fitted to the southern environment. In the Tidewater, the *Arator* system did little to restore depleted soils.

Ruffin remained a Virginian, believing that independence was the cure to whatever ailed him. Rather than rely on farming systems developed by others, he determined to create one for himself, adapting the double-cycle to the climate and soils of his own country. Beginning with a few simple experiments, Ruffin isolated soil acidity as the factor limiting crop growth. He grew enthusiastic when he realized that he did not have to buy commercial lime to correct the problem. Scattered through the Tidewater were beds of "marl," calcium carbonate-rich muds—usually clays and decomposing shells. At Coggin's Point, clover and other crops grew well on the small patches of topsoil that overlay marl beds, and Ruffin quickly set his slaves to work digging up the marl on his land, carting the mud out, and plowing it into his fields. Yields soon increased, and he was able to begin planting clover, rotating crops, and profiting from his farm. Publicizing his discoveries, Ruffin started the first Virginia farm journal, the *Farmers' Register*, in 1824. Assuring his readers that the independent intensification promised by the double-cycle could be saved (and with materials that farmers already owned, no less), Ruffin became the state's leading agricultural conservationist of the 1820s and 1830s.

As his disciples soon discovered, however, Ruffin's gospel of marl had not completely solved the problem of adapting the double-cycle to local environments. The first of his neighbors who tried marling their fields saw no results. As a result, he recalled, "for some years, my marling was a subject for ridicule with some of my neighbors."[35] Even as he publicized marling, Ruffin had to admit that it was a complex and tricky business. Not enough marl, and little benefit came to the soil. Too much marl, and plants suffered even more (and Ruffin was not yet enough of a soil chemist to understand why). Striking a balance was made even more difficult by the wide variations in soil pH that occurred within individual fields, while individual marl beds differed greatly in their lime concentrations. All this left planters hoping to adapt Ruffin's schemes facing great expense and risk as they plunged into the unknown. As unsustainable as traditional southern farming might have been, two centuries of planting in eastern Virginia had given planters a reliable understanding of the region's crops and soils. They remained suspicious of Ruffin's panacea, and marling remained a religion with few converts.

Rather than trying to impose new agricultural ecosystems on their farms, planters preferred to intensify more cautiously, using the plants and animals they already knew. Livestock husbandry was an excellent example of their preference for a tested ecology over an experimental one. A few ambitious farmers imported "improved" cattle and hogs from the North as breeding stock. These animals suffered in the southern climate, though, falling victim to a range of diseases and reproducing slowly, if it all. Observing these failures, Virginia's farmers were confirmed in their distrust of book farming and tried instead to improve their own animals through selective breeding. Practical planters like the Massies and their neighbors remained conservative, sticking with the genetic lines they owned and understood. Improving livestock on the farm was a laborious and slow process, and no dramatic improvements in the size and productivity of the state's livestock were made.

It was never easy to integrate traditional knowledge into the double-cycle, though. The state's traditional crops could not be smoothly slotted into the complex crop rotations developed in England. But planters understood tobacco, and needed the money it still promised, even in the hard years after the Panic of 1819. As Edmund Ruffin recalled of his first years as a planter, "the whole income, and more [of his plantation], was required for the most economical support of a then small but fast growing family; and for any increase of income or net profit, there was no hope." [36] An austere lifestyle had little appeal to an aristocrat who had to display his status through conspicuous consumption. Massie family tradition recalls that Sarah Cocke Massie never entirely forgave her husband for dragging her away from the pleasant upper-class society of Frederick. The move to the Tye Valley may also have been a desperate attempt at self-discipline on Thomas Massie's part—his accounts reveal a taste for expensive liquor, clothing, carriages, and the other accessories of a member of the gentry. [37] Though he built gristmills and grew hard grains in the Tye Valley, the Major also kept clearing new grounds or using the three-field system to plant tobacco in the triangle, as did his son.

When combined with the gentry's hard-pressed finances, declining soils delayed improvement even more. Most early nineteenth-century Virginia planters were like Edmund Ruffin—they had not inherited fertile fields from their fathers. Eroded, exhausted land demanded extensive restoration, and John Taylor of Caroline offered a tough regimen. Take more fields out of cultivation and plant them in clover, he advised the readers of *Arator*. Keep the livestock out so the clover could grow undisturbed, he continued. Then plow the entire clover crop back into the soil as a green manure. Then repeat the process for several years. Facing a pressing choice between bankruptcy and migration, the full measure of Taylor's discipline was too harsh for most planters. Ruffin himself had worried that marling would not be a "practical, profitable remedy," since raising soil pH did not address lack of soil nutrients, leaving him *still* facing the heavy, unrewarded work of raising nutrient levels and rebuilding topsoils by planting and plowing under multiple hay crops. Needing ready money to keep their creditors at bay, most farmers turned instead to half measures that produced half results.

Finally, and perhaps most troublingly, the rugged ecological independence preached by the early southern conservationists could not exist on a real farm. John Taylor of Caroline had seen little problem imposing a complete agricultural ecosystem onto a southern plantation, believing that the relationships of the double-cycle alone were enough to conserve soils. Ruffin had conceded that some adjustment had to be made to the local environment but still wound up arguing that planters could seal themselves off from the outside world and survive on their own. Most planters did not have enough fertile soils to profit from autonomy, though, and they faced a host of competitors for the plantation's biotic productivity that the reformers did not account for. Fences might have been solid lines on plantation maps, but out in the fields invaders made their way in and soils made their way out. Squirrels, birds, and other wandering animals ate the grain; parasitic plant diseases attacked all the crops, while weeds stole water, light, and nutrients from them. Crops shipped to market also took nutrients off the farm, and rainwater carried topsoil away as well. Fighting to hold on to what little they had, many planters doubted that the prosperous independence the double-cycle promised was anything more than a mirage. Others, like the Massies, remained hopeful, but struggled to overcome the many obstacles southern soil conservation faced when applied to the land.

## Pharsalia from Father to Son

When William Massie received the land at the foot of the Priest from his father, he faced all these problems. Major Massie was able to give his youngest son several slaves, a little capital, some cleared fields, and the proximity of family. He could not, however, give William the head start on profitable cultivation that a mature soil under hardwood forests provided those who headed west across the Appalachians. For all his idealization of personal independence, Major Massie had not made the agricultural environment in the triangle ecologically self-sufficient. By 1815, the oak and chestnut forests and rich clay soils Parson Robert Rose had patented were long gone across most of the property. The Roses, their tenants, and the Massie slaves had cleared out the old-growth forest that grew up after the expulsion of the Monacans from the region. They had farmed it in tobacco and corn, using shifting cultivation or the three-field system, exhausting the soils and leaving the fields open to erosion. William Massie's legacy from his father was a denuded environment, a traditional, extensive system of farming, and the culture and politics of the Revolutionary gentry.

During the years the triangle was owned by Thomas Massie, the history of its agricultural environment is obscure. The aging planter dutifully saved his milling accounts and business correspondence, but if he kept detailed records of his agricultural practices, they have not survived. We know a little about the land he bought from John Rose, the deed having been recorded in the Amherst County record books. And William's copious notes give some idea of the state of the property his father gave him in 1815. Between the two, we can make some intelligent surmises about how the area developed before William Massie began trying to organize it into a separate farm.[38]

The triangle was already a mixed forest and agricultural environment when Major Massie purchased part of it from John Rose. The western corner of the area had been purchased from the Roses by local planter Nathaniel Hill. The line between Hill's property and Major Massie's ran south and east from the base of the Little Priest to the low ridge on the southern edge of the triangle. Running roughly parallel with Rocky Run, the Hill-Rose line crossed some of the most fertile land in the neighborhood. By the mid-1790s, it had already been cleared, evidenced by the numerous "pointers" and two fallen oaks the surveyors used to mark the boundary when Major Massie purchased John Rose's property. In contrast, the corners on the low ridge (owned by Nicholas Cabell at the time), as well as those on the lower slopes of the Little Priest, were mostly marked by mature trees. The Roses and their tenants had left them alone while they grew tobacco and corn on the level ground between the creeks below.

Thomas Massie established Level Green plantation at the western edge of his tract. Local workmen and the slaves he brought from Frederick County built him a plantation house, complete with outbuildings, orchards, and a new Massie graveyard, at the foot of the Little Priest a short distance from the banks of Rocky Run. The Major's overseer, George Williams (who had also followed him from the Shenandoah Valley), sent the slaves to lay out Level Green's main fields to the south of the house, clustered in the space between Rocky Run and Muddy Branch. Evidence suggests, though, that they continued the work of clearing and farming on the eastern side of Muddy Branch, in the area the Major gave to William in 1815. Major Massie created Pharsalia as an inheritance for his youngest son by carving off part of the farmland he had been planting for nearly twenty years.

Several preexisting features of the new plantation stood out. Pharsalia rested on a bench between the steep slopes of the Priest and the Tye River floodplain. The side the Priest plunged three thousand feet in a mile and a half to reach the borders of the Massie property. From there, however, the slope dropped two hundred feet across the next mile before reaching the low bluffs that bounded the Tye riverbottom. It was a nice stretch of arable ground that must have been attractive to a young planter surveying the steep, rocky terrain all around him. Like his father, William chose a spot at the base of the mountain that overlooked the entire property and set the family slaves to work building a house and grounds for himself and his young wife, Sarah Steptoe. From the windows of the Pharsalia mansion, he could look out over his new domain, an independent, masterful aristocrat like his father. It was a broad tract of valuable farmland, his own property, worked by people who were his chattels.

The land at Pharsalia was not uniformly level and arable, though. The lines of Major Massie's purchase from John Rose pushed beyond the level ground below the Massies' new homes onto the ridges behind them. Erosion from the mountains above had left rich but vulnerable soils on the slopes just above William's new home. Thomas Massie and his son were unwilling to leave those hillsides covered with oak and chestnut forest. To the west of the Pharsalia house lay Ned's Hill, a knob that jutted out from the lower slopes of the Little Priest, looming some five hundred feet above the house. Rising up the hillside directly behind the mansion lay the Cove, that large hollow with rich black soils nestled between the Priest and Little Priest. To the east of the house, the slopes of the Priest moderated before hitting the bench. This would later entice William Massie to order his overseers and slaves to clear and plant the ground—a tract later referred to as Rambler's Field. The soils of these three spots were undoubtedly rich. Leaf litter washed down from the slopes above deposited a rich, black loam over the clay and gravel. But it was a thin and fragile soil, and terribly vulnerable to erosion in the Blue Ridge downpours.

In fact, rainfall and runoff shaped the topography of the Pharsalia bench as much as the axes and plows of enslaved field hands during the early nineteenth century. Several creeks draining the steep slopes above flowed across the plantation toward the Tye River. The sudden downpours that blew up and over the Priest frequently flooded these streams. These "freshes" tore out crop plants and made the fertile stream bottoms useless for cultivation. Dense grasses, however, could survive most of the brief overflows. By 1815, the banks of one of the Pharsalia streams was already being used as a pasture, although it was probably planted in native rather than cultivated grasses. In later years, William Massie would cultivate a large clover and timothy grass meadow along another creek that ran along eastern edge of Pharsalia in the Tye River bottomlands.[39]

Massie and his slaves were not able to contain the impact of stream bank erosion, though. Muddy Branch had already earned its name back when the Rose family had owned the property. Leaves, soil, and even gravel washed down from the hills above them filled up the beds of this and other creeks that crossed Pharsalia. As they clogged up, their floods spread across the wider areas, saturating the surrounding soils, creating water-logged swamps. Higher rates of erosion from cleared fields aggravated the problem of sedimentation and flooding. With some ingenuity and a lot of hard work, Massie and his slaves found some limited uses for the patches of wetland growing around the plantation. In the spring of 1818, and several times in subsequent years, Pharsalia's owner mentioned using a small "marsh" or "swamp" in the Front Field as a tobacco

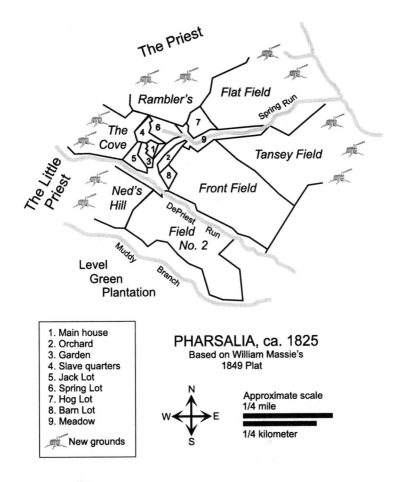

The Priest

Rambler's

Flat Field

Spring Run

The Cove

Tansey Field

The Little Priest

Ned's Hill

Front Field

DePriest Run

Field No. 2

Level Green Plantation

Muddy Branch

1. Main house
2. Orchard
3. Garden
4. Slave quarters
5. Jack Lot
6. Spring Lot
7. Hog Lot
8. Barn Lot
9. Meadow

New grounds

PHARSALIA, ca. 1825
Based on William Massie's
1849 Plat

N
W ← → E
S

Approximate scale
1/4 mile

1/4 kilometer

seedling bed. The larger swamps along Muddy Branch led the young planter in a similar direction, his slaves using them for plant beds throughout the 1820s and 1830s. The threat of flooding remained, though. The field hands were forced to dig runoff channels around the Muddy Branch beds to protect them from inundation. Otherwise, the swamps were abandoned or turned over to uncultivated pasture.[40]

A fair amount of Pharsalia was still covered in woodland when Major Massie handed it over to his son. William Massie sent his first overseer, Bob Mitchell, and his slaves out to clear several stands of timber during the 1820s. In addition to the foothill forests of Rambler's Field, oak trees seem to have survived along the ditches and creek bottoms lower in the property. William's Farm Accounts give some clues, though, that under his father's direction, other areas had already been cleared or at least pillaged for wood. In 1829, the young planter noted that the slaves he had sent to clear additional ground in the Cove above the house were simply "shrubbing" the land. The hollow's timber had already been removed, and years of succession had covered the tract with scrub cedar and other brush. The same appears to have held true for the top of Ned's Hill. It was only fenced in for crops in 1823, after apparently having served as a half-cleared brush land pasture for the Massie livestock.[41]

In 1816, William Massie formally purchased from his father the four-teen hundred acres out of which Pharsalia plantation was drawn. The deed from father to son, as well as the young man's Farm Accounts, give some clues as to how the land had been cultivated during the twenty years since it had been acquired by the family. In the first place, the names given to cleared portions of his new property indicate they had already been farmed. Most likely, the occupants had been tenants who leased farms from the Massies or the Roses before them. A small field at the foot of Ned's Hill was referred to as Old George's Patch well into the 1820s. The headwaters of a stream that fed into the Cove already bore the name Kitty's Hollow when it was recleared by the Pharsalia slaves in the 1830s. The hollow above Castle Creek was named Tarent's Cove. It may also have been rented from the Massies by George Hight, who lived nearby and blazed a trail from it to his house.[42]

Thomas Massie's slaves cleared several hundred acres of the better arable land at Pharsalia. According to a listing of Pharsalia's fields that William compiled in 1832, three large crop fields already existed when he took over the new plantation in 1815. The Front Field consisted of 125½ acres running from the site of the soon-to-be-built Pharsalia main house down to the ridges above the Tye River. It was not completely cleared for cultivation, however. It included "meadow" land along a small creek, as well as some woodland, probably along an unnamed run that drained into Rocky Run at the southern edge of the triangle. Just to the east of the Front Field lay the 117¼ acres of the Tansey Field, which sloped gently down toward the creek bottoms at the southern edge of the triangle. Judg-ing from the erosion problems it gave William Massie during the 1820s, the Tansey Field was the longest-farmed field on the plantation, possibly having been cultivated back when the Roses still owned the property. Just to the north of the Tansey Field lay the 100 acres of the Flat Field. Its name referred to the level tableland that stretched along the meadow run down to the creek that set off the Tye bottomlands from the Pharsalia bench. Several acres of woodland remained on the edge of that ridge before being cleared and added to the Flat Field in 1820. Just across the meadow run from the Front Field were the first clearings that would later become Rambler's Field. Rambler's seems to have consisted of a series of newly cleared patches extending along the length of the Flat Field and running a short distance toward the ridge that separated Pharsalia from the Silver Creek hollow. This steep topography left Rambler's Field vulnerable to sheet erosion and perhaps more serious gullying problems.[43]

These fields became the basis of Pharsalia. Their borders represented the more recent uses of the lands William purchased from his father, though. William's records mention a number of old fields and successional patches, indicating that older clearings had also been made on the property. His deed from his father refers to an "old field" near DePriest Run on the bench lands near the bottom of the original Front Field. In 1827, his crop accounts mention that his slaves were clearing broomsedge from the lower end of the Front Field. Broomsedge was a perennial weed, common and troublesome in depleted Virginia old fields due to its low nutrient and soil structure demands. Massie also reported serious erosion problems on the Tansey Field in the same year. The land between DePriest Run and Muddy Branch, just below Ned's Hill, seems to have been cleared and abandoned before William Massie acquired it. In his records from 1823, the young planter mentioned building a fence through an old field in the area. Another abandoned patch next to it was covered with an ivy thicket. By 1830, the ivy had apparently given way to a briar patch that had to be laboriously cleared and plowed before crops could be sown. In 1826, Massie mentioned that his slaves were cutting and hauling timber from second-growth pine forests at an unnamed location on the plantation. The pines suggest the presence of other agricultural clearings perhaps dating back to John Rose's ownership of the property.[44]

Most of these old fields were concentrated on the southern and western edges of Pharsalia, along the border with Level Green. The Massie slaves had apparently cleared, cultivated, and abandoned them after Major Massie had purchased the property. They had then cleared the three new fields on the far side of DePriest Run to the north and east. These facts suggest that Major Massie was still farming extensively, despite his ambition to make a permanent home in the triangle. He and his slaves continued to plant tobacco during these years. He may have rotated it with wheat or created a three-shift system with wheat, corn, and fallow on fields that were first cleared and planted in tobacco. Clearing new grounds or using simple rotations had depleted the soils between Muddy Branch and DePriest Run. The Major had then been forced to move his plows and slaves onto new grounds farther away from his house. In William Massie's later records, there are some interesting indications of the problems created by erosion and exhaustion. The Massie family renamed several of the creeks that ran through their property after the Major bought it from John Rose. Stoney Creek became Rocky Run, and DePriest Run became Mill Dam Run, reflecting its use in later years. Yet Muddy Branch retained the name soil erosion had earned it throughout these years. Moreover, many of the mentions Pharsalia's owner made of clearing old field colonizers like broomsedge, ivy, and briars from the lands between DePriest Run and Muddy Branch date from well into the 1820s. The young man's records suggest his slaves had not cultivated them in the years since 1815, making them likely survivors of clearings made under Major Massie's supervision. In most simple disturbances of Piedmont forests, like blowdowns or fires, pioneer species last only a few years before hardier shrubs, and soon pine trees, move in. That the weeds dominated the old fields below Ned's Hill for at least a decade is strong testimony to the soil depletion cause by Major Massie's farming. Pharsalia was not a frontier farm, born from the hardwood forests of the western Piedmont. It was a second-generation plantation born from old fields, exhausted soils, and a complex and conflicted gentry culture. William Massie inherited from his father a depleted agricultural environment, a legacy of farming strategies that offered little promise of anything except further impoverishment and a preoccupation with personal independence.

Squeezing a plantation from his father at the tender age of nineteen was William Massie's first assertion of his own will toward that personal independence. His correspondence in the months after receiving Pharsalia dealt mainly with his attempts to hasten the process of establishing a household separate from his clinging father. Major Massie wanted his son to keep a room at Level Green even after his marriage and took time to pepper his son with advice about building a slave force and other business topics. William was in no mood to tolerate "the Old Man's" delays, though, and counted the weeks until he and his wife could move into the barely painted house at Pharsalia.[45] Yet the distance William was putting between himself and his father was really quite small, and not just in terms of the mere mile and a half of wagon road that separated the houses at Pharsalia and Level Green. The economic, agricultural, and personal life William began establishing on his new plantation paralleled his father's. In many ways, Pharsalia's early years were a continuation of the farming done at Level Green. The young planter was slow to try and turn Pharsalia into the kind of independent agricultural ecosystem southern soil conservationists were promoting.

During William's early years managing Pharsalia, he and his slaves continued many of the agroecological practices that had shaped plantations like Level Green. The main house was a substantial two-story wooden structure on a small rise at the lower end of the Cove that took nearly a year to construct. Impressive grounds soon surrounded it. These included a large vegetable garden to the west, slave cabins and carriage houses behind, and eventually barns, tobacco and ice houses, and a variety of other outbuildings. Like most early nineteenth-century planters, William Massie left ornamental gardening to his wife and house servants. He did note that his field slaves established a decorative lawn by "turfing" the yard in front of the house in 1829. He further asserted his independence from his father by adding a family graveyard at Pharsalia to the one behind the house at Level Green. With an intensively managed core of several acres around his house, William had established a traditional gentry home place at Pharsalia.[46]

Like other plantations, though, Pharsalia continued to be marked by a mixed landscape and extensive farming around the house and grounds. In particular, Massie's livestock continued to range freely, grazing in old fields and on forest mast throughout the 1820s. The old native-grass pasture was too small to support the demands of Pharsalia's steadily growing population of cattle and hogs. During most of the 1810s and 1820s, animals were led to the mixed forest and old fields on the top and back slope of Ned's Hill for pasture. A small uncleared cove in the ridge south of Pharsalia was apparently used for forest pasture, and still bears the name Cow Hollow. More importantly, rather than sow hayfields or plant feed corn, for many years Massie relied on the cool woods and glades of his father's Blue Ridge property for summer grazing. Feral hogs bearing Massie's brand continued to wander the woods as well. In 1821, the Pharsalia slaves caught and killed "the wild black spaid sow." Two years later they tracked down two wild hogs who had wandered off into the mountains three years before. Even in the early 1840s, Massie would continue mentioning the slaughter of "woods" hogs separate from the main herds. Intensive animal husbandry was slow to appear at Pharsalia.

In its early years Pharsalia was also called upon to support the gentry's traditional crop, tobacco. William Massie remained bound to tobacco as his primary cash crop for much of the 1820s. A collapse in grain prices following the end of the Napoleonic Wars forced many planters back to their old staple crop. Tobacco's voracious need for nutrients forced an extension of Pharsalia's boundaries to create fresh soils for the main tobacco fields. Massie's accounts from 1832 give a long list of clearings his slaves had made at the plantation since 1815. During these years, he regularly recorded his field hands at work felling and burning timber during the winter months. Most of the Cove above the house, all of Ned's Hill, much of Rambler's Field, as well as a handful of smaller tracts around the plantation were cleared of hardwood, pine, and old field scrub in the 1820s. As late as 1832, Massie was planning to remove 64½ acres of mature white oak forest, probably growing on the lower ridges of the Priest on the edge of Rambler's Field.[47]

Judging from his records, most of these recently cleared fields were committed to tobacco. New grounds supported simple crop progressions—Massie mentioned second- and third-year tobacco grounds on a number of occasions—or incorporated into a modified three-field system. Like the other existing fields at Pharsalia, the Front Field was not fully cleared in 1815. Its remaining woods were gradually cut down and burned over the next ten years.[48] The new clearings were planted in tobacco, as well as corn and other cereal grains. For most of its first decade as part of Pharsalia, two sets of clearings in the Front Field appear to have been rotated in a three-shift system. Corn was planted on the field in 1817, 1818, 1820, 1822, and 1824. Stretches of the field were left fallow in 1819, 1821, and 1823. Completing the cycle, wheat and rye were sown in 1817, 1820, 1822, and 1824. The slaves added to the clearing by planting tobacco on new grounds in the Front Field in 1819 and 1822.

The three-shift rotation in the Front Field adds weight to other evidence that the Massies had abandoned any notion of long fallowing in the triangle. William's accounts periodically mention the Pharsalia slaves clearing sections of pine timber on the plantation. This was a losing strategy if they then planted the land in tobacco before putting it in a three-field system of corn, wheat, and fallow. Timber harvesting on Ned's Hill and in the Cove helped provide lumber for fences and buildings and to feed the plantation's many work and home fires. When it came time to clear those tracts for planting, however, just burning the brush and scrub cedar was not going to provide much in the way of potash and other nutrients. Soils in early stages of old field succession also lacked the aeration and well-drained topsoil tobacco demanded. Pharsalia's main fields were unable to support good tobacco crops under those conditions.

Thomas Massie had come to the Tye Valley with hopes of farming more intensively than the Roses. But the evidence suggests that the many obstacles to improvement had stopped him from joining the first steps of the reform movement. His son, facing the same problems, continued many of his father's habits. But William's own search for independence led the young man to embrace agricultural conservation and try to make Pharsalia ecologically independent and sustainable. During the 1820s, he pushed beyond the systems of farming he had learned as a boy at Level Green. He would soon confront all the problems associated with turning southern conservationists' book farming into practical, profitable agriculture.

### The Double-Cycle Agroecosystem at Pharsalia

Along with Pharsalia, William Massie's inheritance was his place in the gentry—and a share in its struggles. The desperately low crop prices of the 1820s did not repay traditional southern farming. By 1824 he was already referring in his correspondence to "the shattered condition of my finances."[49] Massie did not count his bond to his father in his annual calculations of his liabilities—but still built up debts of nearly ten thousand dollars by the end of the decade. Like other members of his class, the young planter hoped his new estate would ensure his personal independence. And, like them, the promises of the farm conservationists he read in the *American Farmer* or the regional newspaper, the *Lynchburg Virginian*, which also took a frequent interest in farming, turned his head. Bit by bit, he struggled to make the land his father had given him more productive by making it ecologically intensive and independent. But throughout the 1820s, he managed nothing more than half-successful half measures. Pharsalia's soils were already impoverished, and Massie struggled to find the fertility to establish the double-cycle. His lack of understanding of Pharsalia's microenvironments hindered that search even more. He also needed ready cash to keep his young family well-situated and his creditors at bay. This led him repeatedly to commit his agroecological assets to quick fixes—particularly the old troublemaker, tobacco. Pharsalia's agroecosystem intensified slowly and was less than profitable. For all the reformers' promises, William Massie's ideal independence seemed no closer.[50]

In the years after he established Pharsalia, Massie took the first tentative steps to build the double-cycle—particularly the pasture-livestock-manure half of the system. The numbers of hogs slaughtered at Pharsalia steadily increased, from only twenty-one in 1817 to between sixty and a hundred during the second half of the 1820s—indicating a rapid growth in the size of the herd. More importantly, Massie and his laborers cautiously centralized and intensified animal husbandry. The slaves fenced off and developed the soils of a series of "lots" around the main house. These lots were small, intensively managed fields dedicated to livestock husbandry and occasional cropping. The ten-acre Hog Lot was laid out just below the Pharsalia spring east of the main house. A six-acre Barn Lot, including buildings used to house wintering animals, was established just across the road from the Hog Lot. The twelve-acre Spring Lot around the Pharsalia spring was used for many of the same purposes.[51] The slaves responsible for Pharsalia's cattle and swine herded the animals onto these lots to graze and defecate. At the same time, others collected and stored the tassels and leaves of corn plants ("tops" and "blades" in the jargon of the time) as winter fodder for the animals penned up in the new barn. Most importantly, over the years the field hands went to work creating permanent, cultivated hayfields. In 1819, they began replanting the native grass meadow along the run below the house with clover. In the fall of 1820, Massie intensified management of that meadow, sending the field hands out to manure and coulter it after harvesting the hay. In the spring of 1828, they sowed timothy grass on it as well. Finally, in 1830, Mitchell, the overseer, directed the slaves as they fallowed and manured a recently cleared patch of ground along the Tye riverbottom creek. In a couple of years they had established it as a larger, permanent meadow. While developing these intensively managed, durable hayfields, Pharsalia's slaves also cultivated pasture in the various small lots surrounding the main house. These were periodically sown with clover and later timothy, and turned over to the livestock and their feces. The intensification of animal husbandry went slowly, and many Massie animals continued to roam the old fields and hills around Pharsalia. The ones concentrated on the lots at the heart of the plantation, though, contributed not just food, but the most important product of the cycle of animal husbandry: manure. As the dung piled up, slaves spent the late winter months loading it onto wagons and carting it out to the new pastures, the lots around the main house, and the main fields.

In some ways, this schedule was nothing new. Building up soils continued to be a January through March custom at Pharsalia, as "manuring" slowly replaced clearing new grounds. The two chores went on simultaneously for years, though, and animal dung and forest topsoils were the two main concentrations of fertility at Pharsalia. Like other "practical" planters, Massie was torn over how to use his ecological assets. New grounds always went into tobacco, as planters needed the most return from the labor and the quickly exhausted fields. Manure, in contrast, was flexible and renewable, and could be used to build up hay and grain fields. In the 1820s, though, wheat prices were seriously depressed. Throughout the decade, Massie was tempted to commit Pharsalia's manure to the quick expedient of tobacco. Massie turned his animals out into the lots around the main house for much of the year, rather than penning them up. Periodically, he also ordered the wintertime buildup of manure in the barn to be plowed into the soils of the lots, rather than carted out to the main fields. He then took short-term advantage of the spikes in plant nutrients the plowed-in feces created near the main house by ordering Mitchell to plant tobacco, and occasionally wheat. The Hog Lot to the east of the main house was one of the most intensively farmed spots at Pharsalia during these years. After sowing clover for grazing and defecating swine during the late 1810s, field hands planted tobacco on the now nutrient-rich soil in 1820 and 1821, and then again in 1824 and 1825. Intermittently, Massie's commitment to his hayfields also backslid. In 1819 and 1820, and then again in 1824 and 1826, the temptation of the nitrogen- and manure-enriched clover meadow below his house proved overwhelming, and Massie ordered it plowed up and planted in tobacco. Pharsalia's young owner would then "repent," and his slaves would sow clover or timothy the next year.[52]

The growth in the plantation's piles of manure and the restoration of its soils would have been substantially slowed by all this. Plowing up the pastures meant less animal fodder. Compounding the problem, manure that was committed to quick tobacco crops did not go to the main fields, where even less clover hay would have been produced. The results are apparent from Massie's accounts of his annual hog slaughter, in which he noted the number butchered and the pounds of pork preserved. The growing numbers of livestock at Pharsalia, and the greater care given them, were not matched by any increase in their slaughter weights. If anything, the numbers went down slightly during these years, from an average of 150 to 160 pounds per animal in the late 1810s to the several parcels of hogs slaughtered by the end of the decade that only brought 120 to 130 pounds when killed. This decline reflected the increased pressure larger herds made on the halting growth of Pharsalia's supply of hay and fodder.

The temptation of tobacco hit the livestock-manure side of the double-cycle in other ways, as well. For a tobacco farmer, labor was money, and Massie was aggressive throughout this period buying slaves to expand his operations. The growing demand for food to feed these hands was apparent from his records. Plantation hogs were not slaughtered for market sale. Instead they were pickled or smoked on the plantation and distributed to the slaves. Throughout the 1820s, Massie's work notes betray an increasing obsession with his vegetable garden, which was becoming a major undertaking. During these years his slaves expanded the original garden, a small patch on the west side of the main house, into a tract of nearly six acres. Massie began sending some of Pharsalia's field hands there to plant root crops, particularly "Irish" and the traditional sweet potatoes, to supplement their own rations.[53] Still, Massie was forced to buy corn from neighboring farmers, and he fretted over this compromise to his self-sufficiency. He responded by stepping up corn cultivation, another very demanding crop. Tops and blades might go to feed the animals, but the soils could only be built back up with more manure diverted from the double-cycle. The eighty-acre Cove field behind the main house, which was cleared during these years, seems to have become a semipermanent cornfield. Mitchell and the slaves planted other patches around Pharsalia in corn, including several in the Front Field and on Ned's Hill. In the end, Massie still appears to have come up short. The declining slaughter weights of Pharsalia's hogs might also indicate a lack of food, pressuring him to slaughter younger animals. Tobacco fields had to be fed with soil nutrients, and, indirectly, so did tobacco hands. From both directions, plant nutrients were still being diverted from establishing a cycle of healthy, mature livestock grazing on hay cut from nitrogen-enriching clover hayfields.

Despite these problems, Massie also tried to complete the other half of the double-cycle, ordering Mitchell and the field hands to establish complex, grain-based crop rotations with leguminous grasses. It is difficult to discern precise crop rotations from the surviving records of the early years of Pharsalia's existence. Within the main fields, multiple small crop fields, patches of forest, and old fields existed side by side. Massie often recorded several crops being planted on separate clearings within a single field during a given year. The planter would not begin recording crop rotation schemes on a field-by-field basis until the 1840s.[54] Yet Massie's Farm Accounts do suggest that he began experimenting with the new rotation schemes being advocated by southern agricultural conservationists as early as the mid-1820s. For all his desire to turn a quick profit, Massie gradually eliminated tobacco, that great enemy of the double-cycle, from the plant community at Pharsalia. After initially focusing his new plantation's productive energies on tobacco (his slaves planted nearly 150,000

hills a year in the late 1810s), Massie started separating the tobacco from
the grain fields. By the mid-1820s, tobacco had been banished from the
main fields at Pharsalia and was soon excluded from the lots as well. It
still played a role in Massie's finances, but the slaves now grew it exclusively on the newly cleared fringes of the plantation. After 1823, the only
portions of the main fields planted in tobacco were the new grounds on
top of Ned's Hill and on the Priest's foothills in Rambler's Field.

Massie still sent his hands to plant tobacco in the Hog and Barn Lots
until 1826, but he was clearly uncomfortable with using Pharsalia's fertility this way. He chose instead to try to end the plantation's ties to tobacco
entirely. In 1828 Pharsalia's slaves only harvested two thousand "sticks"
(approximately four thousand pounds—the production of five adult field
hands), and by 1830 tobacco was gone from the plantation. In the late
1820s, the efforts of Pharsalia's slaves and the productive potential of
its agricultural environment focused instead on wheat and corn. At the
same time, the planter experimented with alternate crops like rye, oats,
and hemp.

The soils of Pharsalia's main crop fields were thus freed from the nutrient demands of tobacco. This allowed Massie to begin planning more
complex and permanent crop rotations using wheat and particularly
clover. Mitchell and the field hands conducted the first experiments with
leguminous grasses on the Hog and Spring Lots around the main house,
as well as the small meadow. By the mid-1820s, the young planter began
directing them to sow clover on the main fields. For example, after 1824
he seems to have abandoned the three-field system earlier established on
the Front Field. Slaves planted tobacco there in 1819 and 1822, but never
thereafter. Clover made its first appearance on the Front Field in 1825
and was planted again in 1828 and 1829.

Massie also tried to restore the soils of the field depleted by the three-
shift system he and his father had employed. Every year between 1826
and 1829, large stretches of the Front Field lay fallow as the nutrient
and humus content of the top layers of the soil slowly built up. Volunteer patches of clover from seed sown back in 1825 may have aided the
process. The field hands also tried to build up the soil on the Front Field
through generous applications of commercial fertilizer in 1824, 1826, and
1828. By the end of the decade, the fully cleared Front Field appears to

have been operating under a four-, or perhaps even a five-shift system. Wheat alternated with rye, corn, clover, and fallow to sustain the soil's ability to support crop plants. Massie gradually developed similar strategies for the other main fields, particularly the Flat and the Tansey Fields. He also ordered Mitchell and the field hands to sow clover on new clearings in Rambler's Field after they had been farmed two or three years in tobacco. The crop rotations that John Taylor of Caroline and other reformers advocated were not complete at Pharsalia, but Massie and his laborers were working to shift the plantation's ecology in that direction throughout the 1820s.

As with the livestock-fodder-manure side of the double-cycle, several practical obstacles blocked the success of the new crop rotations. As Edmund Ruffin was discovering at Coggin's Point during these years, establishing new agroecosystems required a detailed understanding of the local soils and other aspects of the physical and biotic environment. Massie and his overseers ran into this problem on several occasions during the 1820s. They understood the microenvironments of Pharsalia enough to site tobacco plant beds and meadows near flood-prone streams, and tobacco fields on new grounds just cleared from hardwood forest. But they did not fully recognize the complexities of the land in that corner of the triangle. The newly cleared Cove gave them a great deal of trouble. The Cove's elevation was enough to make it noticeably colder on spring nights than the Front, Flat, and Tansey Fields below. This gave Massie problems in 1829, when a late frost killed an entire field of wheat his slaves had sown there. The Cove's soils also differed from those of the bench below. They were dark and fertile, but thin and easily eroded. Mitchell and the field hands engaged in a confused series of attempts to clear, restore, and plant the Cove's fields throughout the 1820s. They used part of the field for plant beds in 1820, then planted corn for fodder in other areas the next year, followed by a year in clover and oats to replace lost nutrients. Massie then appears to have planted small patches in corn until 1826, when the field hands applied manure and gypsum to the old fields and started a new plant bed. In 1828 and 1829, Massie tried to establish the double-cycle on the Cove, but the field hands had to clear old field undergrowth (a practice known as "shrubbing") during both years. The old clearings, new grounds, and manured patches were then planted in a complex mix of oats, rye, wheat, and more corn. Soil microenvironments in Pharsalia's main fields also confused the planter and his overseers throughout these years. In 1819, corn sown in apparently depleted and compacted soils had to be replanted, even after the ground had been plowed four additional times to loosen the soil structure and bring nutrients to the upper layers. Eight years later, Massie would report that a corn crop planted after tobacco germinated unevenly—"badly missing," as he put it—and also had to be replanted.

Massie's first efforts at manuring and crop rotations also failed to oust all the competing plants and animals from Pharsalia. During these years, a variety of pests repeatedly diverted the plantation's biotic productivity away from the crops. In 1825, tobacco worms hit and nearly destroyed a crop planted in the heavily manured Cow Lot. In the late 1820s, the Pharsalia field hands went to considerable effort to turn Ned's Hill from a tobacco field into a permanent cornfield. They manured the hillsides and planted them in clover in hopes of restoring the field's eroded and exhausted soils. By 1830, though, Massie grumpily calculated that he was losing twenty barrels of corn a year to the savage depredations of the squirrels who congregated along the Mill Road at the bottom of the hill.

A variety of weeds also invaded Pharsalia. His field hands had to contend with ivy and broomsedge when clearing old fields for incorporation into the new crop rotations. Briars also proved particularly troublesome, sneaking into fields all across the plantation and interfering with plowing and seed germination. The weed problems indicated the extent to which Massie began his career as a planter with an already denuded soil environment. His soils had already been exhausted and eroded by John Rose and by Massie's father, and his efforts to restore them to the point they could support clover and grain were confused and haphazard. Manure helped restore soil nutrients, but Pharsalia was not producing enough, and Massie was putting a fair amount into the lots. He was left scrambling to come up with enough fertilizer to make up the gap. Anything at hand that might have been rich in nutrients was used to build up the plantation's soils. Pharsalia's slaves scoured the farm for odds and ends like brimstone from the blacksmith's shop, hen manure from the coops, as well as an unidentified substance the planter called "new milk." When the Pharsalia slaves planted an expanded orchard behind the main house,

INDEPENDENCE AND BIRTH 101

Massie ordered Mitchell and the slaves to fill the tree holes with mud dredged from his father's millpond. By 1828, in an effort to restore the depleted soils of the Tansey Field, his slaves used manure from the barn, as well as hemp shives, as soil additives.

Their efforts proved insufficient, however, and Massie was forced to break Madison's rule of self-reliance by buying fertility. Most noticeably during these years, he supplemented Pharsalia's home manures with "plaster." Plaster (the popular name for powdered, processed gypsum) was a calcium sulfate that boosted soil sulfur content, reduced acidity, and added friability to the upper layers of the horizon. Favored by planters throughout the early national Chesapeake, plaster was not cheap. Farmers untrained in soil chemistry were largely guessing as to its most effective uses. Speaking to the Albemarle Agricultural Society, Madison had sounded a note of caution about gypsum, declaring that its impact on the soil had "yet to be explained" and that "it must be made the source of future manure," a means to establish the more dependable double-cycle, rather than a substitute for it. Massie's "plastering" was confused during these years. He first brought powdered gypsum to Pharsalia in 1824, but used it both to build up the Hog Lot and to restore exhausted soils on the Front Field and on the old fields at the base of Ned's Hill. He returned to it in 1826, this time sending the slaves to plaster plant beds in the Cove, a crop of rye in the Front Field, as well as the Hog Lot and the orchard in front of the mansion. The next year he tried plastering a second-year's ground of tobacco, before using it on a hemp seed lot, a clover fallow, and an old field corn ground the next year. Apparently frustrated, by the end of the decade he had reduced his plastering to eroded stretches of Rambler's Field and the lower edges of the Front Field.[55]

Plaster did little to overcome the damage done by soil erosion. Scrambling to scratch up compacted old field clays to the point that they would take seed, Massie sent Mitchell and the slaves to plow fields with a sharp-edged plow, or "coulter." He also ordered them to "fallow," or plow over without planting, several tracts on the plantation—particularly the easily eroded spots on Ned's Hill and Rambler's Field, as well as the old fields on the Front and Tansey Fields. Their efforts still left Massie struggling to establish stable crop rotations. By 1828, the problems on the Tansey Field had grown so severe that Massie sent Mitchell and the slaves to spread manure and those hemp shives on the galled spots, fallow other patches, and plant clover wherever it would hold. The next year they plastered much of the field. The results were still disappointing. In 1831, as he confronted a miserable yield of five barrels of corn to an acre in a patch planted in the Tansey Field, Massie had grudgingly to admit that it was still "a good crop for the ground."[56]

For all the wonderful benefits its advocates promised, the double-cycle proved difficult for Massie and his overseers and slaves to establish during the first fifteen years of the plantation's life. Years of forest clearing and planting before the founding of Pharsalia had left its soil environments depleted. The ambition of Massie and his young family to be members of the consumer gentry staked another claim to a small supply of nutrients. In the end, the human management that shaped Pharsalia's agricultural environment between 1815 and 1830 wound up being a haphazard compromise. Rather than trying to perfect the double-cycle, Massie first turned his plantation's agricultural environment into an awkward, three-track system. He directed a large portion of Pharsalia's resources—its human energy, biotic productivity, recycled nutrients in manures, and financial assets used to buy fertilizer and grass seed—toward maintaining rich soils in the lots near the center of the plantation. These small fields were then periodically planted in cash crops to keep the Massie family financially afloat. At the same time, he also sent his growing slave force to keep hacking away at the forested edges of the plantation, opening up new grounds for tobacco. These two tactics left Massie fighting to make up for the erosion and exhaustion that afflicted the main fields.[57] The vision of ecological independence promised by the southern reformers remained strong in his mind, though. He hoped and tried to abandon this division of effort and means in favor of an intensive double-cycle during the 1820s. He ordered his slaves to grab every spare resource remaining and plow it back into the main fields. He then cautiously tried to establish crop rotations on them in the recommended hard grains and clover. With so little to commit to the effort, though, the results were not promising. But by the end of the 1820s Massie was desperate enough to abandon the region's traditional extensive farming entirely. By his midthirties, William Massie was a struggling, but committed, agricultural conservationist.

*Pharsalia's Agroecosystem in 1830*

Pharsalia's fifteenth year is a good point to stop and consider the ecological state of the plantation. The information in William Massie's Farm Accounts offers a picture of the landscape at the foot of the Priest nearly a century after Peter Jefferson's survey of the Rose tract. Yet we should be cautious about taking on the planter's perspective. Massie's accounts of farming at Pharsalia were the work of an ambitious, progressive farmer. From the windows of his study, he could look out over the barn lot, the orchard and old meadow, and the main fields of the plantation—but his view of the land would always be shaped as much by what he envisioned as by what he actually saw. To get a clearer image of Pharsalia in 1830, we should consider the landscape from someone else's point of view. The men and women who worked the land at Pharsalia would have experienced the historical changes in the plantation's agroecosystems in a more concrete way than the most "practical" of planters. What would the Pharsalia slaves have seen as they went about the routines of farm labor in 1830? What did the fields of Pharsalia look like from the perspective of a man like Tandy, a field hand in his mid- to late forties?

Beyond a few entries in William Massie's slave lists, no information survives about Tandy. Massie almost never mentioned slaves in his Farm Accounts, recording names, ages, and a few notes in a separate slave register. What we do know suggests that he would have been in a unique position to observe the ways in which the land at the foot of the Blue Ridge had changed over the years. Most of Pharsalia's slave community were relatively recent arrivals at the foot of the Blue Ridge. Major Massie gave him seventeen people to work his new farm, including veteran field hands Chester and Jessee, younger men like Peter and Martin, as well as two families—community matriarch Milly and her four children, and Peter's sister Rachel and her four. The older members of this group had probably come from the Shenandoah Valley with the Major, and Chester and Jessee may have worked on his Tidewater plantations during the Revolution. Massie's father-in-law gave him another eleven people—mostly younger men and women such as thirty-three-year-old Robin, twenty-two-year-old Bill and teenagers Sukey and Sam, as well as Sally and her four young children—all from the Steptoe plantations in Bedford County. Tandy, on the other hand, had probably been born on the estate of the elder Nathaniel Hill at the western end of the triangle sometime in the early 1780s. In 1824, Hill's executors sold the now middle-aged slave to neighboring planter William Massie. Tandy then went to work at Pharsalia, where he remained a field hand until his death in the 1840s. The rest of Massie's slaves had come from the Shenandoah Valley with Major Massie or even more recently from the Steptoe family plantations in Bedford County. Tandy had grown up watching the triangle's forests being transformed into plantations and farms, probably doing a good deal of the work himself. While the property of Nathaniel Hill, he had farmed the land in the extensive manner customary to the southern Piedmont, clearing the oak forest for new grounds, planting rows of tobacco and corn until the soil was eroded and exhausted, then abandoning the fields to old growth scrub and wandering cattle and swine. Being sold to a high farmer like William Massie would have meant major changes in his life. Behind all the theoretical schemes for restoring and conserving soils, intensification meant hard work in the forests and fields building a new agricultural ecology. If we look through William Massie's 1830 Farm Accounts for a year in the working life of Tandy, we can get an idea of what southern soil conservation meant along the streambanks, between the crop rows, and down in the very dirt of Pharsalia.

As a young man on Nathaniel Hill's farm, Tandy would have spent the dead of winter out in the woods just past the worm fences. January and early February were the time to clear new grounds for tobacco, when the dormant oak and pine trees were dry. He and his fellow field hands would have gone into the forest with axes, ropes, and draft animals, cut down a few acres of timber, tied the logs to the horses, and dragged them through the snow and mud to make a few bonfires—around which they would huddle to fight off the cold. Tandy had continued this winter routine when he went to Pharsalia. Back in 1828, he and the other field hands had been out in the white oaks on the slopes of Rambler's Field making a new tobacco field. In 1830, though, different orders came down from overseer Bob Mitchell. Rather than clear more land, all the available hands went to the Barn Lot and began loading cow and pig manure onto carts. Leading the horses across muddy plantation roads, Tandy and the others took the carts out past Rambler's to the stream that ran along the eastern edge of the plantation. They spread the dung out along the cleared stream bottom and dug it in with small plows. It would have been cold, wet, filthy, and noxious work, an unpleasant change from the old routine of chopping and burning trees. It would also have been a change from the old manner of dealing with Piedmont stream bottoms. The creeks flowing down from the Ridge had always been too prone to spring floods to plant in tobacco, so they were mostly left in timber. They would have changed slowly, as topsoil from surrounding fields washed down into them, enlarging swamps in which slash pine slowly replaced oak and hickory. Agricultural reformers like William Massie, though, expected slaves like Tandy to clear the timber and drain the waterlogged soils. Manure and plaster then went into the ground, plowed by slaves through the muck, before they planted the ground in clover or native grasses. As the weather warmed slightly in February, this new work managing the stream bottoms would have intensified. A dozen Pharsalia hands, perhaps including Tandy, built a large dam on the Spring Run up in Rambler's Field. Massie was trying to grow hemp, and he needed large ponds during the dry autumn months to rot the crop. The new pond in the midst of Rambler's Field added to a pastoral vista at Pharsalia but would have evoked mixed emotions among the men who dammed it. Dirt was still washing down into the Spring Run from the slopes from the Cove and the newer clearings in Rambler's. The new pond would have quickly begun to silt up, just like the millpond on the DePriest Run near the main house. As early as 1826, the field hands had to spend some of the cold winter months dredging that pond out to maintain water flows. They would have expected to have to do the same to the new rotting pond in coming years.

As the weather warmed up in March and April, Tandy and the field hands went to work on other denuded environments that their owner refused to let alone. Being owned by a conservation-minded farmer meant that Tandy had to build new ecologies on abandoned old fields in a laborious attempt to redeem them. In early March, the field hands were ordered up Ned's Hill above the main house and the slave cabins with orders to plow it up. The effort must have seemed a waste to a man with Tandy's experience. He had come to Pharsalia the last year tobacco had been planted on the hill. It seems to have been an unrewarded effort.

The front stretch of the field had already been washed by the mountain rains down into Mill Dam Creek and Muddy Branch, and the ground was taken out of tobacco after only one season. The slaves planted wheat the next year, but the results were also disappointing. Massie then ordered a couple of small patches planted in his least demanding crops, rye and oats, but turned most of Ned's Hill over to clover. After cutting clover hay on Ned's Hill in 1826 and 1827, Tandy and the other field hands were apparently ordered to leave it to volunteer clover and native grasses for a couple of years. Massie expected these short seasons of clover and grass fallow to redeem soils. Tandy's reward for having plowed up the hill was to plant a crop of corn and look forward to a hard summer of weeding. During April, Tandy would have gotten more evidence of his owner's unwillingness to seek out the easily obtained plant nutrients under the remaining hardwood forest on the plantation. After two years in tobacco, the 1828 clearing in Rambler's Field was ready to be shifted to wheat, rye, and oats. Instead, Tandy was sent to haul more barnyard manure out to plow into the depleted soils, in preparation for sowing hemp, the new cash crop.

The agricultural rewards for all this work would have been mixed. Seemingly, there was not enough clover and manure to make up the gap between fresh forest soils and the ones Massie hoped to ameliorate. Judging from Massie's notes, Tandy spent most of May and June hoeing the rows of corn and hemp, trying to fight off the weeds that competed so well on depleted soils. In early June, Tandy might well have looked up from the piles of weeds he was digging out of the rocky clay in the Ned's Hill cornfield and surveyed the plantation below. There was plenty of evidence of Pharsalia's denuded environment. The field just below Ned's was still abandoned to ivy and briars. The lower stretches of the Flat and Tansey Fields were still gall'd, or covered with patchy crops of wheat and oats. Scattered around the plantation were several small patches of hemp and wheat Tandy and his fellow slaves had planted, searching for spots still fertile enough to support a crop.

The manure and clover Tandy's owner seemed so obsessed with were starting to pile up at the center of the plantation. To the east, cattle congregated on the Barn and Hog Lots, and some slaves were collecting and piling up the manure once again. Another gang of slaves would have been out harvesting clover hay on the old and new meadows. To Tandy, this success meant more hard work creating new ecological cycles. After the hay and winter wheat harvests in high summer, he went back to work reclaiming abandoned lands in the stifling August heat. There was plenty of work to do—he might also have been sent once more to manure and plow up the meadows. He might have been one of the men sent with sickles and axes to shrub up the undergrowth in the orchard, preparing it to be plowed up and sown in grass. Most likely, though, he would have gone with the plow teams to fallow the "briar land," that stretch of eroded old field at the foot of Ned's Hill. Tandy must have rolled his eyes at this—the land had been abandoned since William Massie had gotten it from his father, and it still only grew useless ground cover more than a decade later. Tandy and the other field hands could already predict what this meant— more manuring in the dead of winter, and more sweaty, hopeless weeding in the summer months.

At one level, Tandy might have appreciated the goal of all this labor. Nathaniel Hill's estate had been broken up after his death, and that included the slave community who had lived and worked there. It is uncertain who might have remained on the old Hill estate, but no wife or children came with the middle-aged Tandy to Pharsalia. For slaves, extensive farming meant migration and the loss of friends and family. William Massie seemed determined to stay put and put more people to work while his neighbors were heading west—or selling slaves over the mountains to pay off their debts. But Tandy would hardly have been secure in his new home. He and his fellows probably had little confidence in the new course their owner was taking. On the soils they were working so hard to sustain, the stands of corn and wheat would have looked patchy and weed choked. At the same time, their owner seemed to have as little idea as they did what to do with the new crop they were growing, hemp. After planting it all over Pharsalia, by November they were having to throw out frost-damaged hemp they had left out too long to rot. The arguments between owner and overseer, and foul tempers all around, would have reinforced in Tandy's mind what a year of work had already told him—Pharsalia and its people were heading into uncharted territory, abandoning the experience of generations for William Massie's odd schemes. Tandy and his fellow slaves would provide the crucial means needed to build the ecological relationships of the double-cycle—aching muscles and sweat. He lived and worked at Pharsalia until his death in the 1840s, but back in 1830 there were no guarantees the plantation would remain his home. Turning Pharsalia back into an extensive southern farm, and sending Tandy back to the forests every winter, would continue to tempt William Massie. The passing years were not bringing a stable maturity to the plantation.

# Pharsalia's Ecological Crisis, 1828–1848

During the 1830s and 1840s, the problems practical planters encountered when building the double-cycle in the south Atlantic nearly overwhelmed Pharsalia plantation. William Massie had hoped that the agricultural system pushed by the leading conservationists of the antebellum South would make his plantation ecologically, and therefore financially, independent. But the shortcomings of high farming's focus on managing soil fertility became clear as Massie and his slaves struggled with the land at the foot of the Blue Ridge. Importing techniques and crops into Virginia's physical environment and agricultural tradition proved difficult. Massie's attempt to replace tobacco with hemp ran aground on this rock—his inability to cultivate and market hemp successfully left him once again grudgingly dependent on tobacco. Worse, the simplified ecology of the double-cycle outlined on paper did not take into account the complexity of real-world environments. Pharsalia's fields were besieged by a variety of pests, weeds, and plant pathogens that competed all too successfully for the plantation's share of biotic productivity. Faced with declining yields, Massie clung tenaciously to the southern reformer's vision of ecological and personal independence, but Pharsalia was no closer to becoming the plantation he hoped in the late 1840s than it had been in 1815.

## Markets and Ecology at Pharsalia

Like many other plantations, Pharsalia struggled in the antebellum agricultural marketplace. Tobacco prices, already low in the years after the

American Revolution, collapsed even further during the early 1820s. With the exception of a brief rise during the mid-1830s, the market value of Virginia's traditional staple stayed low for nearly thirty years. The state's grain crops fared no better—the high prices of the Napoleonic Wars remained a distant memory.[1] Thousands of the state's farmers went bankrupt, and many others left for the western frontier. As he matured, William Massie proved to be a competent planter and a frugal householder. Yet his calling seemed to provide him with little pleasure. As his dreams of independence and mastery evaporated, he became a pessimistic and often bitter man. During the years he was trying to grow hemp, his home and family were thrown into confusion when his first wife, Sarah, died. In quick succession, he married Martha Wyatt, and then Sarah Clarke, both of whom passed away prematurely. He married Maria Effinger in 1834, giving him a stable home and several children. At the same time, though, his father's death and will brought long-simmering tensions with his eldest brother, Doctor Thomas, to a boil. After clashing over the settlement of the estate, the two brothers cut off ties for most of the 1840s, despite living only a few miles apart. William tried briefly to pursue the political career so many Virginia gentlemen aspired to, but that went badly as well. Elected to a single term in the House of Delegates in 1839, he found his arch-Whig sentiments unsuited to the rough-and-tumble of Jacksonian politics. Worse, campaigning and his duties in Richmond cost money he did not have and pulled him away from his struggling plantation. He quickly gave up public life and returned to Pharsalia, trying once more to gain control of his farm. But running his home plantation drove him deeper and deeper into the red—his liabilities had mushroomed to nearly twenty thousand dollars by 1840. Part of this came from assuming his father's debts when he inherited a large portion of his estate in 1834. Major Massie's financial and agricultural legacy was a difficult one, but with a growing number of children to provide inheritances for, Massie felt unable to refuse it.[2] While he was not yet in serious danger of bankruptcy, he desperately wanted to avoid the looming threat of having to sell off large chunks of farmland or slaves to balance his books—and then have to support his household with a reduced income. As the years passed, he wondered if his own career was a failure, or if Pharsalia would survive. "Ruin, Ruin, Ruin," he concluded of his prospects in 1842.[3]

On the surface, Massie's problems during these decades were financial rather than ecological. The planter saw his troubles in terms of his debts and calculated them each year with a scrupulous fixation. Those debts seemed to depend on the fluctuating market prices for tobacco and wheat. After stabilizing his financial obligations after his father's death in 1834, Massie fell deeper into the hands of his various creditors during the agricultural depression that followed the Panic of 1837. During the hard times of the following decade, the fear of debt and of losing his estate lurked behind every one of his letters and his Farm Accounts. On the surface, his cure for his growing liabilities was also financial. "Economy and close cutting" was the solution, he told himself in 1840.[4] Slowly rising crop prices reinforced his penny-pinching after 1843, and he achieved some success in reducing his debts. A cursory glance at the planter's papers suggests that sustainability and independence could be had simply by balancing expenditures and income in the owner's meticulous ledgers.

Yet in other, more profound ways, Massie's financial troubles simply reflected Pharsalia plantation's struggling agroecosystem. Tight crop markets were reinforced by the plantation's inability to generate competitive yields or support a switch to more profitable crops. Pharsalia's ecological instability expressed itself forcefully and visibly in its owner's financial struggles. And by digging into Massie's agricultural papers, we see Pharsalia's more deeply rooted environmental problems emerge as well. In the plantation's youth, William Massie had hoped to build a sustainable soil environment while still farming for profit. As Pharsalia matured, he discovered that he had failed to create the ideal ecological autonomy that promised him both sustainability and profit.

In many ways, the ecological crisis that beset Pharsalia during the 1830s and 1840s was a continuation of the plantation's older problems. The Massie family needed a large income from their main plantation in order to pay for their status among the Old Dominion gentry. But the depleted soil environment made it difficult to build up topsoil and plant nutrients while still sending crops to market. The temptation of extensive cultivation—and tobacco—continued during these years. To make up the gap between productivity and the marketplace, Massie tried to keep practicing traditional agriculture. Massie and Reuben Cash, his overseer during most of the 1830s, searched the plantation for soils that matched the richness of new grounds cleared and burnt in the customary manner. Each winter, Pharsalia's slaves continued to chop away at the margins of the plantation, clearing hardwood and even some younger pine forests to plant tobacco and corn. But the plantation's limited supply of fertile land drove Massie back to the lots around the main house. By the early 1840s, he was using the Barn and Hog Lots to grow tobacco, and even plowing under his meadows for it.

If the crop rotations, pastures, and manuring Massie maintained during these years had actually built up Pharsalia's soils, he should not have had to keep scrambling for quick fixes. Pharsalia's struggles were as much the fault of the agricultural program of the early southern soil conservationists as of Massie's own lack of discipline. As practical farmers had begun to discover after the War of 1812, there were several holes in the theoretical system of men like John Taylor of Caroline and James Madison. The most pressing issue was the way the double-cycle reduced the complex problem of sustainable ecological relationships to simple recycling of "fertility." Two of the old problems with the system of independent high farming grew severe as Pharsalia aged. First, as Edmund Ruffin had discovered at Coggin's Point, transplanting the various parts of the double-cycle from their native habitat into the South was no simple matter. The problem went a little deeper than Ruffin, with his fixation on local soil chemistry, was willing to admit. To build independent and sustainable agroecosystems, farmers had to manage a multitude of interactions between farming methods, animals, plants, and the physical environment. Even though the old tobacco-corn system could not maintain long-term soil quality, its long history gave it a stability that the double-cycle actually abandoned. Creating the double-cycle at a place like Pharsalia meant building entirely new ecological relationships, often between new crops and a now unfamiliar physical environment. Planters had to develop new skills and experience and hand that on to their workers—all the while seeking out new markets. The process was full of an uncertainty and risk that the prophets of high farming tended to brush aside. On the farm, it was all very unstable—a fact that became clear during William Massie's grand experiment with hemp farming. Hemp was attractive because it seemed to offer him a way out of the trap of wheat's low return and tobacco's unsustainability. Hemp prices were high in the late 1820s, and the farm periodicals suggested it could be integrated into successful crop rotations. In practice, though, the problems of adapting this new plant to Pharsalia's ecology, and to the experience and skills of the planter and his laborers, proved overwhelming. For these reasons, Massie was unable to escape from tobacco.

Conservation-minded reformers also promised planters that they would gain perfect control of their plantation's soils, masterfully guiding fertility through the simple steps of the double-cycle. None gave serious consideration to the possibility that other occupants of the environment might break into their system and compete with their crop plants. Yet, in practice, an agricultural ecosystem was only protected by flimsy worm fences and hoes in the hands of overworked and unwilling slaves. As he struggled with weeds, wheat rust, and other invaders during the 1830s and 1840s, William Massie found that the double-cycle could not be isolated from its surrounding environment. Pests swept past Pharsalia's fences and into its fields, diverting soil nutrients, water, and light away from crop plants. In many cases, they were even better adapted to the local environment— the eroded, depleted soils, the regular, heavy rainfall, and the moderate winters—than the plants Massie wanted to incorporate into the double-cycle. He was reluctant to concede defeat in his fight to master Pharsalia's ecology and tried to fight the invaders off with the resources he had at hand. Pharsalia, however, would never mature into the independent plantation he wanted.

## Tobacco to Hemp and Back Again

William Massie struggled on as a reluctant but compulsive tobacco planter during these years. He was hardly alone with his addiction—the traditional staple continued to sound a siren call to the state's farmers. Tobacco prices rose and fell with the crop market but remained somewhat profitable. Assured markets and secure credit comforted many tobacco farmers who might have been tempted to follow John Taylor of Caroline's advice and abandon the crop. And tobacco offered planters security in a more important way than financial stability. The long history of tobacco in eastern Virginia—and that of its partner in the state's customary farming, corn—gave farmers an ecological stability that could not easily be replaced.

The varieties of tobacco and corn grown at plantations like Pharsalia were well adapted to the climate and physical environment of the south Atlantic. Native peoples had been growing both crops on the soils of the Piedmont and Tidewater for centuries. White farmers continued this ancient coadaptation of plant and environment, occasionally using new varieties and improving them within the Chesapeake region.[5] For all the problems they caused, by the early nineteenth century Virginia's staple crops had been adapted to the climate, soils, and pests south of the Potomac— something that could not be said for many of the crops and livestock that made up the double-cycle. Just as importantly, through long experience growing tobacco and corn, the state's farmers had coadapted with crops and environment as well. An enormous body of knowledge was shared between neighbors and handed down from father to son—a keen sense of the best soil conditions; the proper timing of planting, hoeing, topping, and harvesting; and a confidence in knowing when aberrations in the weather and other factors justified deviating from custom. A tobacco farmer had a long familiarity with the local pests that targeted his crops, had selected seed varieties for resistance to them, and knew what more immediate measures might be effective in fighting them off. He also understood the complexities of processing and marketing the sot weed.[6] In his own neighborhood, he could draw on expertise of overseers and slaves who possessed a similar knowledge of the crop, passed on across generations. All in all, tobacco's history in eastern Virginia had built up a reservoir of environmental and human adaptation whose value to sustainable cultivation should not have been dismissed quite as quickly as many high farming advocates did. Replacing such ecological relationships created by the coadaptation of long experience with ones planned on paper created all sorts of difficulties.

Tobacco could not, however, be adapted so easily to the gentry's desire for geographic stability and ecological autonomy. The traditional mode of its cultivation exhausted and eroded southern soils, forcing planters into constant migration. Worse, the double-cycle had been developed without tobacco, and farmers could find no place for it in the midst of cereal grain crop rotations and clover fields. Its hold on the minds and fields of the state's cultivators caused as many problems as it solved. For all their efforts as grain farmers and millers, the Massies continued to plant tobacco during their first three decades on the upper Tye River. Tobacco cultivation in either crop progressions or a three-field system had depleted the soils of several parts of what would become Pharsalia—especially the land below Ned's Hill and large parts of the Tansey Field. Yet the Massie family's dream of stable plantations kept them from abandoning the eroded, exhausted, weed-choked fields and heading west. For William Massie and other planters who tried to reform their farming, the double-cycle was a chance to escape from tobacco into independence and sustainability.

As he pursued the double-cycle, William Massie slowly reduced tobacco cultivation at Pharsalia during the 1820s. In particular, he maintained an impressive discipline in keeping tobacco out of the main crop fields. These were reserved instead for rotations of grain and clover. Low wheat prices challenged his determination to abandon tobacco. Prices hovered between seventy and ninety cents a bushel during much of the 1820s.[7] As a result, tobacco continued to suck up much of Pharsalia's productive potential as Massie tried to stay solvent. The field hands worked to create fertile soil environments for small crops of tobacco. They cleared new grounds where they could, and put clover, manure, and intensive cultivation into the lots around the main house—all while the main fields languished. At five cents a pound, though, tobacco was not doing much to justify this investment. The plantation's strained ecology and his own straitened finances kept encouraging Massie to escape.

Judging from his farm records, he made the leap between 1828 and 1830. In the former year, his slaves harvested a tiny tobacco crop of two thousand sticks (one stick = approximately two pounds). This was probably the work of no more than two or three adult field hands out of a slave force of more than fifty. By 1830, the Farm Accounts make no mention of tobacco. The timing of the abandonment of tobacco did not coincide just with the crop's low market price during the late 1820s. The last years of the 1820s were also the period in which the ecological problems of traditional southern farming struck Pharsalia most forcefully. Massie had committed the lots around the main house to tobacco for much of the early 1820s. After 1826 they seem to have been played out, though, and he set his slaves once again to clearing forest. In the winters of those years the Pharsalia slaves had begun to clear out pine timber and even shrubs and young trees to create new grounds. The property's supply of mature hardwood forests with rich soils was almost expended. In 1828, Massie noted for the first time the terrible problems with galling on the Tansey Field. In 1830, he mentioned the hard work needed to dredge eroded soils out of his millstream. Pharsalia was simply running out of the nutrients necessary to construct the rich soil environments tobacco required. Worse, Massie's ledgers had little to show for his commitment to the crop.

Massie looked for a way to end his plantation's continuing ecological and financial dependence on tobacco. Wheat's low prices during these years made it an unworkable substitute for tobacco—he needed another commercial crop. Yet simply replacing tobacco with another crop that could not be integrated into the double-cycle would continue to divide Pharsalia's productivity. By the late 1820s, Massie was convinced that hemp could both balance his account books and fit neatly into a sustainable double-cycle. Hemp had been a noteworthy part of Virginia's agricultural produce during the eighteenth century. Farmers in the Piedmont and the Shenandoah Valley had grown significant amounts for export to Great Britain. The need for American-made rope during the Revolution had spread hemp cultivation for a few years, but the turn of the century brought on a decline. The spread of hemp farming to the rich soils of the Kentucky Bluegrass, and later to Tennessee and Missouri, combined with competition from Russian and Baltic producers to discourage the crop in the Old Dominion. By the 1820s, however, concerns over the United States' growing dependence on foreign-made rope led to high-level attempts at a hemp revival. Congressional leaders and agricultural journals began agitating for American hemp farmers to abandon traditional dew-rotting techniques and adopt the Russian practice of water rotting. The higher quality produced by water rotting, they argued, would wean the navy and private shipyards off European hemp and secure a market for domestic producers. By 1828, William Massie had determined to jump on the small but noisy bandwagon for water-rotted hemp.[8]

Hemp seemed to offer ecological rewards as well. Conventional wisdom held that hemp did not deplete the soil to nearly the same extent as tobacco. This belief might well have caught the attention of a planter struggling with both soil exhaustion and declining prices. The main problem with tobacco, of course, had been the difficulties farmers encountered integrating it into a rotation scheme. Tobacco sucked up so many soil nutrients that subsequent crops—even leguminous grasses like clover—struggled to grow. In contrast, many hemp farmers claimed to have had good experiences raising hemp in rotation with other common farm crops—particularly corn. In the late 1820s, Massie decided to forsake tobacco in favor of hemp. For much of the previous decade he had been struggling to reconcile his financial and agricultural goals. Growing tobacco on the lots while haphazardly rotating grain crops in Pharsalia's main fields had not been a successful formula. Hemp seemed to offer him the chance to abandon this self-defeating division of his resources by giving him a commercial crop he could integrate into a regular crop rotation.

Massie quickly discovered that agricultural ecosystems were not built out of spare biotic parts that could easily substitute for one another. At the age of fifteen, Pharsalia had become much too intimately adapted to tobacco cultivation for a new species to integrate smoothly or quickly. A number of problems appeared almost immediately. Most important was the lack of understanding Pharsalia's human population had of hemp and the skills needed to grow it for a demanding marketplace. In particular, Massie and Reuben Cash were unfamiliar with the process of water rotting. Before useful fibers could be separated from the rest of the stalk of a hemp plant, the stem had to be left to rot for several days—a process also known as "retting." Traditionally, American hemp growers had relied on dew rotting. Under this method, the harvested hemp was left in the fields. Rainfall and dew provided the moist environment that encouraged the growth of the bacteria that sped the breakdown of the plant. By the early nineteenth century, however, it had become widely accepted that water rotting produced a higher quality fiber for rope. In this technique, the hemp was submerged for a shorter time in standing water to accomplish the same end.

By either method, however, rotting hemp was a tricky operation. Too little or too much decomposition quickly lowered the commercial quality of its fibers. A few of the older Pharsalia slaves like Chester or Jessee who had been with Major Massie during his time in Frederick County might have remembered hemp cultivation from the Shenandoah Valley.[9] Yet it seems most everyone at Pharsalia struggled with the rotting process. Massie initially overestimated the capacity of the three hemp "vats"— ponds dredged and drowned to rot the crop—his slaves had dug. Some of the crop went to waste for want of rotting space. In 1830, his slaves built another dam on the Spring Run at a cost of more than a hundred dollars, but it too proved insufficient. In 1832, the field hands had to try and rot hemp in another pond behind the small "shop dam" after the vats failed to contain the crop. Predicting the amount of water washing down the sides of the Priest into Pharsalia's streams proved to be the flip side of the coin. In 1829, low flows in those streams left the slaves unable to fill one of the three hemp vats. As late as 1834, the last year of large-scale hemp cultivation at Pharsalia, the crop once again overflowed the rotting vats.

The time needed to rot the harvested hemp was also a mystery to Massie and his workers. He trusted Cash less than himself when it came to hemp rotting. When business kept him absent from Pharsalia during these years, he demanded detailed letters accounting for the water-rotting work. Yet he too remained unsure about the process. Throughout these years, Massie peppered other planters, merchants, and rope-makers with letters asking for information on hemp processing. Even at the end he still seemed to be stumbling blindly. In 1834 he noted in his Farm Accounts that he would in future have to *double* the rotting time he had been using to get the crop processed properly.[10]

The intricacies of growing hemp also seem to have vexed Massie, Cash, and the slaves of Pharsalia.[11] Finding or building suitable soil environments was the object of continual experimentation during the seven years hemp was grown at Pharsalia. Massie knew from his reading that hemp demanded rich soils. As a result, he began hemp farming as he had tobacco cultivation, with intensive amelioration of the lots around the Pharsalia plantation house. He established a hemp seed lot near the house and also committed a large part of the Barn Lot to growing hemp. In both places he apparently left the ground fallow in 1827, then ordered his slaves to sow plaster of paris to maximize their fertility. He continued the intensive management of hemp fields in coming years. Many progressive soil-management practices and technologies made their first appearance at Pharsalia in support of the hemp crop. By 1831, Pharsalia's slaves were using large plows designed by Robert and Cyrus McCormick to cultivate the hemp fields more deeply. Slaves were also harrowing the soil, sowing hemp seed with a cultivator, and rolling the ground flat—all activities Massie had avoided before. But the wide variety and erratic application of his experiments suggest he was not making an educated adoption of progressive methods. These were stabs in the dark.

The reason for experimenting with hemp was not just to replace tobacco in the manured lots. Massie also wanted to grow the crop on the main fields at Pharsalia. He clearly hoped that hemp could become a commercial crop integrated into a stable crop rotation. Yet extending hemp cultivation beyond the intensively managed confines of the central lots was not a smooth process. Two questions immediately presented themselves: What constituted good soil for hemp, and how could it be rotated with other crops in the double-cycle? Massie was unable to find conclusive answers to either challenge. The years between 1828 and 1834 were a period of experimentation in cultivation techniques. They were also a period in which the planter searched throughout Pharsalia for suitable ground for a hemp-clover-wheat rotation. In addition to the lots, his slaves planted hemp on the main fields at Pharsalia, especially the Tansey and Flat Fields south and east of the main house. They also sowed new grounds on the plantation's fringes and made experimental plantings on hillsides like Ned's and in mountain hollows like the Cove. In particular, Massie and Cash struggled to find a balance between soil nutrients and drainage. Hemp's need for rich ground drew the planter's attention to the silty and organically rich swamps that bordered Pharsalia's main streams. He planted hemp in the first meadow near the main house, as well as along the Spring Run between the Flat and Tansey Fields. It took Massie several years to discover that many of these soils became too waterlogged from mountain rains to support hemp. In 1831, he noted in his Farm Accounts a need to limit hemp fields to parts of the stream bottoms where he was certain he could keep the growing plants reasonably dry. That same year the plantation slaves dug out a ditch in the hopes of draining the Spring Run swamp, but apparently to little avail. Finding ways to integrate hemp into his crop rotations was also the subject of extensive experimentation, and few easy answers emerged. During these years, he planted hemp on new grounds, second-year grounds, third-year grounds, old fields, and cleared hillsides. In various years and on various fields he ordered wheat and clover planted both before and after hemp. He planted hemp after demanding crops like tobacco and corn, then after a restorative one like clover. He tried following hemp with undemanding wheat, then tried clover as a restorative, then turned back to oats, a less demanding crop than wheat but hardly a legume. Yet from all this puttering, no workable system emerged.

Massie and Cash also struggled to time hemp harvests at Pharsalia. Naval rope–quality hemp had to be gathered at a precise point in its maturity. Like tobacco, immature or overripe hemp declined dramatically in price. In the case of tobacco, Pharsalia's managers and laborers were drawing on generations of experience growing the crop in Virginia. They also had several decades cultivating it in the specific environment of the level triangle at the foot of the Priest. When it came to hemp, however, they were flying blind. In 1828, the first year of large-scale hemp cultivation at Pharsalia, Massie reported that the crop had a "bad turn out," primarily due to "great waste before gathering." The next year he noted that most of Pharsalia's hemp crop had been stacked and housed too late in the season and much of it had been damaged. In 1830, two stacks of hemp were damaged by sitting too long in the fields. Late autumn rains destroyed more of the crop the next year, leading to another in a string of "poor turn out[s]."[12]

The troubles Massie faced integrating hemp into Pharsalia's agricultural ecosystem led to poor commercial returns. He tried to market the crop to the U.S. Navy and private shipyards through a variety of merchants in Richmond, Lynchburg, and Norfolk. Unable to obtain high prices, or on occasion even to sell the crop, these men reported back complaints about the quality of Massie's hemp. Pharsalia's hemp was often improperly cleaned or else too dark for U.S. Navy rope. These criticisms all reflected Massie's lack of experience growing and processing the crop. Frustrated by these failures and other reverses, he abandoned hemp after 1834. Despite the long-term ecological problems, he turned Pharsalia's fields back to tobacco and wheat in hopes of restoring his commercial income.[13]

Massie was desperate to make Pharsalia both ecologically stable and commercially profitable. Adapting new crops to the physical environment at the foot of the Priest was as hard as inserting them into the double-cycle, though. The failure of the hemp venture showed how difficult it would be to re-create the plantation's ecosystem while making it sustainable. By the late 1820s, the skills of Pharsalia's field hands had already been long adapted to a narrow range of crops, particularly tobacco and wheat. Pharsalia's soil environments were also adapted to the production of those crops. The plantation featured well-plowed and manured lots supplying the high nutrient and soil structure demands of tobacco. The main fields beyond were rotated to meet the lower nutrient demands of wheat. This arrangement divided Pharsalia's productive potential, of course. The nutrient demands of tobacco made the plantation's ecology and economics unstable and unsustainable. Yet many of Pharsalia's other species and its physical environment were tied to tobacco farming. In these circumstances, hemp was an alien invader that did not adapt to the existing community. It disrupted the plantation's farm routines while driving the Massie family deeper into debt. In the end, Pharsalia's owner was unable to spend the time needed to adapt hemp to the intricacies of its environment and its inhabitants, and vice versa.

Having failed trying to introduce hemp, Massie was for a time reluctant to experiment with other imported crop species with which he and his bondsmen were unfamiliar. No answers appeared from within Pharsalia's existing biotic community either. With considerable reluctance, he and his plantation turned back to their troubled relationship with tobacco. Tobacco cultivation, briefly abandoned in the late 1820s, began to expand. A brief rise in tobacco prices in the mid-1830s encouraged him to commit more of his plantation to the region's traditional crop. The host of problems that tobacco created for Pharsalia's ecology soon reemerged, though. As one farmer from next-door Amherst County explained in 1835, "The present rise in the price of tobacco will be of serious disadvantage to the small spirit of improvement that exists amongst us. All the manure on the farms, which should be applied to reclaiming the worn out parts of the land, so that the clover would take, is now applied to tobacco."[14]

By this point, of course, Massie understood that trying to integrate tobacco into the crop rotations of the double-cycle was impossible. His initial planting strategy also seemed to acknowledge that the sot weed did not repay the commitment of so many of Pharsalia's plant nutrients to the lots around the main house. Instead, he retreated to the oldest of to-bacco farming methods, clearing and burning forest timber to create new grounds with momentarily rich soils. In the winter of 1833–34, slaves were hacking away at the trees on the benches above the Tye River on the eastern margins of Pharsalia. These may well have been old fields already covered in small pine that his slaves were clearing. Pharsalia al-most certainly had run out of fresh stands of hardwood timber from which to create new tobacco grounds. Massie's Farm Accounts are fre-quently vague as to the location of tobacco fields during the 1830s. A couple of passages, though, give a clue that the axmen were going back to Pharsalia's old fields in a stuttering attempt to sustain tobacco cultivation on "long fallowed" fields. For most of the later 1820s and early 1830s, his records omitted mention of the fields along Muddy Branch below Ned's Hill. Given the problems with rampant ivy mentioned in 1823, it seems likely that the field had been abandoned for nearly a decade after years of heavy cultivation by the Major's slaves. Yet after several years of silence, tobacco fields along Muddy Branch appeared again during the mid- to late 1830s. Massie hopefully christened the ground Field Number Two in the new rotations he was drawing up in his study—but tobacco fields on eroded clays and scrub pine were not an auspicious start. A similar process seems to have been at work above Field Two on Ned's Hill. In 1838, Pharsalia's field hands went up to "break" some of the Ned's Hill tract for tobacco. Massie's slaves had been farming Ned's Hill almost since the establishment of Pharsalia plantation. It seems probable they were breaking the knob's old fields and scrub for tobacco, rather than clearing new ones from mature timber.

Clearing, burning, and planting partially regenerated old fields did not interfere with attempts to maintain the double-cycle elsewhere on the plantation. Yet it was hardly a sustainable proposition, either. A single decade was not nearly enough for a mature hardwood forest to emerge and build the soil beneath it. Even the somewhat higher crop prices of the 1830s hardly compensated for the poor crops that were grown from eroded, sterile soils. In 1839, when tobacco prices dipped back below five cents per pound, Massie dramatically reduced tobacco cultivation at Pharsalia. Slaves at Pharsalia planted only 28,000 hills that year, compared with the 150,000 to 200,000 they averaged in more ambitious years. Their efforts were reduced even further in 1840, when they only seeded 20,000 hills.[15]

Yet this restriction of tobacco seems more to have been an act of resignation than part of a positive response. On the main fields across the plantation, Massie ordered his new overseer, John Harvie, to plant rye on fallow ground. Rye's market prices could have done little to sustain his finances, though. Pharsalia's other main commercial crop, wheat, provided particularly poor yields in these years. By 1841, as his debts began once again to mount, Massie turned in desperation back to tobacco, sending his slaves out to plant 100,000 hills. This action revealed the continuing lack of biotic options at Pharsalia, since the tobacco market was doing little to recommend this move. Tobacco prices had fallen markedly as the depression of the early 1840s gathered force. The five and a half cents a pound tobacco had commanded in 1839 tumbled to an average of four and a half cents a year later.[16] Slaves would continue to plant tobacco at Pharsalia in subsequent years, even as prices plunged below three and a half cents. There was simply no other crop that could return a profit on Pharsalia's soils while still integrating with its biotic and human environment.

Massie seemed unable to respond creatively to the gathering agricultural depression. Yet his planting strategies did acknowledge that Pharsalia's not-quite-so-new grounds were failing to produce quality tobacco crops. He tried one last time to plant tobacco on depleted grounds on Ned's Hill and along Muddy Branch in 1841. The crops were haphazard at best—"dreadfully missing," as he put it. Faced with exhausted tobacco fields, he returned to fertilizing the lots near the main house. That same year, Pharsalia's slaves planted tobacco in the Jack Lot and in the newer meadow at the eastern edge of Pharsalia. Massie expanded this practice in 1842, committing the Hog Lot, Barn Lot, and Jack Lot to tobacco. Only one small patch of old tobacco ground in Field Number Two was strung along for another season.

Other problems also appeared. Tobacco prices continued to fall, and in 1843 a large crop on the Hog Lot was devastated by horn worms. Yet these frustrations paled in comparison with the difficulty of creating rich soil environments on the lots. Even in the face of unfriendly markets and hostile worms, Massie refused to abandon his most reliable commercial crop. Instead, he banished its cultivation from the sustainable rotation systems he hoped to establish at Pharsalia plantation. The field hands planted tobacco in two small tracts at the foot of Ned's Hill and in the newer meadow in 1844. Yet for the most part they had only planted to-bacco in several smaller mountain hollows. The darker soils of the Cove were too exhausted by this point to support tobacco. By 1843, the field was covered with bushes, weeds, and briars. The Pharsalia slaves could only coax a crop of rye and oats from it with a potent combination of plaster and ashes. But Massie also owned a number of smaller hollows elsewhere in the neighborhood. These included Ginseng Hollow in the ridges on the other side of the Tye River, and several nooks and crannies of his father's Montebello property just behind the Priest. Both locations were mentioned prominently as tobacco fields during the mid-1840s. Yet even these rich, dark soils could be exhausted by the demands of the sot weed.

By 1846 the field hands were back manuring and planting the Hog Lot and the Jack Lot in the crop Pharsalia could not seem to escape from. Even then, the yields and quality were disappointing, as Pharsalia still seemed to be short of soil nutrients. The 1846 crop was judged poorly on the Richmond market and brought below-market prices. Massie's Richmond agent commented, "I . . . do not know, why your strong lands don't pro-duce richer Tobacco & of *better texture*. . . . It ought to produce nearly as good quality as the *Virgin soil*." [17] Even the return to the lots did not reconcile the demands of the marketplace with Massie's hope for sustain-ability and independence. He had occupied the better part of two decades with convoluted and frustrating attempts to find a sustainable way to grow tobacco. Yet steadily declining commercial returns had been the main result. With tobacco still "being in bad taste" with the buying public in 1847, Massie threw up his hands and abandoned the crop entirely. [18]

Massie was trapped trying to tap into two different sources of eco-logical sustainability. The double-cycle promised to restore and sustain soil productivity but demanded that planters abandon tobacco. Tobacco, however, promised stable credit and a moderate income, rewarding the long coadaptation between the crop, the southern Piedmont's physical environment, and its agricultural population. Crop rotations and clover could not replace this stability. Without a crop that was "native" to Pharsalia's agroecosystem, Massie tried importing hemp to plug the commercial hole in the double-cycle. But the planter, his overseer, and his slaves could not adapt hemp quickly and easily, and Pharsalia remained a tobacco plantation. The old crop's familiar frustrations meant it was never a smooth relationship, though. Massie still tried to maintain the double-cycle alongside the tobacco fields while periodically trying to abandon the weed. But the confusion and division of resources during these years drove Pharsalia's productivity down.

## The Boundaries of an Agroecosystem

Abandoning traditional ecological adaptations was not the only way the double-cycle oversimplified the relationships between agriculture and the environment. To conserve soils and use them in the most efficient manner, a farmer must monopolize them. The farmer tries to drive other occupants of the ecosystem away and replace them with ecological relationships that direct biotic productivity toward crop plants and domesticated animals. The key to efficient, intensive agriculture, then, is boundary maintenance. For intensifying farmers, nothing can be allowed to get out of the agroecosystem—not wandering livestock, not eroding soils. Nor can anything be allowed to get in—wild herbivores and predators, weeds and other old field pioneers, plant and animal diseases—all must be kept out. Natural ecosystems never achieve this kind of efficient independence, though. Core networks of climate patterns, soil types, plants, herbivores, predators, and other species may have roughly common ranges and close ecological associations that define a geographic ecosystem. Yet these communities always coexist with others that inhabit niches that cross that common range.

Compared with the world outside the fences, agricultural ecosystems are very simple, and the double-cycle proposed by Virginia reformers particularly so. That basic set of relationships between soils, plants, and animals hardly occupied every ecological niche in the Piedmont. Other species—like the marauding squirrels who filched the Ned's Hill corn—

found space to survive and divert a share of a farm's productivity. In addition, a farm was an extremely small ecosystem—even a big plantation like Pharsalia. A multitude of plants and animals occupied the southern Piedmont, and William Massie and Pharsalia's field hands could not control the whole biome from behind the worm fences in the triangle. All sorts of flora and fauna that preferred red clay soils and a temperate climate laid perpetual siege to Pharsalia, looking for an opportunity to reclaim it. In the end, all Massie could do was send his overseers and slaves out to maintain the agroecological relationships he wanted to establish, preserve the boundaries of the plantation, and hope that with a little help his crops and livestock could outcompete the hordes of would-be invaders. Plenty of early national Piedmont plantations had their biotic productivity commandeered by soil erosion, weeds, pests, wandering livestock, and a host of other forces. If these losses went unchecked at Pharsalia, Massie realized, the agricultural ecosystem would produce few crops and bankrupt its owner. Judging from their usual silence on such matters, southern farm reformers assumed victory would come easily once the double-cycle had been established. But as Massie discovered during the 1830s and 1840s, the means he could muster were not enough to shore up Pharsalia's borders and conserve its soils.

The crisis in wheat cultivation best illustrates the inability of the double-cycle to seal off Pharsalia's ecosystem. Calculated in terms of grain harvested relative to grain sown, wheat yields at Pharsalia ranged between 8:1 and 12:1 during the first fifteen years of the plantation's existence. These yields were low by national standards. Yet they were typical of the long-cultivated red clays of the Piedmont. Following a break in the yield calculations recorded in 1834 and 1835, wheat harvests collapsed dramatically. Ruinous returns of 4.2:1 for 1836 and 3.75:1 for 1837 were followed by a brief rally in 1838 and 1839. The 1840 wheat crop, however, repaid barely two bushels harvested to one sown. Yields remained desperately low throughout the rest of the 1840s, barely inching back to six or seven bushels to one in the last two years of the decade. For a decade and a half, Pharsalia's main fields were unable to provide yields of one of the plantation's main crops worth the labor invested in cultivation, to say nothing of commercial returns. This predicament kept Massie hovering on the brink of having to sell off much of his landed estate and slave community throughout the decade. It was also the main reason he kept trying to force Pharsalia's ecosystem to support tobacco.

The cause of the collapse in wheat yields did not emerge from *within* the structure of the Pharsalia agroecosystem, as the long-term problems of tobacco had. Yields had been stable and acceptable throughout the 1820s and early 1830s. The establishment of the double-cycle on the plantation's main crop fields had been slow, to be certain. Yet the rotations of wheat and clover on grounds like the Front Field were working. While Massie might have hoped for better, there was nothing in Pharsalia's agricultural ecosystem that would have caused the collapse of the late 1830s. Instead, the crisis that hit during those years came from outside the plantation's borders. The main cause of tumbling grain yields was wheat stem rust. "Rust" was the common term for a variety of fungal diseases of the genus *Puccinia* that attack the leaves and stems of cereal grains.[19] Massie first mentioned one of his wheat fields having been attacked by rust in 1828; he then faced a small recurrence in 1832. In 1836, though, stem rust exploded across Pharsalia's grain fields, cutting wheat yields in half. For more than a decade following, Massie anxiously watched the wheat crop every spring. As summer approached, though, he reported with despair the sudden yellowing of the growing plants that signaled the reappearance of the fungus. "It really is distressing," he wrote to himself in 1841, "to see all ones labour & expense in preparing & making a crop waisted [*sic*] & all hopes totally annihilated. My wheat crop which was very promising indeed 10 days ago, is now of a filthy ochre colour from rust, & if not destroyed is nearly so. . . . The rye . . . must go by the board—as must the oats if this flood of desolation continues."[20]

Rust fungi infesting wheat plants reduce yields in a number of ways. Fungal colonies take up nutrients the plant would ordinarily use to produce grain. The colonies form pustules inside the plant that, when grown, burst through the skin. The holes they create inhibit the respiration and metabolism of the wheat plant. Weakening of the stems can also cause plants to fall over in wind and rainstorms. Particularly bad infestations of rust have devastated cereal grain crops throughout the history of human agriculture. Several types of wheat rust have been associated with grain cultivation in excavations of sites dating back to 1300 B.C. English colonists brought wheat rust spores to the New World with the first shipments of seed for hard grain cultivation. The various fungi soon established themselves as an ongoing threat to wheat crops throughout Britain's North American colonies. Rust proved particularly devastating in New England, crippling the region's grain production during the late eighteenth century.[21]

Like most pest populations, though, wheat rusts fluctuated widely in scope and severity in response to a variety of factors. While present in Virginia for most of the Revolutionary and early national periods, wheat rust seems to have been a minor problem. Southern grain farmers were much more concerned during this era with the Hessian fly (*Mayetiola destructor*), an insect that laid its eggs on wheat stems and whose larvae fed on the cells of the growing plants. The Old Dominion's early soil conservationists had little constructive to say on the issue of rust. John Taylor of Caroline took only enough time to blame rust problems on insufficient plowing—a less than perceptive analysis indicating little serious thought. During the late 1830s, however, rust made a dramatic return to the Piedmont, this time in the form of a yellowing blight that seemed much worse than the previous red rust.[22] It remained a problem throughout the 1840s, cutting wheat yields throughout the region and devastating the fields of Pharsalia plantation.[23]

This resurgence in the populations and effects of wheat rust fungi had a number of sources. All of them took advantage of Pharsalia's limited size and porous ecological borders. Of most significance, central Virginia was hit during these years by a series of warm, wet summers. Stem rust in particular is favored by warm weather (above 80°F). Its spores need free water, either from dew or recent rainfall, on wheat plant stems to germinate. During these years Massie began to note the connection between extended stretches of warm, rainy weather in June and July and the devastating explosion of wheat rust in his grain fields. "Rain is the cholera of this region," he opined; "it is our awful scourge." "Rain is without a doubt my greatest enemy on Earth," Pharsalia's owner concluded in 1846.[24]

Weather, of course, crosses the boundaries of farm ecosystems with no regard to the efforts of farmers to control it. Pharsalia was particularly vulnerable to rainfall, sitting as it did at the foot of the Priest and Little Priest. With the predominant wind coming from the west and west-southwest, warm, moist summer air from the Shenandoah Valley was pushed up over the Blue Ridge. The result was heavy afternoon rains that fell on the fields at the eastern foot of the mountains. Late summer rains in the 1840s repeatedly soaked and rotted unthreshed grain lying in Pharsalia's fields after harvest. Worse, rainfall in June and July left standing pools of water and soaked growing wheat stems, a perfect environment for stem rust spores to multiply.[25] Summer after summer during the 1830s and 1840s, showers blown up over the mountains behind the plantation swept across Massie's property lines and over his fences, drowning Pharsalia's grain fields. Massie looked with dread at the threatening summer skies behind the Little Priest, calling it the "stinking putrid Hell Hole the W S W."[26] In the face of his inability to keep summer rains and stem rust spores out of Pharsalia, Massie fell back on farmer's ancient fatalism, alternately cursing fate and placing himself in the hands of God. "A man dependent on weather is but a Poor Dog," he wrote, "indeed an existence in this World is a very poor Dogs privilege."[27] The only answer he could suggest to the stretch of inhospitable weather was abandoning wheat cultivation at Pharsalia entirely.

Other factors in promoting wheat rust epidemics operated on a smaller scale than long-term weather patterns. But they too crossed Pharsalia's poorly defended borders to blast the wheat growing in the main fields. Most visibly, spores of the various rust fungus species passed between neighboring wheat fields as the disease spread. Massie dreaded early summer rides around the neighborhood, suspecting he would see the first signs of rust on a neighbor's land and know that it would soon hit Pharsalia.[28] Just as importantly, Pharsalia's grain fields were so close to the borders of the plantation that rust spores could lurk right along the plantation's fences. Before wheat rusts can infect growing plants, they must go through earlier stages of spore development after overwintering. The most common host for these stages in the fungus's life cycle is the common barberry bush (numerous species of the genus *Berberis*). The barberry was imported into North America by European colonists who recognized its value as a hedge shrub and found other uses for its wood and leaves. Soon, however, Euro-American farmers recognized that rust attacks were particularly severe in areas of fields near barberry shrub fences. This connection was well enough understood in New England during the later eighteenth century to prompt the passing of several laws banning the planting of barberry bushes. As part of the widespread attempts by reforming planters to abandon shifting cultivation for the double-cycle, permanent crop fields were established with more stable fence lines that would have served as a hospitable environment for barberry bushes. While never specifically mentioned in William Massie's farm records, barberry might have become established along the edges of Pharsalia plantation. On the fence lines it would have been just clear of the plows and hoes wielded by the plantation's enslaved fieldworkers. It would also have been close enough to quickly spread *Puccinia* spores to the growing grain just a few yards away.[29]

At first, Massie treated the stem rust problem in a similar manner to his attempts to escape from tobacco cultivation. With wheat yields collapsing, he went looking for substitute crops to replace it. In the grain fields, at least, there were plants on the plantation like rye and oats that could fit smoothly into the double-cycle. Massie's custom during the 1830s had been to sow wheat on a clover fallow. But in 1840, overseer John Harvie planted rye on large fallows laid out the previous year in the Flat and Tansey Fields. By 1843 and 1844, Massie was experimenting extensively with oats, ordering them sown in the Cove, the Front Field, and Field Two below Ned's Hill. These crops turned out well, and yields, while rarely recorded, drew no complaint from the planter in his accounts. Yet they could not replace wheat in the commercial balances of Pharsalia plantation. Widely grown in America's rural areas, and with a limited consumer market elsewhere, rye and oats commanded low prices throughout the antebellum era. These typically ranged between fifty and eighty cents a bushel for rye and between twenty-five and forty cents for oats. These were both less than the ninety cents to one dollar and twenty cents wheat drew even during the depression of the 1840s. Experiments with these crops amounted to little in the end. More desperate attempts to secure Pharsalia's wheat fields against the rust were unsuccessful as well. Massie quickly turned back to tobacco to save his estate in the early 1840s.[30]

After the failure of rye and oats to replace wheat, the problems of boundary maintenance grew clearer. Traditional cultivation practices did not prevent plant competitors from invading crop fields. A variety of weeds overran the plantation's fences and established themselves inside

Pharsalia during these years. Massie's laments about weed infestations were pointed and frequent in the 1840s. In June 1841, he complained that "the weeds and crab grass are taking the Tobacco & corn." Sassafras bushes were infesting the wheat in 1845. The next year his "corn fields and tobacco ground grassy, & sodded." Cheatgrass (*Bromus tectorum*) established itself in the grain fields in the early 1840s, and infested the seed grain from year to year.[31]

Plants that farmers pejoratively term weeds are usually opportunistic. They have developed a low need for soil nutrients and a rapid and prolific rate of reproduction. These qualities help them successfully colonize recently disturbed or denuded areas. The soil disturbance that is the starting point of most agriculture provides weeds with an ideal habitat. In biological terms, of course, most crop plants are weeds themselves. Being useful to humanity, though, they are not plowed under, dug out, or poisoned like their less-appreciated competitors. Yet most agricultural clearings do not create a perfect boundary between cultivated ground and the surrounding mature forest. Old fields, roadsides, and small patches of cleared land around and outside the fences offer a disturbed microenvironment where weeds can flourish free from pesky plows and hoes. From the farmer's point of view, undesirable weeds lay a perpetual siege around crop fields. They take root and thrive just beyond the fences. From there they send their plentiful windblown seeds inside year after year to sprout in the midst of the crop plants and steal moisture, nutrients, and light from them. Farmers could set up boundaries around their farms, but the proximity of weed-infested habitats along the edges of the agroecosystem made the crops vulnerable to invasive competition. The survival and success of agricultural ecosystems depended, then, on the ability of farmers to defend their ecological borders against invaders from those edges.[32]

Briars and cockle, the bane of Piedmont farmers, were especially well-adapted weeds. The briar, also commonly known at greenbrier and catbrier, encompasses a variety of species of the genus *Smilax*. Many nineteenth-century farmers also used the term to refer to any weedy plant with thorns and a thick, woody stem. *Smilax* was a particularly hardy invader of grain fields. Active plants sent out shoots to form clusters of underground bulbs at a distance from the original plant. One of the bulbs in these clusters sprouted aboveground to photosynthesize and then continued the process of sending out bulb colonies. Making this plant particularly hardy when competing with crop plants were the other briar bulbs belowground. When the sprouting plant died (or was killed), the dormant bulbs in the underground cluster activated and sent up a new sprout, renewing the plant. Briars, once established in a field, were incredibly difficult to eradicate by traditional weeding methods because of this redundancy. In an infested field, briars took up soil nutrients and water, shaded sprouting plants, and interfered with their root systems underground.[33]

Briars colonized crop fields by being adapted to prosper from endless soil disturbance. In contrast, cockle (*Agrostemma githago*) used another survival strategy common to weeds—profuse reproduction. Cockle, a frail annual that sprouts two to three feet high before producing a beautiful pink and purple flower, also generates thousands of tiny black seeds. Taken up by the wind, these seeds can spread miles from the original plant before settling down to sprout. For nineteenth-century grain farmers, briars at least had identifiable and compact colonies that could be attacked and at least theoretically eradicated. No fence or hoe, however, could keep cockle out of the wheat fields once it had established itself in the disturbed patches of a regional ecosystem. Once in the fields, cockle plants competed somewhat successfully with the growing wheat, although never becoming as dominant as briars could if left unchecked. More troubling were the seeds, which are mildly toxic to humans and many species of livestock. Flour contaminated by ground-up cockle seeds inhibits yeast rising and gives a disagreeable taste. Consumed in sufficient quantities, it can even cause unpleasant, if rarely deadly, reactions. Both plants, as a result, represented a serious weedy threat to the cultivation of cereal grains in the Piedmont. Keeping them out of the fields was a continuous challenge.[34]

At Pharsalia, the long-term battle against weedy plant species took on two forms. First was the hand weeding with hoes that had been part of the seasonal labor of servants and slaves since the seventeenth century. Every summer, as tobacco and corn plants began to grow, field hands were sent out in gangs to hoe up the nameless assortment of weeds springing up in and between the hills and later rows of crops. Hand weeding was labor intensive and never entirely successful. It did give colonial Virginia's staple crops enough of a competitive advantage to mature profitably, though. The practice was still so ubiquitous by the early nineteenth century that it rarely merited a mention from Massie in his Farm Accounts, except when bad weather or other circumstances forced his overseers and slaves out of the regular routine.

One change was slowly emerging, though. Like other Chesapeake area slave owners, William Massie had grown concerned about the amount of labor needed for successful hand weeding. He periodically fretted about the high percentage of his slaves hacking away at the little sprouts in the crop fields while other vital tasks went undone. Tobacco and corn planters had begun abandoning hill cultivation of their crops for row planting during the late eighteenth century. This allowed them to facilitate weeding by horse- or ox-drawn plows and cultivators. While not as thorough as hand weeding, mechanical cultivating had the advantage of dramatically reducing the labor needed for weeding, and expanding the acreage a plantation's labor force could farm.[35] In 1842, Massie wrote to the Richmond-based *Southern Planter* that he had moved on to fighting the briars with an "August mowing, followed by an immediate deep plowing." His Farm Accounts mentioned other minor developments in weeding practices at Pharsalia—the introduction of new technology, where and when it was used, and the like. Yet weeds still became a major problem for the plantation. Massie concluded his letter to the *Planter*, saying of the briars, "nothing I have done has proved effectual."[36] The failure of an already considerable investment of labor and equipment designed to keep weeds out reveal declining agroecological stability on the plantation. Invaders from the plantation edges were able to overwhelm even more modern means of defense. As he lost control of his fields, Massie's fatalism grew. "O this World," he dashed into his notes as he saw the weeds spreading, "Where are its attractions & Great Providence what did you put us here for?"[37]

Developing permanent fields at a place like Pharsalia meant dealing with old fields. Abandoned fields provided wonderful environments for weeds. Their bare and typically exhausted soils supported little competition for hardy invaders. Clearing these old fields for new cultivation meant hacking away at various weeds and bushes. These disturbances spread their seeds throughout the newly exposed and loosened soil. Massie first referred to the process of clearing early successional old fields for permanent cultivation as "chopping bushes." He later moved on to the term "shrubbing" for the rest of Pharsalia's lifespan.[38] Slaves went out shrubbing the old fields in the Cove and the Front and Flat Fields during the early 1830s, then again during the early 1840s as weed problems came to a climax. Certainly there were advantages for crop growth in the development of old field succession. By the time clearing took place secondary successional species like cedars and perennial grasses had forced out many of the weeds. At that point, the accumulating biomass of the old field could be burned or plowed back into the soil. Yet the old fields below Ned's Hill, in the Cove and the Flat Field, and elsewhere on the plantation continued to be the kind of unmanaged edge habitat that nurtured weeds that could invade and disrupt the crop fields.

Hoeing, plowing, and shrubbing were not the only ways in which farmers tried to give crop plants a competitive advantage over invading weeds. Through long adaptation to agriculture, crop plants have grown to depend upon farmers to provide them with nutrient-rich and friable soils. When those things are lacking in an agroecosystem, the seeds of weed species better adapted to take root in difficult soils and take up scarce nutrients can outcompete the crop plants. During the early years of Pharsalia's existence, weed problems do not seem to have exceeded the capacity of spring and summer hoes and the occasional plow cultivation. Around 1830, this began to change. In that year, Massie first described part of his crop fields as "briar land."[39] The very next year, he mentioned heavy labor investment in weeding cockle from grain fields in the Cove for the first time. He repeated the complaint in 1833. The timing of this minor outburst of weed problems coincides suspiciously with the problems of erosion and galling that became serious enough to demand amelioration in 1828 and 1829. In particular, the fields mentioned in association with the briar and cockle problems included the Cove and Field Two below Ned's Hill. The Cove appears to have been seriously eroded, judging from the heavy and almost annual work Pharsalia's slaves were having to do to clean out the millrace on the streams that flowed out of it. Throughout these years, Massie also mentioned repeatedly having to send his slaves out shrubbing in the Cove to clear opportunistic bushes from the cornfields he hoped to plant. Field Two was largely an old field of ivy and exhausted soils rarely used for cultivation during this period. Both fields had been exhausted by the farming practices of Major Massie and his son's early years as a planter. Labor and biomass had been committed to the lots around the house while shifting cultivation was still practiced on the main fields. It seems probable that the depletion of the soil on the outlying fields during the 1820s opened the door to weed invasion.

This suspicion is reinforced by the second explosion of weed problems that occurred during the 1840s. By 1843, the Cove was choked with weeds and briars. By 1845, the briar problems had spread to Field Two, the Front Field, and various other spots around the plantation. "My soil . . . ," Massie wrote to the *Southern Planter*, "is more inclined to put forth brier bushes . . . than any other I have seen."[40] Cockle also reemerged as a serious problem in Field Two and the Cove. Again, the timing of this outbreak of weeds is noteworthy. It came in the depths of the depression of the early 1840s, and shortly after Massie had recommitted his farm to tobacco. In particular, the weeds exploded in Pharsalia's fields after the large-scale return to tobacco that commenced in 1841. While tobacco was generally not planted in the main crop fields between 1841 and 1843, much of Pharsalia's biotic assets were dedicated to the crop. The lots around the house were intensively fertilized with manure and clover to prepare them, while the main fields appear to have been slighted. The problems began in Field Two and Cove, which had long lagged behind the fields between the main house and the Tye River in nutrient levels and soil structure. With labor and biomass being diverted to growing tobacco, the marginal fields were left exposed. The commitment of Pharsalia's agricultural ecosystem to tobacco during these years was great enough that the rest of the double-cycle was also being jeopardized. By the middle of the decade the cockle and briars were making inroads into the other fields as well.

The attempts of Pharsalia's field hands to drive cockle and briars back to the borders of the plantation met with limited success. The various species of the genus *Smilax* thrived on the kind of disturbance that hand weeding and plow cultivation created. The efforts of the slaves probably helped the plants spread from the Cove and Field Two across the rest of the plantation. Massie responded by stepping up efforts to eradicate them. In 1843, he sent most of the field hands out on a special mission to pull briars up from the wheat crop in the Front Field. The next year, fearing an outbreak in his corn crop, Massie ordered Harvie to have the ground plowed thoroughly before planting. He then worried some more and sent his slaves to "list" the corn ground—a deep and heavy plowing with a double-moldboard, probably with some manner of subsoiler attached. The extra efforts seem only to have accelerated the growth and spread of the briars. In the middle of the summer, Massie surveyed them growing throughout the cornfield and gave up. He sent the field hands out to chop the growing corn plants for cattle fodder before even attempting to hand weed, commenting, "the Briars drive me to this."[41]

Alarm over the possible impact of the briars on his finances seems also to have pushed Massie toward an earlier and more profound concession to the weeds. By the early 1840s, he was apparently unwilling to put wheat plants, one of his key commercial crops, right up on Pharsalia's defense lines against the briars. All but one of the mentions of briar problems during these years came in connection with the plantation's main subsistence crop, corn. This suggests that the field hands planted only the less valuable crop near the growing colonies of *Smilax*. Certainly the corn crop's battles against the briars would have done little to make Massie and John Harvie hope for a positive outcome to the practice. The experience of watching the briars attack the wheat crop of 1843 in the Front Field, leading, along with wheat rust, to a terrible yield of only just over four to one, seems to have cemented the practice, however. For the next several years, the only recorded troubles created by the briars were with the corn crop.

The battle against cockle was equally frustrating. Unlike the briars, which sprouted a relatively small number of large, easily identifiable plants from underground shoots, *Agrostemma githago* spread its lavish production of seeds on the wind. The result was early spring wheat fields full of cockle sprouts that could only be removed by hand weeding. Judging from the Farm Accounts, the task overwhelmed even the abundant labor resources of a large slave plantation. The first mention of cockle problems in the Pharsalia wheat fields focused on this problem. In 1831, the slaves weeded the cockle sprouts from a single grain field, but "a tremendous job it [had] been."[42] The theme continued in Massie's accounts during the 1840s. His laments culminated in 1845, when weeding a small wheat field in the Cove "took two weeks with all but plowers and ox drivers, sometimes all hands."[43] Pulling field hands away from the plantation's other work to clean up a small portion of the wheat crop was an impossible commitment to sustain.[44] In subsequent years the practice of hand weeding was largely abandoned in the Pharsalia grain fields. Instead, Massie joined most other prosperous farmers in spending the extra money to purchase a number of cockle sieves.[45] These newly developed contraptions of wire mesh on frames separated the larger wheat grains from the smaller cockle seeds in the harvested crop. This kept the poison out of Pharsalia's flour. But it also surrendered a substantial portion of the water and nutrients in the grain fields to the cockle, which was still spread from wild plants growing in the old fields and on the margins outside the fences. It also allowed the cockle to reappear year after year without any hope of eliminating it. The weed continued to drag down the double-cycle for the remainder of Pharsalia's existence. Even when the rust crisis eased with the return of drier weather in the late 1840s, wheat yields at Pharsalia never returned to the levels of the 1820s.

## Pharsalia's Last Struggle for Independence

By the middle of the 1840s, the inability of John Harvie and the Pharsalia slaves to seal off the agroecosystem's boundaries and intensify it had driven William Massie to distraction. Rigid domestic economy was allowing him to cut slowly into his debts. Yet his journey to solvency was taking far too long for a planter who expected to live a luxurious life and pass the same onto a large and growing brood of children. Low crop prices were being reinforced by his agricultural ecosystem's failure to continue producing adequate yields. Despite the efforts of its owner, overseers, and slaves to seal the plantation off from the outside world, Pharsalia remained connected and vulnerable to the physical and biotic realities beyond the fences and property lines. But Massie was not quite ready to abandon his dreams of building his fortune on ecological independence. Between 1845 and 1848, he made a last, desperate stab at resolving the crisis in wheat production brought on by wheat rust, briars, and cockle. He still saw the ecological problems he was facing as reflecting internal weaknesses in the agroecosystem he and his slaves had created. Like the founders of the southern farm reform tradition that he followed, Massie seemed to reason that if only he could conserve his plantation's soils, problems of boundary maintenance would disappear. Self-reliance was the key.

Massie concluded that the solution to the difficulties of Pharsalia's wheat crops lay in solving two inherent flaws he saw in the plantation's agroecosystem: unimproved grain seed and a poor understanding of his plantation's microenvironments. Both stemmed from the planter's continuing desire to intensify his farming while remaining independent. In the first case, Massie blamed rust problems on a stock of wheat seed he thought deficient. When dealing with seed-bearing crops, nineteenth-century planters and farmers retained part of the harvested crop each year for planting the next. This left them with a narrow genetic range in their main crop plants. This long-term homogeneity helped planters learn through long experience the personality of the seed they were dealing with. On the other hand, they were left with few alternatives when the weaknesses of the varieties they were using were exposed. When problems did emerge, farmers were reluctant to abandon the understanding they had of their seed by importing new varieties. Instead, many tried to solve the problem with careful experiment and genetic selection from within their own seed stock, maintaining their adaptation and their independence. This mind-set can be seen in the way Massie reckoned grain yields at Pharsalia. Eighteenth-century planters figured tobacco yields in pounds per hand, revealing the greater value of labor over land. Intensifying farmers reversed the calculation and began measuring yields per acre. Massie, in contrast, calculated a ratio of grain harvested relative to the amount sown—the productivity of the seed was an even greater concern than that of the land or the labor.[46]

Throughout the first three decades of Pharsalia's existence, most of the wheat population had been drawn from two popular varieties, Yellow Lammas and Mediterranean. Both had been selected and spread in the late eighteenth and early nineteenth century for success in resisting the assaults of the Hessian fly. Their shoots were extremely vulnerable, however, to stem rust in the warm, moist weather that hit the region during the summers of the 1830s and 1840s. Yet Massie and his hands were accustomed to these varieties, their characters and seasonal patterns. Through-

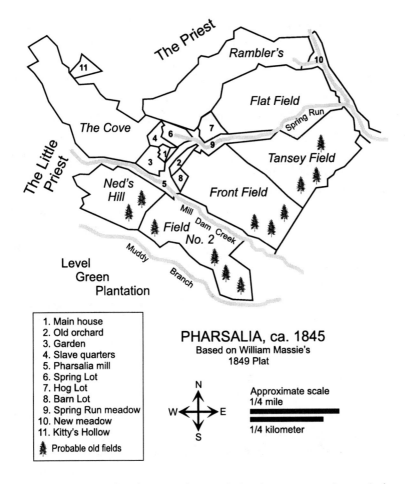

PHARSALIA, ca. 1845
Based on William Massie's
1849 Plat

1. Main house
2. Old orchard
3. Garden
4. Slave quarters
5. Pharsalia mill
6. Spring Lot
7. Hog Lot
8. Barn Lot
9. Spring Run meadow
10. New meadow
11. Kitty's Hollow
🌲 Probable old fields

Approximate scale
1/4 mile

1/4 kilometer

out these two decades, he was slow to bring in new genetic stock from the outside, even when the troubles with rust and weeds became serious. In 1828 and 1830, he made small experiments with Mexican and New York White Flint varieties, but by 1831 he limited himself to experimenting with some seed from Montebello, which had the advantage of being "of my own make." Massie made several small experiments with other kinds of wheat during the late 1830s and early 1840s.[47] Yet he never strayed far from the base of ecological experience Yellow Lammas and Mediterranean gave him. Massie never went out of the immediate region in his search for new seed stock. Instead he used varieties obtained from neighbors with soils "of similar character, in the same range of country" to experiment with during the early 1840s. At the same time, he largely abandoned Mediterranean to focus on the older standby, Yellow Lammas.[48] By 1845, he seems to have given up even these limited efforts and was back to planting Pharsalia's old varieties. Rather than buying grain from New York dealers, Massie believed that careful selection and improvement from within his existing stock of seed would produce a strain hardy enough to withstand the rust.

Pharsalia's slaves had begun attempting to improve the plantation's seed stock as early as 1831. Massie had ordered Reuben Cash and the Pharsalia slaves to select ten and a half bushels of "picked wheat" seed from the previous year's harvest and plant it in the Hog Lot near the main house.[49] To improve the yield of this crop for planting the next year, the lot was liberally manured and cultivated. He apparently repeated the process the next year, but then abandoned it for the next decade. Massie was evidently satisfied with the improvements made to his seed, or else he was unwilling to commit more of Pharsalia's biotic assets to an unrewarding effort (yields showed little meaningful improvement in coming years). Wheat planting was confined to the main fields in rotation with clover, rye, and oats in the double-cycle. Yet by 1843, in the lowest ebb of the wheat rust crisis, Massie suddenly returned to planting grain in the well-maintained lots around the house. After a dozen years committed to grazing and manure-enriched tobacco cultivation, he directed Pharsalia's slaves to plant wheat in the Hog, Spring, and Barn Lots. While Massie did not mention this shift in strategy specifically as an attempt to improve seed stock, he did blame "worthless seed" for the miserable wheat crops on a number of occasions during these years. As he jotted down these comments, he had grown desperate enough to abandon his crop rotations in the hopes of saving his wheat crops. He was still trying to find a solution from within the plantation's existing crop population.

The second approach Massie took to the wheat rust crisis was to look for a better adaptation of Yellow Lammas wheat to the vagaries of the plantation's many microenvironments. The double-cycle had been an attempt to use managed crop succession and rotation to reconstruct the soil environments of the plantation's main fields. It was unable, however, to eliminate all the local variations created by topography and drainage. During the 1840s, Pharsalia was still dotted with silted-up stream bottoms, eroded hillsides, and old fields in varying states of succession. Those microenvironments had given his hemp crops problems a decade earlier, so Massie seems to have reasoned that the source of the wheat rust might lie in the same local misadaptations. If the right combinations between the plantation's fields and its seeds could be established, he hoped, Pharsalia's ecological autonomy could be secured.

In 1842, Massie analyzed the stem rust problems in these terms, breaking the severity of the rust problems down by plantation and fields. He was clearly looking for soils on the plantation that would help his plants resist the rust. He did stop to note that all Pharsalia's failures should not be blamed on the ground, though. The seed, he believed, was "for the most part originally mean."[50] After the wheat crops of 1843 and 1844 failed, Massie abandoned the double-cycle he, Reuben Cash, and Harvie had loosely maintained in the main crop fields since the 1820s. Instead, Massie's new overseer, Nelson Munroe, and the field hands went out to plant wheat in desperate experiments at diverse spots all around the plantation in 1845. All the main lots except the Barn Lot were seeded, along with parts of the Cove, the old orchard in front of the main house, Field Two below Ned's Hill, the newer meadow on the eastern edge of the plantation, and three different plots within the Flat Field. Drier weather helped return Pharsalia's grain yield to five and a half to one, but the results of the experiment fields were still discouraging.

The next year, Massie tried looking for other spots, abandoning the lots and the Flat Field and sending the field hands to plant seed in the Front Field, the Tansey Field, and Rambler's. Yields crashed to two and two-thirds to one and faced the additional insult of a temporary influx of the previously absent Hessian fly. In 1847, he continued looking for the magic combination of seed and field that would fend off the wheat rust. Munroe and Pharsalia's field hands went back into Field Two and Field Six, as well as into the Cove, Kitty's Hollow just off the Cove, the Front Lot, and even Ned's Hill, where they had not planted for many years. The results were just as discouraging. Briars invaded the three tracts planted in Field Two, and the seedlings on Ned's Hill died and had to be replaced with corn. Yields remained at a dreadfully low three and a half to one, and a "new bug" Massie could not identify also assaulted the wheat crop.[51] But even as late as 1848, he was still not ready to declare Pharsalia's seed stock and agricultural ecosystem defeated. He ordered plots seeded in all the main fields except Field Two, even returning to Ned's Hill. He also thought of another internal source of defense, ordering part of Field Six to be prepared for wheat sowing with an eclectic mixture of home manures including ashes from the plantation blacksmith's shop and mud dredged from one of his millponds. Drier weather restored yields at Pharsalia to five and a half to one, still an unprofitable level. Much of the 1848 crop had been attacked by cheatgrass, which crowded wheat plants out, competing for water, light, and soil nutrients.

Massie was so obsessed with independence that he was even prepared to find some virtue in the cheatgrass that volunteered to occupy Pharsalia's fields. Ever since the 1810s, Massie had been sending his slaves to plant clover in Pharsalia's lots, meadows, and fallow fields. Yet during the mid-1840s, high seed prices appear to have driven him to abandon clover for less effective varieties like herd's grass. Trying to maintain Pharsalia's independence, Nelson Munroe and the slaves even pillaged the cheatgrass infestations that were plaguing the wheat fields to sow the fallow pastures. Massie also dug in his heels about commercial fertilizers. After many years of supplementing Pharsalia's crop rotations and manure with plaster, he abandoned the fertilizer at the same time he gave up on clover. Instead, he sent Munroe and the field hands looking for odds and ends to sustain the plantation's soils. Even though grain prices were starting to inch upward after 1845, Massie nearly broke apart the double-cycle in his failed quest to make Pharsalia ecologically independent.

William Massie was convinced that when his crop plants struggled against parasites and competitors, the source of the problem lay in a mismanaged agroecosystem. Perfectly engineered adaptations between seed stock, cultivation techniques, and farm microenvironments were supposed to leave no room for outsiders to muscle their way in. Agricultural reformers had promised that soil conservation would lead to independence. Yet all the efforts to turn Pharsalia into an ecological fortress failed. The double-cycle could not easily be adapted to the soils and climate of the southern Piedmont, and the plantation's borders remained open to invasion. But as his problems grew worse, Massie looked even further inward. He seemed to hope that in the smallest details of Yellow Lammas wheat characteristics or in tiny differences between patches of ground on the plantation he could find the key that would lock the Pharsalia agroecosystem into a sustainable place. He never found it, though, and his career as a wheat farmer and an advanced practitioner of the double-cycle stuttered to a standstill. As early as 1844, when wheat yields at Pharsalia barely cleared two and a quarter to one, the planter reported, "It is in fact discouraging and makes me almost despair of ever making a crop of wheat again. . . . Gloom—Gloom—Gloom," he concluded of his prospects.[52]

With Pharsalia's grain fields and crop rotations failing during the 1830s and 1840s, Massie went looking for other ways to make ecological independence turn a profit. He tried to increase the quality of Pharsalia's brandies and hams in the hopes of turning them into real moneymakers rather than merely items for local consumption. In each case, he was reluctant to bring in new animals or trees to quickly increase yields or quality. Instead he directed his overseers and slaves to improve the plantation's existing stock of plants and animals.

Fruit brandies were a regular item in antebellum house cellars and country taverns. Farmers who wanted to tap into this local market had to develop large stands of productive fruit trees. In the 1810s and 1820s, many ambitious Virginia distillers built up their old apple orchards by acquiring improved trees from a number of firms based on Long Island. Massie had joined in this investment, purchasing cherry, apple, and peach trees in 1826–27 for an expanded orchard in the Cove. In 1833–34, he bought more apple and plum trees from the famous Long Island nurseries of William R. Prince & Company. But from that point forward, the planter backed away from alien trees. Pharsalia's orchards still suffered from diseases, poor soils, weather, and other problems, but Massie did not make up the losses, or expand any further, with new imports. In 1835, Pharsalia's field hands grafted apple trees with old stock, while planting pear saplings acquired from a Nelson County neighbor. In 1837, Massie concluded of the Cove orchard: "The missing trees, or those that may not live, can be replaced by Home grafts of the same kind, in so much as I have plenty."[53] To improve production, Massie tried to accumulate a detailed knowledge of the relationship between the Pharsalia ecosystem and its orchard trees. For years, he had recorded casual notes on apple production in his Farm Account books. At the same time he stopped buying imported trees, he started an obsessive accounting of his orchard, cluttering the Farm Accounts for several years. He then started a separate orchard book that recorded details of pruning, grafts, fertilizers, and other efforts on a tree-by-tree basis. The result of all this effort was distilled brandy, and Massie's papers show regular production of apple, peach, and occasionally pear and plum brandy for sale to merchants in Lynchburg and Richmond.[54]

Massie also tried to make Pharsalia's old stock of half-feral hogs into a moneymaker. Massie had never committed much effort to breeding and fattening these animals for market sale, using their meat instead for home consumption. Throughout these years, the Hog Lot was more often planted in tobacco and hemp than clover pasture for the swine. As the slow but steady expansion of the region's urban centers created a market for higher-quality meat, Pharsalia's owner, like many other planters, pursued this opportunity, joining the growing trade in salt-cured hams. He was successful enough to make Massie hams a recognized "brand" in Richmond.[55] Even more rigorously than with the plantation orchards, though, he tried to intensify hog husbandry using Pharsalia's own animals. The planter's records make no mention of purchasing breeding stock from off the plantation. Instead, slaves culled the plantation's herd more aggressively, built new pens and barns, and expanded clover pastures during the late 1830s and early 1840s. Pharsalia's slaves and overseers separated higher-quality animals from the lean and stringy pack descended from the "piney-woods rooters." Massie still claimed ownership of a few semiferal hogs roaming the ridges below Pharsalia near Massie's Mill and above it in the hills around Montebello. Yet mentions of "sandy hill," "wild," and "woodland" hogs soon disappeared from his Farm Accounts.[56]

This kind of independent intensification did not fulfill his hopes, though. Massie began producing brandy and Virginia ham by slowly and laboriously transforming Pharsalia's agroecosystem. Deeply in debt after the death of his father in 1834, the planter felt he could not afford another failed experiment with an exotic crop. Over the next decade he ordered the Pharsalia overseers to improve the commercial qualities of the existing genetic stock, requiring all the hard work of breeding, culling, and intensive care. In practice, intensification did not provide planters with both independence *and* wealth. In the first place, it all moved too slowly—years of patient selection, experimentation, and simple trial and error had to underlie any self-started improvement in the marketable qualities of crops and livestock. That long-term commitment left planters unable to adapt their farming to quickly shifting markets. Intensifiers were also adapting their flora and fauna to the same environments and the same regional markets as their neighbors. As all of them marched slowly forward, they flooded the area with similar products, depressing prices. Hog meat in particular never achieved the kind of price increases that would have rewarded intensification of Virginia herds.[57] As a result, profits did not flow in nearly fast enough. In the fall of 1842, Massie concluded of some of his unrewarded efforts that "at that rate distilling brandy is a very loosing [sic] business."[58] Massie was able to reverse his plantation's slide toward a forced sale by cutting spending and reducing investment. But his climb up out of the red was threatened by Pharsalia's depleted agricultural ecosystem. Independence did not prevent the plantation's productivity and profitability from stagnating.

## The Failure of Independence at Pharsalia

If one were to walk in the shoes of a visitor to Pharsalia in the late 1840s—say, perhaps, Matthias Law, a carpenter from neighboring Rockbridge County who built a gristmill on the banks of the Tye for William Massie in the spring of 1847[59]—some stark contrasts to the landscape surveyed by Peter Jefferson a century before would be apparent. To talk business with Pharsalia's owner, Law would have followed the farm road from the mill site at Tyro to the Massie's house a couple of miles away. He would have crossed the newer meadow on the fringe of the Tye River bench on his way into the plantation. Farther on, he would also have passed by the older meadow on his left. Tamer and fatter cattle and hogs would have been grazing inside enclosures, tended by at least somewhat watchful eyes. The wild shoats of the early nineteenth century would have belonged to poorer farmers and been consigned to the hillsides above, kept out of Pharsalia's fields by wooden fences. The extensive cultivation of the eighteenth century had become more focused, with William Massie and Nelson Munroe working more slaves on less land.

As he neared the main house, Law would have found himself in the midst of a bustle of ambitious activity—a far cry from the scattered shacks and small clearings of the eighteenth-century triangle. On his right, he would have passed the Hog Lot and the Spring Lot, where the slaves were planting corn and tobacco on rich soils. The stench of manure from the barns and the small fields would have been heavier than on nearby small farms that let their animals run loose in the woods. Surrounding the house would have been a complex of buildings—barns, springhouses, smokehouses, and a large slave quarter. Numerous slaves would have been toiling away in the lots and the large orchards in front of and behind the main house, as well as in the large garden nearby. Having passed thirty years of age, Pharsalia was a radical transformation of the local environment. It also carried an air of permanence that the squatter clearings and isolated quarters of the mid-eighteenth century had lacked.

Law came from the prosperous grain-farming country across the Blue Ridge in the Shenandoah Valley. He was also a Virginia German, a group who maintained their cultural independence in the Old Dominion through agricultural conservation.[60] Unlike the slave Tandy, Law would have appreciated the rewards that might come from the hard work of intensification. But he would doubtless have noticed the flaws in Massie's control of the agricultural environment at Pharsalia. While a far cry from the slash-and-burn farming of the previous century, the plantation's crops and livestock were still not monopolizing its productivity and delivering high yields—intensification was still limited. Nor would the plantation have seemed quite as stable to him as visionary high farmers might have hoped.

The meadows he walked by would not have been as lush as those in the valley. Instead of a regular sowing of top-quality commercial-grass seed, the pastures would have consisted of some shabby volunteer clover interspersed with cheaper herd's grass, local cheatgrass, and a variety of wild grasses and weeds. For their part, the animals inside the fences would still have carried an air of their ancestors' feral life in the woods of the triangle about them—a quick, suspicious eye toward the passing Law, and long, lank bodies that promised tough, lean meat fit only for long boiling.

The main crop fields around the plantation would have shown signs that the double-cycle had met its match in the surrounding environment. A fair proportion of the main fields would not have been under the plow. Beyond the Flat Field to Law's left as he entered the plantation, the Tansey Field would have consisted largely of old fields covered in weeds and brush. While a small clearing had been sown in rye, bare patches of galled red clay probably still poked out under the scrub cedar in the rest of the field. The small stream that ran down from the plantation spring would have been drowned in the mud that had flowed off Rambler's Field and out of the Cove, leaving small swamps on either side. As he ascended the road, Law would have seen small patches of Yellow Lammas wheat seedlings dotted around the plantation. Later that summer, the German builder could have predicted, all would be attacked by the rust. Nearby patches would have been abandoned to corn fodder and briars. As it approached middle age, Pharsalia plantation would have seemed a paradox to Matthias Law. A wealthy and powerful man's vision of independence, prosperity, and permanence was resting uneasily atop a struggling agro-ecosystem in which people, weather, crops, animals, streams, weeds, and pests fought for dominance with uneven results.

Following the lead of his Revolutionary-era father, William Massie had searched for a personal independence built on the back of an ecological independence. Like other early nineteenth-century planters, he tried to make Pharsalia's agroecosystem both intensive and sustainable by turning it into an autonomous realm. But the inability of the plantation to live up to its owner's ambitions would have been clear to Matthias Law. Pharsalia was simply too small and its borders too porous to keep its soil nutrients in and various trespassers out. Rainstorms, weeds, fungal spores, even the local squirrels competed with Massie's farming schemes for control of Pharsalia. Indeed, they often competed with notable success. Steadily losing its already denuded biotic and physical assets, Pharsalia's ecosystem was being pulled in several directions. With productivity declining, again and again Massie was forced to search for quick profits at the expense of his schemes for sustainability. Yet his search did not include radical changes in the dysfunctional farm environment Pharsalia had become. The double-cycle was compromised; the plantation's labor, organic matter, and nutrients were spread too thin; and adequate conservation measures could not be taken. As a result, Pharsalia could not be sustained as an independent agricultural ecosystem. Its owner began to search for new measures to achieve his agricultural and personal goals. This search would transform the Pharsalia environment over the next decade.

William Massie, ca. 1840.
(Courtesy of the Flippin family;
photo by Barbara Massie Kurek)

Maria Massie, ca. 1840.
(Courtesy of the Flippin family;
photo by Barbara Massie Kurek)

Maj. Thomas Massie's house at Level Green, 2005. (Photo by author)

The plantation house at Pharsalia, 2005. (Photo by author)

The Front and Tansey Fields, seen from the main house, 2005. (Photo by author)

The Front Field and Field Number Two, seen from the main house, 2005. Field Number Two is to the right, covered by trees. (Photo by author)

The Cove, 2005. In William Massie's day, the field was cleared much farther up the hollow. (Photo by author)

Ned's Hill, seen from the Flat Field, 2005. The plantation house can be seen in the center. (Photo by author)

Part of Rambler's Field, 2005. The dirt track leads over a dam on the old Spring Run. (Photo by author)

Mill Dam Creek (originally the DePriest Run), 2005. (Photo by author)

Remains of a rock levee built in the 1850s by William Massie's slaves, 2005.
(Photo by author)

The Tyro Mill, 2005. Originally built by Matthias Law, it was operated by Hope Massie after the Civil War. (Photo by author)

# Capitalism and Conservation at Pharsalia, 1848–1862

As the double-cycle fell apart during the mid-1840s, William Massie took bold measures to raise the productivity of Pharsalia's agricultural ecosystem. He abandoned his pursuit of ecological independence and brought new resources into the plantation's ecosystem to increase productivity quickly. His new strategy began Pharsalia's capitalist intensification and revealed a new outlook on his part and that of other nineteenth-century southern soil conservationists. Capitalist farmers were prepared to abandon tested ecological relationships if they saw the possibility of greater profits. If any part of their agroecosystem was not maximizing production, the capitalist planter tried to replace it. Since Pharsalia's soils were nutrient poor, Massie bought fertilizer. Since its livestock were scrawny and mean, he bought breeding stock. Since its crops were yielding poorly, being killed off by pests and plagues or just not bringing top dollar at harvest time, he bought new varieties. This readiness to remake his farm's agroecology over and over did not mean Massie abandoned the goals of conservation, though. The cost of his investments and the lure of long-term profits pushed him to renew his efforts at fighting off soil exhaustion and erosion.

The success that planters like Massie had during the 1850s defined the new ambition of southern conservationists—intensive, sustainable ecosystems, but ones transformed by their interaction with the global marketplace. Pharsalia's middle-aged rebirth as a capitalist farm did not fully reconcile it with the ambitions of southern aristocrats like William Massie, though. He still longed for security, and the constant ecological upheaval of capitalist farming was threatening. He wanted financial independence but had to go into debt to invest in intensification. He aspired to be the masterful patriarch but saw his authority over Pharsalia's ecosystem and finances challenged by the world market's power, his slaves' resistance, and his neighbors' hostility. Capitalism ended Pharsalia's ecological crisis, but the perfect gentry plantation—secure and independent, as well as sustainable and profitable—remained Massie's ambition, not Pharsalia's reality.

## Capitalist Agricultural Ecology

The collapse of the double-cycle could be seen on Pharsalia's Front Field during the 1840s. The ground between the old orchard in front of the main house and the southern edge of the plantation had always been the focus of Massie's attempts to build fertility through crop rotations and manuring. Major Massie's slaves had cleared a good deal of its timber, and the soils in its clearings were probably already depleted when William took over. After Pharsalia was founded, he promptly put the Front Field into wheat and clover in rotation. With few exceptions, he kept tobacco out, instead giving the ground what manure and fallow time he thought he could spare from money-making crops. When he sat down in the 1830s to draw up a new plat of Pharsalia and plan out longer crop rotations, he started with the Front Field, renaming it Field Number One in a six-field scheme.

The results of nearly a quarter century's effort at soil restoration were disappointing, though. By 1846, the Front Field was further from the high farmer's vision of a well-managed soil fertility cycle than it had been when Massie had taken it over. In that year, the planter was searching for a soil that would give Yellow Lammas wheat a competitive advantage against the threats of wheat rust and briars. He ordered wheat planted in four separate spots on the Front Field in the hopes that one or two might flourish. With *Smilax* spreading across the field, two patches of corn were planted around the briar colonies. With little confidence in the wheat crop, the planter also ordered Nelson Munroe to plant a few bushels of old rye seed near one of the sediment-drowned stream swamps at the lower end. Massie had reached the point of just trying to squeeze a little return from the marginal resources of the plantation—old seed and damaged soils. The results of this mishmash of plantings were next to worthless. Stem rust and the unwelcome return of the Hessian fly cut the yield of the Front Field wheat to a miserable two and two-thirds to one. The battle to restore soils and intensify cultivation was being lost as the field's already meager resources were being eaten up, washed away, or left untouched by crop plants.

Just eight years later, though, the Front Field's agricultural environment had been transformed. After the disastrous season of 1846, Massie and his overseers had banished corn (with one exception) and old seed from the field. Instead, the slave hands fallowed the soil for several years. They then planted bluegrass and experimented with improved wheat and rye varieties Massie bought from national dealers, reestablishing the crop rotations with new plants. In the fall of 1853, the slaves planted the Front Field entirely in White Poland wheat. With its seeds growing in nitrogen-enriched soils, the new variety had greater success fighting invaders for soil nutrients. This planting became, when Massie surveyed it the next spring, "the finest field of wheat . . . I ever had in my life." A yield of thirteen and a third to one more than doubled the average on other fields around Pharsalia. He made no mention of either stem rust or briars causing problems with the grain. He responded to the thriving crop on the Front Field by investing more in its soils. That summer he purchased guano and phosphate of lime, and sent the slaves out to dig them in, in preparation for another crop of White Poland.

After rugged independence had failed, Massie's embrace of new varieties of grain, grass, and fertilizer had redeemed the Front Field. But his new farming strategy required a change in his mind-set about managing farm ecology. After all, importing new crop varieties was exactly the approach that had failed him so badly during Pharsalia's misadventure with hemp two decades before. But in the midst of the worst ecological crisis in Pharsalia's history, he rushed headlong back into importing new crops and experimenting with new planting methods. Massie remained a disciple of high farming, and his new way of looking at the land was a reflection of a broader shift in the views of southern soil conservationists.

How and why had reformers' ideas about the nature of successful farming changed, that they were now ready to revisit an unsuccessful approach and convince their followers to do the same?

The depression that followed the Panic of 1837 was a heavy blow to Virginia's farmers. Crop prices crashed to historic lows and did not begin to recover until nearly a decade later. Another wave of planter bankruptcies swept across the eastern part of the state. Some took the old escape route across the mountains to the western frontier, but many were so strapped for funds they could not afford the move. In an effort to save their cherished independence from their creditors, big planters like Massie tried to retrench by growing traditional crops for local markets. Smaller farmers throughout the south Atlantic retreated even further, subsisting on worthless lands in the pine forests, swamps, and mountains.[1] Massie encountered their desperate stand against low crop prices on his father's old property in the mountains around Montebello. "When I have rented [mountain land] for a monied rent," he recalled in 1850, "it has been more trouble to collect than it was worth, & at last had to be for the most part taken in truck—as cabbage, turnips, mast fed pork, and etc."[2] During the depths of the depression in the early 1840s, small farmers in the Tye River region dodged local tax collectors by abandoning their land and hiding in the caves up in the Blue Ridge.[3]

The depression also prompted a change of heart on the part of the region's agricultural conservationists. High farmers had intended the independent agroecosystems they had designed to provide prosperity and a secure home—not some stringy pork and a cold seat in a mountain cave. Starting with depleted lands and facing numerous ecological obstacles to importing the double-cycle, southern high farmers had been unable to intensify their farming quickly enough to profit. They might have kept just ahead of their creditors, but hard labor and tight living were unappealing. When crop prices bottomed out, that approach was unsuccessful as well. Antebellum conservationists responded by rethinking their commitment to independence, both financial and ecological. Writers in the Chesapeake farm periodicals backed away from the strict republican virtue endorsed by John Taylor of Caroline. Edmund Ruffin continued to preach the old faith of hard money and self-reliance, but he was increasingly seen as an elder statesman with eccentric views.[4] In order to profit from intensification, farmers had to find ways to speed up the increase in the productivity of their lands. The more reflective reformers agreed it was risky, as one correspondent to the *Southern Planter* admitted: "There are in every county many industrious, hard-working men, who know that they cannot afford to risk anything upon wild experiments. They have a growing family to support, taxes to pay, lands perhaps on which money is due, or they are straining every nerve to make their crops build a barn, that the barn may hold their crops."[5] Such calculations made getting ahead of the game next to impossible. If the region's agricultural land was too poor to support the double-cycle, reformers concluded, farmers needed to find agroecological wealth somewhere else.

By the 1840s, outside resources were more readily available to southern farmers than they had been when Madison and Taylor were counseling self-sufficiency thirty years before. Agricultural developers were beginning to provide producers with one of a farmer's most valuable assets, ecological adaptation. Market-oriented agricultural improvers were turning their attention to problems that plagued farmers across wide stretches of the Atlantic world. New products that promised to instantly overcome stem rust, low yields, soil acidity, soil erosion, and a host of other difficulties were tantalizing when the solitary efforts of William Massie and his slaves went unrewarded. Imported ecological resources could potentially solve an indebted planter's problems by quickly turning his agricultural ecosystem into a productive, profitable investment.

At the same time, these developers promised to overcome the other problem facing would-be high farmers—adapting intensification to fit the demands of buyers. Rather than laboring for years to prepare crops and livestock for an unstable market, a planter could immediately bring in-demand organisms to his farm. The expanding Euro-American economy of the nineteenth century created a larger field of ecological exchange. A farmer could find seed, animals, nursery trees, equipment, fertilizer, and the like, all designed or bred to the current demands of the marketplace. When Massie tried to intensify through his own resources, he struggled just to improve his own ham and brandy to meet a regional demand. By the 1840s and 1850s, the southern farm journals he subscribed to were filled with advertisements for seed, fertilizer, new machinery, and improved livestock. Soon, he began to receive nursery and seed catalogs in the mail, as well. High-quality organisms meticulously bred for the most lucrative markets were now just a letter and some money away.

Moreover, the letters traveled faster and the prices were cheaper than ever before. New steamships, canals, and railways brought all these new ideas and new materials to the doors of rural farmers and connected them with distant markets at lower costs. William Massie had always had to ship Pharsalia's produce by wagon down to New Market on the James River, there to be loaded into batteaux for the slow and risky trip downriver to the warehouses of his Richmond agents. By the early 1840s, though, the James River & Kanawha Canal had been extended up past Nelson County, dramatically cutting shipping rates. During the early 1850s, the tracks of the Orange & Alexandria railroad were built from Charlottesville down to Lynchburg, offering Massie and his neighbors even greater opportunities. Combined with the progress in agricultural science, improved transportation reduced some of the ecological and commercial risks that had undermined experimental farming at Pharsalia and encouraged Massie to try remaking the ecology of his plantation again.

There were still risks, of course. If farmers wanted to take advantage of outside resources, they had to abandon their ideals of independence. They still had to take on some ecological risk when importing new resources and techniques into their agricultural systems. At the same time, they had to buy all these imports, usually on credit, and redeem their investment by selling their produce in demanding, uncertain markets. During the hard years of the 1840s, many Virginia farmers, especially those in the lower classes, had little access to credit and saw no point to such investments with crop prices so low. With typical self-assurance, antebellum conservationists began condemning their stubborn unwillingness to embrace new opportunities. As one farm journalist put it, "Ask of all these wretched managers . . . and you will learn that every one is assured that if he could 'find time,' or 'spare money,' to adopt some particular improvement to sufficient extent, that he could make a large profit, say twenty per cent. and often much more. . . . And yet all these persons are, in various ways, devoting far greater amounts of time or expense to other labors on their farms, which do not bring them 3 per cent. clear profit, if indeed, any."[6]

A new division in the rural landscape of the Chesapeake region emerged during the 1840s, as stark as the one created by the first farm fences thrown up in the triangle a century before. Wealthier planters, influenced by the advice of leading conservationists and their periodicals, dramatically intensified their farming, while their poorer neighbors lagged behind. Two available measures of intensive agriculture—the value of farm equipment and livestock in probate inventories in the area around Pharsalia—show the change. Up through the 1840s, the assessed value of equipment and livestock in the area increased slowly, and did so quite evenly across economic classes. This is not surprising—farmers at all levels were guarding their independence and intensifying with their own resources. From the 1840s to the Civil War, though, the agricultural estates of wealthier men shot ahead. Men with means were now buying new farm machinery and importing improved breeding animals—risky ventures poorer farmers shied away from. It was a strategy high farmers soon extended to all aspects of Virginia farming.[7]

The contrasts between the Front Field in 1846 and 1854 or between Pharsalia's fields and those of poorer men on the surrounding hillsides were made by a capitalist farmer. Calling what Massie was ordering his slaves to do on the Front Field "capitalism" calls for a different understanding of the term, though. Academic definitions of capitalism revolve around market involvement and labor system. Capitalists produced goods for the market and/or used free labor to do so, while noncapitalists did not. Yet neither sense of the word helps to grasp the problems facing southern agriculture at a place like Pharsalia. In the first place, the change in Massie's farming after the later 1840s did not reflect any new commitment to commercial agriculture on his part. He had always grown crops for sale in international markets—like most all his countrymen up and down the James River. He had always managed Pharsalia to make money. Indeed, the southern agricultural reform movement itself never intended its followers to abandon market farming. Ecological self-sufficiency was supposed to be a path to a secure income, not a road to local subsistence. Importing resources was just a new way to achieve an old goal.

Second, this new agroecology did not result from any change in the labor system at Pharsalia—Massie stuck with slavery. Some southern conservationists did think planters would do well to sell a few slaves to acquire capital to invest in their soils, but Massie never followed their advice. And reformers never seriously questioned the peculiar institution—

in fact, regional periodicals like the *Southern Planter* or the *American Farmer* rarely addressed it at all. Their lack of concern should not surprise us too much, despite the insistence of many outside observers that southern agriculture was entirely the result of race slavery. Historically, major shifts in southern farm ecology have not accompanied major transformations of the region's labor system. Slavery was no more a driving force here than a sudden embrace of the market.[8] To understand what Massie and the other farm reformers were doing at midcentury, we would do well to consider alternatives to the assumption that the capitalistic elements in southern thinking about agricultural intensification must have entered through changes in the region's socioeconomic system. We need to think about capitalism in agroecological terms.

In the simplest sense, a capitalist is someone who invests capital. This is a tautology, of course, but it does shed light on the causes of the transformation in Pharsalia's environment. How did Massie begin to think of the ecology of his plantation as capital to be invested? Up through the 1840s, he kept falling back on tested ecological relationships that provided him with fertility—the relationship between tobacco and newly cleared forest soils enriched with wood ashes, between allied crops like corn and oats and the depleted soils of old tobacco grounds, between free-ranging hogs and the pine roots and acorns of the second-growth and mountain forests around his plantation. Bringing the double-cycle to Pharsalia had been a break from this strategy, but for Massie the main appeal of wheat, clover, hay, and manure had been the promise that they would interact well and free him from having to migrate to the distant western forests. When the new system struggled in the Piedmont, he revealed his underlying motivation. He kept sneaking back to plant tobacco, tried to improve his own fruit trees and hogs, and stuck doggedly with Yellow Lammas wheat while trying to fight off rust and briars by searching for protected microenvironments on his estate. Tested relationships between plants, animals, cultivation, and soils were a security blanket to Massie, keeping afloat his dream of intensifying and maintaining a stable independence.

To take advantage of the new opportunities of the 1840s, though, he had to cast the old agroecology of the Piedmont aside. A capitalist accepted the risks of disrupting old adaptations—and the financial risks of buying imported resources, usually on credit. In exchange, he hoped to speed up intensification enough to see a profit. To do that, the capitalist farmer had to stop thinking of his farm environment as a set of ecological relationships that preserved fertility. In his mind, he had to be able to separate the elements of his agroecosystem. They still had to interact with one another and the physical environment, but to the capitalist intensifier, they became removable or replaceable parts—resources. A resource was measured not by the stability and longevity of its ecological relationships but by the productivity it created when inserted into a carefully managed system. As one farm journal author put it in 1843, "How often do you see an individual with limited capital embarking in the profession of a farmer, expend it all in the purchase of his land; which is about as reasonable as it would be in a merchant to sink his whole capital in a warehouse, without leaving any for the purchase of goods."[9] If landed property was just a warehouse, then what were the "goods" stored there, waiting to be sold—the equipment, seed stock, animals, fertilizer, and the like? This author, and many others, made it clear—the various inhabitants of an agricultural ecosystem were capital. The South's first conservationists had always measured intensification by the independence it gave to farmers, a calculation that favored local experience and adaptation. By the late 1840s, though, they were measuring each element of their farm system as investors—calculations that favored importing resources to intensify their farming.

As Pharsalia reached the lowest point of its ecological crisis, William Massie joined this push to bring outside resources to the Piedmont. He took his first steps in this direction in 1845, during his last, desperate attempt to make Pharsalia an ecologically independent wheat farm. Intensive grain cultivation required plants that could do a number of things: take up the nutrients available throughout the soil, convert their growth into grain, and resist competition for nutrients and water from weeds and disease. In all these areas, Yellow Lammas wheat was falling short. With Pharsalia's soils already nutrient poor, a successful double-cycle could not afford to waste resources. His varied experiments with microenvironments and home manures during the mid-1840s did not produce results quickly enough. While he kept searching Pharsalia for resources to save his wheat crops, Massie also began looking beyond the plantation's fences for answers.

In 1842, a minor sensation swept through the American farming community over news of the phenomenal yields being produced in western France by a new strain of rye. Multicole rye (Massie also referred to it as Polish rye) got rave reviews from agricultural journals in both Britain and the United States. Correspondents cited not only extraordinary yields but also its apparent resistance to stem rust. It was doubtless the latter quality that most caught William Massie's attention. Just two years after the U.S. patent commissioner reported importing a few bushels for prominent improvers to experiment with, Massie got hold of a half gill of the new strain and planted it just above the old orchard in front of the house. The return on these fertile soils exceeded his wildest expectations, yielding from seed at a ratio of 756:1. With that result in hand, Massie began hoping Multicole rye could help him establish successful crop rotations on less promising ground. The next year, the Pharsalia field hands planted the seed on the eroded ridges of Rambler's Field and received a yield of 45½:1. Multicole rye flourished in a year when stem rust and Hessian fly cut wheat yields below three to one on the Front Field. After this success, rye quickly took the place of wheat in some of Pharsalia's crop rotations. Only low rye prices reserved a large place in its ecosystem for Yellow Lammas. Slaves planted Multicole rye in the Cove in 1847 and then on the plantation's main fields below the house during the next two seasons. Massie also spread the seed among his neighbors and in the mountain hollows above, in hopes of drumming up business for his struggling gristmills. By the 1850 agricultural census, a large clutch of rye farmers were at work within a day's ride of Massie's Mill.[10]

This success convinced Massie to unlearn the harsh lessons of his failures with hemp. He quickly went on to try to intensify other aspects of Pharsalia's ecology with imported resources. In 1849, he broke with Yellow Lammas wheat, purchasing a new variety, Early Purple Straw, from a dealer in New York state. The marketers of this strain promised it would defeat the attack of stem rust by maturing earlier in the season. This schedule gave Pharsalia's field hands a chance to harvest the grain before Virginia's summer heat and the hard rains at the foot of the Blue Ridge could provide a nurturing environment for the fungus. Massie also experimented with a recently developed variety known as Goose wheat. The next year, two new varieties, Kloss White and Kloss Bluestem (the latter derived from Early Purple Straw), arrived at Pharsalia. In 1851, they were followed by experiments with White Poland, another import from France. These new strains increased wheat yields just enough that the planter finally abandoned Yellow Lammas. Pharsalia's grain crops were dominated by Early Purple Straw and White Poland over the next decade. While never reaching the stunning yields of Multicole rye, these new varieties combined with slightly drier summers to help inch Pharsalia's wheat yields back to profitable levels—on average between eight and nine to one in most of Massie's calculations during the 1850s.[11]

Massie began investing in imported crop varieties in other aspects of the plantation's agroecosystem at midcentury. During the mid-1840s, he had abandoned clover for cheap, native pasture grasses. This left Pharsalia's main fields nitrogen poor and provided the stock with meager feed at a time when the double-cycle was struggling. In 1849, he went in the opposite direction, purchasing several bushels of Italian rye grass seed from a dealer in New York and switching the plantation's hay meadows over to the new variety. In 1851, timothy reappeared on the list of imported grasses, and clover also returned to close the double-cycle on Pharsalia's old and new pastures. Massie also bought small amounts of some of the more exotic grass varieties being marketed at the time, including Evergreen and Velvet grass. To take advantage of this pasture, he then purchased improved livestock, including the Cotswold rams present at Pharsalia by 1849. Massie was particularly aggressive in bringing in new varieties for the Pharsalia vegetable garden, now a large tract to the west of the main house. In 1848, brown mustard and several other unnamed seed varieties came from dealers in New York. In 1853, he stuck more closely to Virginia markets, buying several varieties of seed sweet potatoes from contacts in Richmond, an act he would repeat in 1856 and 1857. A major rush of experimentation came in 1857, as he sent his slaves to plant Wiyandot corn, and Ice Cream, Japan Honey, and Hunley watermelons, as well as Christiana muskmelons purchased from Briggs & Co. of West Macedon, New York, in Pharsalia's fields and gardens. That same year, beardless barley, cranberries, "Japanese" peas, and "Mexican" potatoes came from a New Haven, Connecticut, dealer named Trowbridge. The Pharsalia garden continued to serve as Massie's experiment station until the Civil War closed off the national seed variety trade in 1861.[12]

Nor was he willing simply to turn these valuable new crop varieties out to make their own way in Pharsalia's depleted soils. Beginning in 1849, Massie abandoned his former pursuit of an idealized independence in nutrient fertility and began investing more heavily than ever in mineral fertilizers. At the close of the 1840s, he got caught up in the international craze for guano. Nitrogen depletion and lack of soil phosphates were two of the leading causes of soil exhaustion in the southern Piedmont. Guano, the fossilized buildup of bird dung, provided a major boost to soil nitrogen levels and was the most concentrated source of phosphates available in the mid-nineteenth century. Mined from islands off the coast of Peru and across the rest of the Pacific, rock guano was pulverized and shipped to markets in the developed world. Spread out and dug into crop fields, the new fertilizer provided a chemically similar burst of fertility to what frontier farmers had been able to get from cutting and burning the oak-hickory forest. By the end of the 1840s, Pharsalia's stands of mature timber had been cleared and the plantation's soils were struggling along. Massie must have longed for the rich new ground soils his father's slaves had created for tobacco crops back in the old days.[13] Like thousands of other farmers across the nation, Massie rushed to buy guano. Overseers and slaves began spreading the powder around Pharsalia with abandon. A purchase of twelve hundred pounds in 1849 grew to fifteen tons two years later. Massie kept buying the new fertilizer until the national craze drove its prices to ruinous levels later in the decade. The more established commercial fertilizers also returned to Pharsalia. During the mid-1850s, Massie started buying large amounts of plaster again and added lime to both plaster and guano in various amounts and mixtures. By the 1850s, soil fertility was a capital investment, rather than the result of a strictly independent agroecology.

At a more limited level, outside expertise and equipment also began to transform the Pharsalia ecosystem. In 1845, Pharsalia's slaves seeded the grain fields "in the new fashion," sown on top and then plowed under. Overseers and slaves practiced deep plowing much more aggressively, digging nutrients from lower soil horizons up into the eroded and exhausted topsoil. By 1852, the plow hands were "subsoiling" and "listing" the main fields. The plantation blacksmith made a renewed effort to attach coulters to all the plantation's big plows, to aid in deeper cultivating.

Massie supported these tentative steps into more intensive farming techniques with new equipment purchases. He continued his long-standing interest in new plows even after his old friends the McCormicks left Rockbridge County for Chicago. By the time of Massie's death in 1862, numerous heavy, two- and three-horse plows had replaced the scratch plows that had cultivated the triangle's soils in earlier decades. An expensive threshing machine arrived in the hopes of saving valuable midsummer time during the grain harvest. Since the hard work of hand weeding cockle from the grain fields had proven unprofitable, the Pharsalia slaves received cockle sieves to sift the weed seed out at threshing time.

In the years after 1845, this new ethic of capital investment remade the ecological relationships of Pharsalia plantation. Massie's battle to intensify with his own resources had been slow, laborious, unprofitable, and ultimately unsuccessful. Buying new crops, fertilizers, and equipment got the process of directing Pharsalia's productive potential toward crop plants rolling again. Backed up by more aggressive tillage and fertilizing, new varieties proved more successful at competing with the pests that invaded the ecosystem. Wheat rust disappeared from Massie's records until a brief return in 1858.[14] Drier weather helped somewhat, but there was enough rain still coming in from "the putrid rotten hole" behind the Little Priest to support the fungus.[15] Early Purple Straw wheat seems to have been filling its advertised promise of maturing early enough in the year to beat the rust. Hessian fly destroyed a small field of beardless barley in 1857, and joint worms attacked the wheat crop in 1861, but did very little damage. Both were making only passing appearances at Pharsalia.

The absence in the planter's Farm Accounts of complaints about weeds is even more striking. After trying to drive sassafras, cockle, cheatgrass, and briars out of the fields with hard hoeing work, Munroe and the field hands had tried to avoid particularly infested areas during the experiments of 1846 and 1847. After that, though, Massie sent them back to troubled places like Field Two, the Cove, and the Front Field armed with large plows, plaster, and guano. The imported technology and imported fertilizers seem to have given Pharsalia's new grain varieties enough help to outcompete the weeds for water, space, and nutrition. Certainly Pharsalia's owner did not give up on the hardest hit areas. After its eroded fields had been infested with cockle, briars, and colonizing shrubs during the early 1840s, Massie lavished plaster and guano on the Cove after 1850. By the latter half of the decade, it had been integrated back into the double-cycle, supporting wheat, corn, and clover pasture in successive years. Successful intensification increased yields and brought in profits, albeit at the expense of abandoning independence. By 1854, the only dark spot on the intensification of the Front Field was the three acres of grain near the run in the lower end that were lost to "swamps," the saturation of soils as the sediment-choked stream flooded its banks.[16] With crops flourishing and profits rolling in, Massie turned his attention to regaining control of those troublesome spots on his plantation. That attempt revealed an alliance between investment and conservation that typified capitalist farming in the South.

## Capitalism and Conservation

It might seem incongruous that Massie's new capitalist ethic refocused his attention on resource conservation. Environmental historians have typically argued that capitalists are defined by their willingness to see the natural world as a collection of commodities, ready to be sold out of their natural setting.[17] As a result, supposedly, capitalists use up these commodities with no thought for their ecological role, destroying the environment and moving on. Yet if we once again rethink our definition of capitalism a bit, the southern farm reformer's new determination to break down the natural world by profit potential plays a different role. Capital investment in intensification was the partner of natural resource conservation, not its enemy.

Across the antebellum Piedmont, it was not the wealthiest, most commercially oriented planters who wore out their fields and headed west. Instead, migration was the choice of struggling men, an alternative to putting assets they did not have in reform schemes that did not work—or retreating into subsistence farming in the hills, swamps, or pine forests. Farmers in the long-settled areas of eastern Virginia were caught in a trap. On the one hand they lacked resources—their lands were depleted from decades of extensive cultivation, and years of low crop prices had drained their finances. On the other hand, they needed an income from their farms. Members of the gentry wanted to spend and consume like aristocrats, while men of the middle classes were hard-pressed just to stay afloat. These two factors came together to encourage short-term thinking about increasing the productivity of land. Wanting money, but having little to invest to make it, southern farmers squeezed their land and their slaves as hard as they dared. One frustrated high farmer described their thinking this way: "The first and generally the only questions asked to decide on the good or bad management of any individual, are, 'How many laborers does he employ?'—'How many acres does he cultivate?'—'What amount of crop does he make?'—By such estimates, is the practice of most of us entirely regulated."[18] Land plus labor equaled annual crop—men with more debt than capital could not afford to think beyond this calculation when trying to intensify the ecology of their farms.

Faced with the crisis of the early 1840s, prominent conservationists began trying to think differently about intensification. Those who chose to invest in intensification wound up thinking about agroecology and finance in terms that encouraged soil conservation. Capitalist intensification demanded so much investment, and had such an uncertain short-term return, that the farmer had to stay put on his property. For starters, the purchase of resources from off the farm did not give planters an immediate permit to print money. For all the achievements of agricultural improvers, the risks of rebuilding farm ecosystems with alien imports remained. New York seed, tree, fertilizer, and equipment developers could attack some of the environmental problems afflicting their southern customers. Yet many regional and local factors were still beyond their experience and skill. Even breeders and tinkerers based in the Chesapeake could not perfectly adapt their creations to the specific circumstances of every local environment. Results were not always immediate, and farmers often had to experiment with imports for several years before their full benefit might be had. The summer storms that blew up over the two Priests and drenched Pharsalia created unique microenvironments in the plantation's mountain hollows, swampy stream bottoms, and eroded clay ridges. William Massie and the people who worked for him still had to figure those out on their own.[19] "There is no subject the phenomena of which are so mysteriously concealed, or so slowly developed, as those attendant upon agriculture," one farm journal author conceded; "they are discernable only to the practical farmer; and to him only when endowed with powers of the greatest patience and investigation."[20] A planter bringing in a new crop, animal, fertilizer, or piece of equipment took on great short-term risk. Under these circumstances, it made little sense for him to squander the other resources of his agricultural ecosystem. For instance, a capitalist intensifier could hardly gain a clear sense of the profitability of new seed varieties if he planted them in old fields depleted by tobacco and erosion. Nor could he assess the value of guano, plaster, or lime dug into those soils if they were washed away in the Piedmont's spring and early summer thunderstorms.

Besides, all these imported resources did not come cheap. Capitalist planters had to be ready to use credit—after climbing out of the red during the early 1850s, William Massie plunged himself back into debt later in the decade, adding land and importing new resources to Pharsalia. His borrowing kept going, as he experimented with his new purchases, exchanged unworkable ones for new options, and kept buying to keep up with the market. That kind of investment demanded a return—a large return. The biggest profits, though, did not come from quick expedients. Businessmen earn the most by investing a lot of capital in the hopes of reaping rewards over a long period of time. Innovations that returned a percentage on investment season after season were the ones that put the most money into a planter's pocket. Yet to get that return, he had to make sure that the other resources in his farm's ecosystem would still be around to deliver on increased productivity years down the road. Resource conservation increased a farm's ecological capital and its commercial value. In 1843, one agricultural author defended the unmarketable clover meadows in those terms. "Pasturage," he wrote, ". . . creates, as it were, a savings bank, in which their products are deposited; therefore, all that increase of wealth, which accrues from the improvement of the farm, may be offsetted . . . against twice the amount obtained in *money*."[21] Long-term productivity not only brought in an income but also increased land values, which in turn won more credit for further investment. In 1843, a planter from neighboring Amherst County writing in the *Southern Planter* drew on an old folk tale of "rational greed" to explain the wisdom of investing in conservation: "Equally silly is he who is killing his land, to fill his purse, with him who killed his goose to get the golden egg."[22]

The effort Massie's slaves put into conserving Pharsalia's resources in the years before the Civil War made it clear that their owner now intended to keep the goose laying golden eggs as long as possible. His first conservation effort during these years was to make crop fields at Pharsalia permanent. With half an eye still on the western frontier, even intensifiers tended to avoid work that made it difficult to abandon depleted land. Virginia's worm fences were the best example of this kind of thinking. Easy to assemble, they required little labor to set up and maintain. Easy to move, they did not tie a planter to a field that might be eroded or exhausted long before a more permanent fence had outlived its usefulness. Worm fences rotted quickly in a warm, humid climate, though. By the 1820s and 1830s, improving planters were beginning to complain about the cost of timber in the Chesapeake. Petitions began going up to the Virginia legislature, asking them to save timber by changing the fence laws to require livestock owners to fence their animals in, rather than farmers having to fence them out. A more aggressive solution was the construction of stone barriers between fields or the cultivation of live fences—hedgerows of sturdy, fast-growing shrubs like osage orange. Beginning in 1849, Massie took advantage of Pharsalia's location at the rock-strewn foot of a mountain. During the slack winter months, slaves went out to build stone fences around the plantation's main fields. The work appears to have gone on for several years. In 1857, the field hands made major improvements to an expanded network of stone barriers, as well as planting locust bushes for live fences. [23]

This kind of effort was a tremendous expenditure of labor that otherwise could have been committed elsewhere. The only way to make all this work pay was to ensure the long-term productivity of the fields inside the stone walls and hedges. To do this, Massie returned to the double-cycle, still hoping to take advantage of the promise of soil fertility recycling. After the desperate experimentation of the second half of the 1840s, Massie and his overseers worked to reestablish crop rotations on Pharsalia's main fields. They also cut back on experimental wheat plantings in 1849. Instead, Massie ordered large plantings of new varieties like Early Purple Straw in the main fields. He replaced cheap, ineffective herd's grass and cheat with leguminous grass varieties to restore nitrogen and slow erosion. During the early 1850s, the main fields at Pharsalia were back in a five-shift rotation of wheat, leguminous grass, oats or multicole rye, grass, and wheat. The reestablishment of the clover fields was also reflected in the growing amount of manure collected at Pharsalia. During the 1840s, Pharsalia seems only to have had enough dung to fertilize the lots for grain experiments and tobacco. By 1850, the field hands were able to start hauling large amounts of manure out to the grain fields and pastures, as well.[24]

Massie's confidence in his new grain varieties—and his need to make them pay off—also led him to attack Pharsalia's long-term flooding and erosion problems. In 1852, particularly bad spring rains washed down from the Little Priest and left large stretches of Pharsalia's fields covered with gravel. "The DePriest Run," Massie reported, "has done awful damage . . . changed its bed in many places + cut furrows from 6 to 40 feet wide + from 2 to 6 feet deep." The flood combined with the regular heavy thunderstorms to deepen the many gullies already present on the plantation. Massie ordered his overseers to make a major effort to repair the damage, but he also began considering more permanent remedies for the flooding problem.[25] That same year, field hands began building large stone levees along the banks of flood-prone streams, an effort that continued for the rest of the 1850s. Before some of Pharsalia's streamside fields could be protected, though, they had to be reclaimed from the erosion-induced swamps that covered places like the bottom of the Front Field. Beginning in 1854, Pharsalia's laborers made their first effort to dry out the streamside swamps, digging trenches and burying drains. In 1860, the Pharsalia slaves were back in the old Flat Field, digging drainage ditches along the old meadow run. Massie's accounts also mentioned efforts to straighten streams on his property, including the ever-troublesome Muddy Branch.

Pharsalia's owner invested a great deal of work and money to make other permanent improvements to the plantation. Fretting about the cost of labor and materials, Massie had limited construction work at Pharsalia for nearly twenty years. After midcentury, he began adding to the plantation's farm buildings again. In 1852, he hired workmen to build a large cattle shelter, and in 1856 he invested in a major expansion to the main barn. Pharsalia's labor also went toward other long-term improvements. During the winters of the early 1850s, slaves made extensive repairs to the plantation's roads along with their fence work. The field hands also followed up their efforts at repairing flood damage by working to fill in erosion gullies across Pharsalia. In 1860, the planter, his overseers, and the Pharsalia slaves capped this work with a major push to repair the gullies on Field Number Two, that long-eroded and exhausted tract at the foot of Ned's Hill.

Reclaiming the soils in Pharsalia's now-permanent fields, however, was not enough to set the double-cycle at a profitable level of productivity. Massie also started investing in long-term improvements to the fertility of the plantation's main fields. His purchases of guano, plaster, and lime grew to levels well beyond short-term expedients. He backed up all the fertilizer with deeper plowing to slow soil erosion. In 1852, the Pharsalia blacksmith attached newly purchased listers to some of the plantations deep plows to throw up even larger between-furrow ridges to channel runoff. The plantation's plow hands then went to work protecting the expensively fertilized soils of steep or long-cultivated tracts like the Tansey Field and Rambler's from destructive erosion. By the end of the 1850s, Pharsalia's main fields were approaching the early southern conservationist's dream: well drained, well tilled, well fertilized, well rotated—and profitable.[26]

The road up to the plantation house in 1859 would have presented a much different prospect from Matthias Law's walk a dozen years before. The worm fences bounding the road through the Flat Field had been replaced by stone fences and, in some places, quickly growing live hedges. The fields behind these fences would have had a different appearance as well. The galled patches on the Tansey Field to the south would have been covered by fields of oats and new grass breeds. On the other side of the road in the Flat Field, rich clover and timothy meadows would have been growing. Beside the meadows, fields in four-shift rotations would have been planted in oats—two new varieties the planter had just purchased called Poland and Prince Edward Island. In particular, most of the old fields of scrub and cedar would have vanished, as Pharsalia's owner concentrated his growing workforce back onto the main fields. The old Barn Lot had been wholly turned over to penning livestock. The Jack Lot would have been largely taken over by the increasingly large, productive, and exotic Pharsalia garden.[27]

All in all, Pharsalia plantation would have looked like an expanded, prosperous version of what Law might have seen in 1847. The fields would have been bigger, the crops more plentiful, the cattle fatter, and the buildings newer and larger. An unmistakable air of permanence and human control would have hung over the landscape. In 1847, the triangle's native plants and various successional weeds were persistently finding places to thrive at Pharsalia. By 1859, humanity would have appeared more in control of the plantation's ecology. Cockle, briars, and other nuisances would still have been nibbling at the plantation's edges. More labor and better fertility were making it difficult for them to get a foot inside the intensively managed agroecosystem, though. A German carpenter from Rockbridge might still have felt uneasy in the social world of a Tuckahoe plantation. But he would have been much more impressed with the level of "improvement" the plantation displayed. This transformation had come through William Massie's willingness to sacrifice both this year's profits and his own autonomy for long-term investment in imported resources. The focused productivity of Pharsalia's agricultural ecosystem was the result more of his new capitalist ethic than his inherited love of personal—and ecological—independence.

## Capitalism and William Massie's Lost Mastery

Pharsalia's new career as a capitalist farm ended any possibility of the plantation becoming ecologically independent. First, Massie gave up on the idea of being able to fight off outside invaders using only the double-cycle and the older agroecological relationships in the triangle. Then he broke Pharsalia's already flimsy ecological barriers wide open by importing a host of new resources. He kept trying to conserve soils and achieve self-sufficiency in food, but shipped out cash crops at an even greater rate than before. If he could neither cut off Pharsalia from the surrounding environment nor profit from independent intensification, Massie seemed to reason, then he would have to manage the passage of resources back and forth across the plantation's fences. In the face of Pharsalia's grave ecological problems, Massie's response was not so much a greater respect for the natural world but rather an even greater effort to manipulate and control its workings. His drive for mastery reflected the ideals in Massie's world that had driven his desire for ecological independence in the first place—his need to prove himself a southern aristocrat by establishing authority over his chattels and his environment. The first southern farm reformers had promised planters they could achieve this by sealing off their plantations and managing them more intensively. When that system failed, they adjusted, embracing a capitalist approach to intensifying agroecosystems. They now assured men like Massie that they could perfect their control over their farm environments, confidently measuring their ecosystems against the yardsticks of production and profitability, then exchanging one resource for another until results improved. Southern conservationists still hoped to make capitalist intensification the salvation of the plantation gentry. For William Massie, the greatest praise for all his hard work "improving" the environment of Pharsalia plantation came when one correspondent asking for agricultural advice admiringly called him "the Beau Ideal of a Gentleman Farmer."[28]

Yet this new mentality, which seemed so well suited to banishing the Old Testament fatalism that seemed to rule his view of his environment, did not do much to lift Massie's spirits during the 1850s. Capitalist intensification, while it did fend off some of the threats to his aristocratic mastery of Pharsalia, left others unchallenged, while opening the gates in new and threatening ways. Mastery and conservation were difficult to reconcile—planters did not have the power to manage their resources as perfectly as they would have liked. As he approached his death, Pharsalia's owner remained gloomy and defensive in his notes and accounts, keenly aware that he had not achieved the kind of control he wanted. "Did what things I could, consistent with my great depression of spirits," he concluded of the 1860 crop year, his mood dragged down not just by "the alarming condition of the country," but also "the succession of dramatic losses and afflictions that have been heaped upon me."[29]

Some of these afflictions came from the regional transportation improvements that had made capitalism possible at a remote plantation. Massie had pushed for the extension of the James River & Kanawha Canal, buying stock in the company and lending the project his family's political support. He also helped the Orange & Alexandria extend its line through the Tye Valley and got a depot located a few miles down the road from Pharsalia at Arrington. Yet these new outlets began to shut the triangle off from the market, rather than connect it. By the early

1850s, Richmond merchants were more interested in the mass of south-side Piedmont, Shenandoah Valley, and upper east Tennessee produce flooding into the growing town of Lynchburg. Canal boats rushed past the warehouse settlement at New Market, leaving Tye Valley produce sitting—and sometimes rotting—for weeks on end. The canal company also built a dam across the James River just below the Tye River's mouth. The mouth of the Tye silted up, and boats could not get enough draft to reach New Market. Local merchants and warehouse owners were then forced to cart their goods three-quarters of a mile down to the canal. The backed-up waters of the Tye also regularly flooded out New Market during the 1840s and 1850s, including Massie's small warehouse. The canal company seemed unconcerned by the damage and inconvenience, and refused to aid in the move of the New Market warehouses down to the canal at the new town of Norwood, despite Massie's angry protests. The rail line proved equally frustrating to him. Service to the sparsely populated Tye Valley was as poor as that of the canal. In February 1860, Massie had some goods shipped to him by rail from Charlottesville, and he sent one of his slaves down to the Arrington depot with a wagon to pick them up. The train arrived several hours late and then did not stop. The conductor yelled to the wagoner that they had to make up time to Lynchburg and that Massie's goods would be dropped off on the return leg. As the train pulled away, the conductor recalled that they had some letters for Massie, and tossed them into the trees on down the line.[30]

Unable to counter the power of distant capitalists, Massie was also downcast about the vulnerability of his finances. The heavy investment demanded by capitalist intensification opened the doors to the very debt and dependence he had spent his adult life trying to escape. It is not easy to determine precisely what Massie had invested in trying to intensify Pharsalia's agriculture during the 1840s and 1850s. He did not clearly account for his new ecological investments, continuing to track income and expenditure in his customary way. The best measure of the change in the scope of his investments comes from a figure he regularly calculated, his annual "plantation disbursements/expenses." This number included over-seer, miller, and laborer's wages, purchases of equipment, seed, fertilizer, and other agricultural necessaries, as well as some other miscellaneous outlays for all his farms. While he did not isolate Pharsalia plantation in this account, the number does give a general picture of his agricultural and financial strategy.[31]

During the period when he was strictest about maintaining his ecological independence—the crisis years of the 1840s—Massie zealously kept those costs under twenty-five hundred dollars a year. This stern "economy and close-cutting" enabled him slowly to reduce his overall debt (and his dependence) even as Pharsalia's crops faltered and prices fell. Yet as he had discovered, comfortable living and generous bequests to his descendants demanded a higher income than his impoverished fields could provide. Reasoning that he had to spend money to make money, he allowed his estate's annual disbursements to climb steadily. These peaked at well above five thousand dollars by the middle of the 1850s, a big increase, even factoring in inflation. Some of this money came on credit. In 1848, the last year he was still trying to squeeze a profit from Yellow Lammas wheat, Massie had nearly ten thousand dollars in outstanding debt for land he had purchased over the past twenty years. He took advantage of good prices in the next few years to whittle that down, but he continued to receive loans from the merchants he did business with. Richmond factors John Jones & Company, William Hambleton, and Hunt & Brothers all extended Massie additional credit to finance his efforts at intensification. Only the steadily improving crop prices of the early to mid-1850s kept Massie's overall indebtedness going down. In 1857, though, he dived back into debt, buying some prime Tye River bottomland to expand and consolidate the farms he wanted to hand down to his children. He was also spending money that year bringing in a host of new crop varieties to Pharsalia's gardens and fields.

Indebtedness increased his vulnerability to marketplace demands. Much of the success of his investments in capitalist intensification had rested upon the high crop prices of the 1850s. Massie had stoically refused to go back into tobacco farming, planting only small amounts between 1854 and 1856, and foregoing the weed entirely in 1857 and 1858. Yet his virtuous adherence to the double-cycle was thrown off by the Panic of 1857. Grain prices slumped, but tobacco held its own, dropping only slightly during 1858. Unable to resist because of his debts, Massie contributed to a surge of tobacco planting across Virginia the next spring. After all his successes since the 1840s, he once again diverted a large part of Pharsalia's assets back to tobacco. The Front, Ice Pond, and Cow Lots, along with much of the plantation's manure, were put back into the sot weed. The field hands even headed out to a few spots in hill hollows Massie owned elsewhere in the neighborhood to clear new grounds. He could now add outside resources like guano to support the new plantings, of course. But money spent to buy guano for tobacco grounds would not go to buy grass seed and new crops that could be integrated into the double-cycle. Labor spent cultivating tobacco could not go into building fences, draining swamps, repairing gullies, and carefully maintaining arable soils. In 1860, tobacco, infamous for accelerating erosion and exhaustion, was planted on some of the most vulnerable soils at Pharsalia— Ned's Hill. Capital investment demanded repayment, which could only be had on terms set by the marketplace.

At the same time, Massie also struggled with the fact that the agricultural development market had not fully replaced the old virtue of local ecological adaptation. In fact, the pressure for profits often pushed farmers to buy new resources before their uses and benefits were well understood. Imports kept destabilizing Pharsalia's agroecology, a problem illustrated by William Massie's struggles with commercial fertilizers. Many farmers began using guano as a cure-all for their complex problems of depleted soil fertility. Developing manure- and clover-based rotations to restore exhausted native soils demanded painfully slow and expensive labor. Guano, on the other hand, was only a cash or credit purchase away and promised immediate returns on the money invested. Its oft-reported effectiveness in quickly reviving productivity made it an enticing investment for capitalist intensifiers. Pharsalia's field hands dug guano into the soil of just about every part of Pharsalia during the early 1850s.[32]

Yet it soon became apparent that guano was not an easy resource to master. First, buying it on the world market left planters dependent and vulnerable. In the early 1850s, the world's best guano deposits were all claimed by Peru. The Peruvian government realized the value of the ground rock to the burgeoning capitalist agricultural systems of the United States and northwestern Europe. Its officials moved quickly to establish a state monopoly and to license agents in foreign countries with exclusive contracts to market Peruvian guano. In the United States, that agent was the firm of Felipe Barreda & Brother, a partnership in Baltimore headed by an expatriate Peruvian. To the endless rage of popular and agricultural editors, Barreda was not above taking advantage of his monopoly and rapidly raised the price of the precious fertilizer. Indeed, prices increased so rapidly that William Massie swore off guano after 1855, only returning to it in 1859. Yet planters were so desperate for rapid intensification, and guano hysteria so consuming, that the Barreda monopoly appears not to have destroyed the market. There were still plenty of men willing to bet against Massie and assume they could still make the investment turn a profit. The South's newspapers heaped endless columns of praise on guano as the salvation of the region's agriculture, economy, and political power. As Massie himself put it, criticizing guano in the 1850s was like "sing[ing] psalms to a dead horse. . . . The rage is up."[33] But prices kept climbing, and the guano craze's initial euphoria soon turned into desperation.[34]

The fact that the sources and prices of guano lay so far beyond the mastery of the plantation gentry was galling to independence-minded southerners. In 1856, frustration had mounted to the point that a number of influential Chesapeake and mid-Atlantic planters and merchants convened a Guano Convention in Washington, D.C. They discussed several options for dealing with rising prices, including both quixotic hopes of organizing a boycott and a little wild-eyed talk of using military force against the Peruvian government. In the end, though, the delegates were forced to agree on their own impotence and concluded that the only course available to them was continuing gentle remonstrance with Barreda and the Peruvian ambassador. This helplessness in the face of unchallengeable commercial prerogatives infuriated planters. In place of effective action, editors chose instead to heap abuse upon Barreda—an editorial strategy that never seemed to fail to sell papers to rural readers. Massie's own opinion, "what better could you expect than treachery from the Spanish, or anything tainted with the Spanish," was among the milder insults out of Virginia. Few essays on the guano trade passed without Felipe Barreda being likened to the Prince of Darkness.[35]

Even when they were able to get guano onto their plantations, capitalist farmers encountered problems. Reports of guano's miraculous effects were so common that its use spread with little hindrance from popular suspicions of "book farming." But the guano craze, in addition to bringing southern planters to their knees commercially, offered them little opportunity to experiment cautiously with the new fertilizer. Planters using guano could not be entirely sure what the fertilizer was doing to the soil, other than making more crops grow. Despite considerable advances that had occurred during the preceding two decades, agricultural chemistry was still primitive in the early 1850s. And even the knowledge acquired by a few scientists was slow to make it to ordinary farmers in an age before agricultural extension and government-subsidized soil testing.[36] Apart from complaints about prices, the essays and correspondence on guano in the agricultural papers during the 1850s consisted of reports on the wide variety of experiments (stabs in the dark in many cases) planters were making in using the product with their various crops and soil types.

At Pharsalia, Massie kept searching for its most profitable uses. He fiddled with guano on different fields, in different quantities, on different crops, in different combinations with lime, plaster, and manure, rolled seed in guano, and on and on. After first using guano in 1849, the planter even ordered his slaves to mix it with salt and lime on some of the small lots. In 1852, he thought he could use guano to revive eroded land, ordering several tons plowed into "all the Pharsalia ridges." The next year, he was back mixing and matching with guano, ordering the Pharsalia slaves to, "sow a mixture of 4 parts guano and 1 part plaster on all the Pharsalia fields except the old tobacco lot." In 1854 Massie tried yet again to revive hill and ridge land with guano. In 1855, he spread guano all over the plantation's main fields, experimenting with mixing it with lime on several plots. Whether guano did much to increase the yields of Pharsalia's wheat crop remains unclear. There seems to have been little correlation between increases and fertilization. The outstanding crop of White Poland on the Front Field came a year before the first recorded application of guano there. Wheat's main limiting factors at Pharsalia remained competition from cockle, briars, and the annual onslaught of stem rust. Pharsalia's owner concluded of guano, "I have never been able to discover the least advantage from its use, but on thin ridges."[37]

In 1852, Massie had ordered his overseers and slaves to make a third of a ton of "artificial guano,"[38] whatever that was. He probably was not sure himself. Guano buyers felt their ignorance most keenly when they considered the possibility of the fertilizer being adulterated by an unscrupulous

Peruvian government, or its American agent, or any of the various commission merchants who sold it. Southerners were completely unaware of
what the "proper" physical and chemical composition of guano might
be. In desperation the state government appointed a guano inspector to
test and certify imports. Yet, as officials of the State Agricultural Society
reported in the pages of the *Southern Planter*, the inspection was of little use. Accurately determining the phosphate and ammonia content of
imported guano, it was disclosed, required a complex series of managed
chemical reactions well beyond the means and skill of the state's guano
inspector, to say nothing of ordinary planters. Occasional experiments in
thorough testing revealed enough dramatic frauds to keep the readers of
popular and agricultural periodicals fearful.[39]

All these problems made Massie cynical about guano and helped him
decide to abandon it for a time. Yet by the end of the 1850s, he had
returned to it. The tensions and unease created by the guano craze were
part of the process of creating a capitalist farm economy. The ecological
effectiveness and profitability of guano were uncertain in both the short
and long terms. Guano left planters at the mercy both of purveyors of
information beyond their expertise as well as the importers and dealers
of a product in whose market the only serious competition was among
the purchasers. More importantly, it upset the stable relationship between
farmers and the agricultural ecosystem that capitalist intensifiers hoped
to create. The torments guano put its buyers through revived the old al-
lure of strict ecological independence. Right up to the Civil War, a small
group of farm reformers hewed to the old line of independent intensification. The purpose of high farming, they still assumed, was to reduce
the debts of land-owning cultivators by maintaining and improving soil
fertility. Since high-priced guano encouraged debt and dependence, they
insisted that planters should instead go back to making the most efficient
use of their plantations' own resources. In 1854, a reformer told one of
Virginia's regional agricultural clubs that, despite the promise of guano,
"we must not depend on the use of this, as the settled policy of farming, *to
the neglect of our home manures*. It is opposed to every principle of political economy, to send as far as half the circuit of our globe for guano, and
neglect equally, or even more, valuable manures, on our very premises,
and in our neighboring cities."[40] A number of correspondents and essay-

ists responded to the growing guano craze among southern farmers by defending the double-cycle, extolling the competing virtues of the leguminous cowpea when planted in the old rotations. Others continued to advocate the self-sufficiency strategies used at Pharsalia in the mid-1840s. They heaped praise on on-farm manures like marl, green sand, night soil, and marsh mud whose use was even more in line with the ideal of ecological and financial autonomy.[41] In the end, they had little impact, though. The independent, prosperous farms promised by the first southern conservationists had failed to be either. Southern farmers tried instead to master guano's workings as quickly as they could. Correspondents to the farm journals reported and questioned experiments with rolling seed in guano, mixing guano with wood ashes, salt, or both, using guano on old corn grounds, on tobacco plant beds, and so on. The obsessive public discussion of guano claimed more attention than a few sermons on ecological self-reliance. In 1859, Massie gave up on his virtuous abstinence and bought several tons of guano. He then sent his slaves to dig it into, of all places, the new grounds they had cleared for tobacco in the hill hollows around Pharsalia. Buying overpriced fertilizer he did not understand how to use summed up Massie's weakness in the capitalist world he had entered. At the close of the 1850s, capitalism had breached the stone walls and hedgerows of the new Pharsalia and turned him from a would-be master of natural resources into a frustrated servant of the marketplace.

## The Human Challenge to William Massie

While his inability to control the international market compromised his ability to control Pharsalia's resources, the threats to William Massie's mastery also came from closer to home. For the southern gentry, personal independence was based on their domination of human chattels and the deference they received from the surrounding community. Yet planters were never able to win that kind of authority and faced constant challenges that threatened their ability to manage their own property and resources. Their slaves fought against attempts to turn them into another managed plantation resource. Poor white farmers refused to give political and economic deference and threatened capitalist intensification by continuing to pursue their old subsistence strategies. William Massie's control of Pharsalia's resources was contested by the triangle's human population, both inside and outside the plantation's fences.

The labor of the Massie slaves turned Pharsalia into a capitalist farm, proving that the new ecology and the peculiar institution were not incompatible. Indeed, Massie and other southern conservationists did not see slavery as any more of an obstacle to conservation than to capital investment. Along with the general assumption that southern agriculture was almost exclusively shaped by the peculiar institution, recent scholars have also argued that slavery was an obstacle to agricultural reform. Either the cost of slaves kept forcing planters into extensive farming, or slaves themselves were unable or unwilling to participate, or the conservative culture of the slave-owning South prevented planters from embracing innovation.[42] Massie, however, seems to have wasted little sleep adapting his labor force to his new agricultural ideas. During the 1850s, Pharsalia's slave hands completed the slow transformation in their work routine that Tandy had begun back in the 1820s. They largely abandoned the annual trek out into the forest to clear new grounds and plant cash crops. Instead, they were sent to work at the core of the plantation, restoring and conserving soils and adding to a permanent infrastructure. Massie made a few calculations of labor efficiency in several farm chores during the late 1840s, but soon set them aside to concentrate on extracting the maximum long-term return from his land. He seemed more concerned about the effectiveness of the white overseers, millers, and occasional day laborers he hired—few of whom seem to have carried out his instructions or offered him proper deference. By 1851, he had not concluded that his slave hands were inefficient but simply that "my labor is . . . insufficient for my lands"—his solution was to stop buying land (with one notable exception six years later) and wait for his younger slaves to grow up.[43] This is not to say that much of a positive correlation existed between the peculiar institution and agricultural reform, despite the predominance of wealthy slaveholders among the early southern conservationists. Some historians have suggested that the paternalism of upper-class masters came to encompass a similar duty of care for the land.[44] Massie does not seem to have fit this model, either. Although he was a careful slave owner, little emotional content shows through his letters and records—his interest was in efficient, productive labor. At the same time, he showed no emotional connection to the fields and forests of the triangle or the mountains that surrounded it. For an area whose beauty has attracted so much appreciative attention in recent decades, Massie had little good to say. His "respect" for the natural world was the fear and anger he directed at flash floods, gullies, swamps, rust spores, weeds, and marauding squirrels, and at times the angry God who sent them all to afflict him. The farming advice he read told him to overcome all this by manipulating and mastering his surroundings. High yields and high profits were the beauty this soil conservationist hoped to see in the southern landscape.

While it was not a decisive factor either for or against intensification and conservation, race slavery did introduce conflict into Pharsalia that Massie struggled to manage. He was never given to general reflections about slavery, but his papers do reveal that he fought throughout his life to assert control over his bondsmen and -women. As he did with the ecology of his plantation, Massie tried to control his laborers by isolating them from the surrounding world. Pharsalia may have been physically isolated in a back corner of the Piedmont; yet in the end all his attempts at fending off the broader realities of race slavery were unsuccessful. Slavery remained a hostile relationship in the South, with battle lines that ran across plantation boundaries. Pharsalia's slaves never became the insulated, orderly, and productive labor force Massie and other planters envisioned, and their resistance to his mastery threatened his ability to control natural resources, as well.

During his early years as a planter, Massie bought—and sold—slaves frequently, trying to build up a labor force large enough to undertake his intensification schemes. Parents and children were separated by these sales, and Pharsalia developed a pronounced gender imbalance as Massie purchased adult men to put more labor in the crop fields.[45] The triangle's black population was unwilling to accept this treatment, though, and hoped to establish a community with stable families. Influenced by racial conflicts that stretched back into the colonial era and across the American South, Pharsalia's slaves resisted Massie. Judging from the outbursts of frustration and anger he occasionally wrote down, they repeatedly stole food and other supplies. In 1827, they moved on to more serious actions, when "Old Indian John" set fire to a tobacco house, causing

$150 in damage. In the wake of Thomas Massie's death and estate set-
tlement after 1834, the disruption of black life in the triangle sped up
as slaves were shuffled between William Massie's plantations, sent off to
estates of the Major's other sons, or sold away. As the threat to their
community increased, so did the arson. In 1836, a Pharsalia slave named
Sam burned the plantation stable, costing Massie several hundred dollars
for the building and its contents.[46] More of the plantation's outbuildings
went up in flames in 1838 and 1839, torched by unknown arsonists. This
campaign may have culminated when another slave, "Saint" Peter, allowed the Pharsalia mill to burn down. Faced with a loss of more than
$5,000 for the mill—and enough ongoing discontent that he created a
special record of slave insubordination for the next four years—Massie
rethought his approach to managing his labor force. When the stresses
created by the breakup of his father's estate severely disrupted his plantation, he reversed course and cut back on his buying and selling of slaves—
even though it left him, as he later admitted, short of labor to pursue his
various intensification schemes.[47] The stabilizing family and community
that resulted from this concession reduced the strife at Pharsalia, but it
never disappeared. In 1844, slaves set fire to one of the plantation's barns,
burning up more than three thousand pounds of tobacco leaf. Another un-
explained fire destroyed another of Massie's gristmills in 1860. This kind
of rebelliousness threatened more than just his position as a slave master.
Field hands who burned up the plantation's infrastructure and crops diverted resources away from the double-cycle and the crop market—and
undermined their owner's finances. Massie understood the threat of slave
resistance to agricultural improvement and tried to maintain control over
people at Pharsalia with the same zeal for independence he applied to the
conservation of soils.[48]

His withdrawal from the slave trade suggests that—at least at a sub-
conscious level—Massie accepted that Pharsalia's bondsmen and -women
were resisting their condition and relationship with him. Most of the time,
though, he clung to the idea that the master-slave relationship at his plantation was being disrupted from the outside. In the end, Massie saw the
danger to slavery coming from beyond Pharsalia's fences, not from any
contradictions within. In 1847, he hired Mathias Law, the German carpenter from Rockbridge County, to build him a new mill near the Tye

River. While working in the triangle, Law was apparently shocked by the brutality of Massie's overseer, Nelson Munroe. Word reached Pharsalia's owner that Law had spoken freely in the neighborhood about Munroe's "cruel and barbarous treatment of slaves." Massie stewed about this challenge to his authority more than any danger to his local reputation Law's gossiping posed.[49] He cautioned Law that he "would render [himself] exceedingly unpopular among slaveholders" if he questioned their mastery, and went on to warn him that "if you work in this section in the future . . . be more guarded in that particular."[50] Privately the planter wrote in his weather memoranda (and perhaps repeated to friends): "This day Law finishes the Tyro Mill. God damn him."[51] Trying to explain his unpleasant dealings with Law, Massie chose to blame the man's Shenandoah Valley origins. It was an interesting choice—Massie had attended school in the valley, had business dealings there for decades, and made a German girl from Harrisonburg his fourth wife. Yet after ridding Pharsalia of Mathias Law, Massie returned to the Virginia planter's old prejudice against the strange, dangerous Cohees who lived on the other side of the Blue Ridge from respectable Tuckahoes like himself. When forced to hire a new miller from the valley in 1850, Massie grumpily wrote to a friend, "I greatly prefer a man raised on the east side of Blue Ridge to one raised in the Valley nor would I have employed this man, except for his being part Tuckahoe. He was partly raised in Amherst, & married first in a good stock of that county."[52]

Massie was disappointed, though, in his hope that other whites did not pose a threat to Pharsalia's social order because of their shared culture. When his overseer caught a field hand named Pollard stealing grain from one of the mills, Massie tried to get the man away from Pharsalia. He hired Pollard out to a businessman named Charles Scott in distant Wytheville, Virginia, in the hopes that Scott would buy the unfortunate slave. Massie quickly reversed himself, though, when Scott set Pollard to work on a railroad crew in the southwestern part of the state. Close association with the hired-out slaves and free laborers on the crew, Massie feared, would further infect Pollard with the germ of independence. He promptly began demanding that Scott purchase him immediately or send him back so Massie could sell him elsewhere. Closer to home, he fretted about the influence of his neighbors on his slave community. Hemming and hawing during the 1850s over purchasing some local land with a dubious title, he panicked when a white man "of most infamous character" threatened to occupy the property on the basis of a competing claim. Worried that "by trading with my negroes [he would] greatly injure me were he to get in there,"[53] Massie embarked on several years of costly and time-consuming litigation to obtain the property. In the end, he had to acknowledge that the race issue crossed plantation boundaries, and he began involving himself in fights between owners and slaves on nearby plantations. In the early 1850s, Bob, a slave belonging to neighboring planter Lemuel Turner, escaped across the Blue Ridge and lived for a time in Harrisonburg. Massie concluded that "all of [my slaves] (that were old enough) certainly knew that this man Bob had been there as a free man unmolested for near two years & would naturally conclude that there was nothing between them & any of my neighbors['] negroes and freedom but to go to Harrisonburg and be free." "To break them of this example," Massie carried out a chancy scheme to seize and return Bob that eventually landed him in court.[54] Throughout his life, Massie struggled to keep pernicious outside influences at bay, thinking he might thereby keep his slaves safe from any corrupting thoughts of freedom.

In the end, Massie's defense of Pharsalia's social boundaries did not banish notions of freedom from his slave community. In the summer of 1864, a party of Union raiders under Gen. David Hunter passed Pharsalia on their way down the Tye River, and several of the Massie slaves ran off with them. Even when two returned voluntarily, neighbors complained loudly enough about their presence in the neighborhood that Maria Massie, now managing the plantation, quickly hired them away. Her nephew John Ott appreciated the difficulty she had controlling slaves while the temptation of liberty lurked at the edges of the plantation. "Freedom once tasted," he wrote his aunt, "is enough to disturb the equilibrium of most negroes. The bitterness of actual and prolonged experience is only sufficient to change their minds, and when the change does take place, you run the risk of their having come to a condition little better than absolute worthlessness."[55] The taste for freedom was something the Massies were never able to exclude from Pharsalia with stone fences and mechanical cultivators.[56]

The people who surrounded Pharsalia threatened Massie's mastery over the plantation's resources in other ways, as well. He discovered during the antebellum era that capitalist agriculture needed the nonslaveholding whites who owned small farms or rented land in the creek hollows and mountains around Pharsalia. When they chose not to invest in the intensification of their lands, they gave local businesses less trade, dissuaded transportation companies from extending service to the neighborhood, and discouraged capitalists from providing credit in the area. When they refused to abandon their traditional extensive subsistence, or to accept Massie's attempts to intensify Pharsalia's ecology, they challenged him for control of natural resources and authority within the community. White farmers around the triangle refused to acknowledge Massie's mastery and threatened the success of his attempt to be an aristocratic capitalist.

At midcentury, southern conservationists were frustrated by the refusal of so many ordinary white farmers to participate in their plan for capitalist intensification. In the first place, property owners who were unwilling to intensify the ecology of their lands made things more difficult and expensive for those who were. Free-ranging livestock forced planters to fence in large crop fields, requiring an enormous amount of timber. At the same time, many otherwise valuable tracts of rich bottomland were being "turned out to be trampled into mortar [by foraging livestock], producing neither corn nor grass, because they [were] too long and narrow to be fenced," while geometry often forced planters to fence in and farm "the bad land with the good."[57] Furthermore, planters interested in draining those rich stream bottom soils for hay meadows or crop fields were left dependent on the voluntary agreement of their neighbors. Mainstream channels could be affordably straightened and levied—but if one property owner along the watershed refused to participate, others would be forced into the prohibitively expensive task of ditching back up the side creeks as well. William Massie was able to levy off and drain many of his own stream swamps, but the larger Tye riverbottom was left open to the mountain floods. Like the rest of the Piedmont's low grounds, they were probably "a wilderness of weeds and rubbish growth of all kinds" until well into the 1840s.[58]

Farmers with unproductive land also hindered the local economic development needed to sustain the finances of the capitalist intensifier. The Massies came to the Tye Valley as planter-millers, and both father and son continued to grind grain for the community and sell goods and extend credit in exchange for the local crop. Yet profits were always hard to come by. In 1826, the Major and his youngest son had founded the Tye River & Blue Ridge Turnpike Company, which built a toll road that connected the triangle with the Shenandoah Valley across the Blue Ridge and with the main Nelson County roads down the Tye River. Business was always sparse, though, as mountain hollow residents growing corn and running hogs in the woods had little to sell and less ability to buy. Eventually, William Massie was forced to agree with the other investors to cut their losses and declare the company bankrupt.[59] He was still struggling to build up the area's commercial economy in the late 1840s, when he eagerly distributed Multicole rye seed to his neighbors in the hope that the new variety would help them wring a nice grain crop from their poor soils. Any intensification of these lands was a blessing to local businessmen. In fact, one of the major reasons midcentury farm reformers had for pushing the legislature to change the fence and drainage laws was to force small property owners to intensify their holdings. As one advocate of fence law reform explained, "Each farmer having to maintain his own cattle, would keep a smaller number, and confine them generally to a permanent pasture well enclosed; and by being necessarily reduced to one-fourth of their present numbers, and treated as well as the change of system would permit, the livestock would yield more products of every kind . . . than at present."[60]

This struggle between reformers and common farmers to control the landscape of the south Atlantic was brought on by capitalist intensification—a fact revealed by the political debates of the time.[61] Opponents of the coercion of property owners were the ones who made the best rhetorical use of Virginia's republican tradition of personal independence. Conservationists complained that politicians were frightened away from the cause by what one author termed "that bug-bear 'infringing property rights.' "[62] As one essayist put it: "We should hear the plan denounced as an invasion of the 'sacred rights of property,' and the denunciation maintained by so many arguments (or what would pass for arguments) that the advocates would be glad to retreat from the wordy inundation." Until the late 1850s, bills to change the traditional fence laws were beaten back with the charge that closing the open range would make it impossible for poor white men to find a subsistence, and thus force them into servitude. For their part, capitalist reformers tried to defend the rights of property against wandering livestock, but mainly fell back on their confidence that capital investment in intensification was the modern path, and that their opponents were "orphan children . . . old women and contrary and obstinate men."[63]

In the triangle, Massie butted heads with the old women and obstinate men who let valuable ecological resources go to waste. During the 1850s, every trip he made down to his mills near the Tye presented him with a particularly annoying scene: precious bottomland just across the river being planted in tobacco and corn by tenant farmers. The property was owned by Nancy Coffey, the common law widow of a local yeoman, who leased it out for a quick income. "[She] has rented all the flat part of the land to Dick—Tom & Harry," Massie fumed, "who have skinned & abused it horribly & suffered Tye River to break in & wash away several acres on one side, & Cub Creek which traverses it has been permitted to run wild & tear it up in every direction." For a long time he cast longing eyes on the tract, being "exceedingly anxious to get possession of it." But for years he was frustrated by Coffey, who "would neither lease nor sell to [Massie] on any terms, from the fact of her looking on me with jealousy."[64] She finally agreed to give Massie a life lease, albeit at a rate the new tenant thought highly inflated. He quickly sent in his slaves to build massive rock levees—still standing today—to protect it from river and creek floods.

This was not the total extent of his troubles with the Coffeys and other local farm families, though. Even when he had legal title to property, the resentment of his poorer neighbors frustrated Massie's attempts to intensify its ecology. Small farmers resisted labor and capital-intensive agriculture throughout the South, defending traditional ways of exploiting the environment. Up and down the Blue Ridge, especially, white settlers held fast to notions of common rights in the fields and forests. They burned mountain timberlands to improve pasture and hunting and ran cattle over the free range. Both of these activities compromised Massie's attempts to recast the environment of his properties and the surrounding neighborhood. Woods-burning was a particular problem—small farmers set fires in the mountain forests above Pharsalia with little concern for control or property lines. Massie hoped to make profitable use of the mature timber outside his fences and was also worried that mountain residents' fires could easily jump those fences. One 1853 fire on the Little Priest worked its way down into Massie's timberland and then hopped the fence into the Cove. "The damage it has done is immense," Massie seethed, "probably 800 to 1000 panels of fence for me . . . & 500 to 1000 acres of Timber land has been burned over, including the immensely fine timbered hollow at the head of muddy branch. . . . It also blew over into the West fence of my Cove Orchard, got into the logs there & I fear has killed 9 or 10 of my Lady Sweetening apple trees."[65] Massie reserved his greatest wrath, however, for "that long bunter of wench Tyries wife who let it out."[66] The people who thought of the woods as a source of family subsistence were unmoved by his fulminations. The fires were a recurring spring event, and Massie ranted helplessly. In 1841, he accused small farmer Garland Henderson and his neighbors of firing the woods in the hills above Pharsalia to help themselves to the chestnuts. For this crime, the planter named them "the Hell cats about Old Shingleheads."[67] Another woods-burner named Hudson was simply "the maniac."[68]

Many local farmers seemed similarly unconcerned with Massie's claim to his fences, pasture, and crops. In 1836, the constant use local cattle and hog owners made of a large woodland pasture Massie maintained in the ridges just below Pharsalia drove him to fence it off and put a gate up on his mill road.[69] In the mountains, even fences were not enough to keep poorer planters from foraging their livestock in his fields. In 1850 Massie advised a business acquaintance, wealthy Richmonder John Thompson, against buying lands for sale in the Blue Ridge for this reason. "My overseer and slaves," he told Thompson, "have been run to ruin [trying] to keep horses, cattle, and hogs out of my grain. The population [there]about . . . is such that no sooner are their backs turned than down come the fences and in goes the stock."[70] Such trespassing was an ongoing problem for planters in the neighborhood, who faced repeated invasions of their properties in the form of small clearings made in the woods for crops and timber poaching, along with the clandestine livestock invasions. In 1850, absentee landowner Richard Pollard sent Pharsalia's owner a note asking him to look into whether the Fitzgeralds,[71] another local farm family, were still intruding on his land. He asked Massie to have them arrested, but was frustrated enough that he also offered just to sell him the land and wash his hands of the business.[72] Conflicts over similar invasions were a backdrop to the planter's later difficulties with Nancy Coffey. In 1844, his contract with Nelson Munroe instructed the overseer to protect Tyro plantation "from intrusion—particularly intrusion from the Coffey gang."[73]

For their part, local farmers met Massie's ambition and anger with similar animosity. Local farmers were reluctant to allow "a few rich men . . . to dictate to the County," as Nelson County Democrats put it in 1841 (a jibe perhaps aimed at the county's recently retired legislative delegate).[74] At a local election meeting in 1844, Massie was accosted by a drunk who charged that "the Massies were poison, that they had land and slaves, and that they wanted to oppress and sell white men as slaves."[75] Capitalist intensifiers like the Massies were not satisfied with investing in their own properties; they demanded the support and participation of their neighbors, as well. Lacking capital, wanting to avoid the market, and having their own dreams of personal independence to defend, common whites dug in their heels. Fighting the spread of intensification across the southern landscape, they nibbled away at the upper class's mastery over ecological resources. In the triangle at the foot of the Priest, Massie's neighbors and his slaves broke open the borders of Pharsalia and the farming system of its owner. He had intensified the plantation's ecosystem during the 1850s and profited handsomely from his efforts. But as he neared the end of his life, William Massie could not feel confident that he had gained a secure mastery over the natural and social environment.

## The Peak of Capitalism at Pharsalia

After a debilitating intestinal infection that lasted for several months, William Massie died on July 28, 1862, at the age of sixty-seven. Although the Civil War was threatening its continued existence, Pharsalia was at the high point of its capitalist intensification and material prosperity. Shortly after Massie's death, the Nelson County Court designated three of his wealthier neighbors, Charles Patteson, Henry Loving, and James Penn, to take a probate inventory of the estate, which they completed in late August. The lengthy inventory gives a remarkably detailed picture of the human technology that shaped Pharsalia's mid-nineteenth-century agro-ecosystem, and the material life that environment supported.[76]

Pharsalia's owner was a very wealthy man at the time of his death. The total appraised value of his estate was enormous, even considering the influence of wartime inflation—$234,320.11, the equivalent of nearly $4 million dollars in today's money. And that did not include the value of the land at Massie's various plantations, estimated in the 1860 Agricultural Census at more than $100,000.[77] The appraisers went room by room through the Pharsalia house and recorded the consumer affluence of a southern gentry family. Massie and his family lived surrounded by sets of imported china and rockware, expensive beds, wardrobes, mirrors, and side tables, silver plate worth $500, casks of Madeira, sherry, and aged whiskey in the cellar, along with the proverbial silver spoon—several dozen of them, in fact.

Even with all this spending, Pharsalia's overseers and slaves had still been outfitted with some of the best agricultural equipment available. Old plowshares, moldboards, and plow points lay rusting in the lumber house, while steel hoes and shovels were in the hands of fieldworkers and gardeners. Down at the blacksmith shop sat several two- and three-horse hillside plows, as well as a land presser. Cultivators and harrow teeth were also stored there, waiting to be refinished for the next season's soil maintenance. Several double- and triple-tree plows rested in the stable shed. Pharsalia's pastures now fed a full eight yokes of oxen to help the horses pull those big plows. A large corn sheller, a mechanical thresher, and all the various accouterments of milling, distilling, tanning, and the like made Pharsalia the triangle's industrial center. The plantation's molasses cellar had some homemade blackberry wine and pokeberry bounce, reminders of Massie's push to make himself self-sufficient in orchard products back in the 1830s and early 1840s. Mostly, though, it was full of cans of machine oil to maintain all this equipment.

After more than a year of war, the market had swung away from tobacco and back to supporting the crop rotations of the double-cycle. The Confederate government needed meat and bread for the troops, and oats and hay for cavalry and draft horses. Pharsalia's barns were filled with 100,000 pounds of oats and 1,200 bushels of wheat. The clover and grass fallows at the plantation had produced 70 tons of hay. The system was prepared to sustain itself as well. More than 500 pounds of clover seed were left over for the next planting season. Anticipating a wartime shortage, the late planter also had an equal amount of other varieties of grass seed bagged away. The lime house and the Pharsalia mill were full of expensive commercial fertilizers. Even after spring plowing, 230 bushels of lime and 15 tons of plaster of paris were stored at the plantation. The war had cut off supplies of guano, but Massie still had half a ton socked away. All this effort at pasturage was apparently successful, since Pharsalia's livestock herd was prospering. Even with wartime demands, there were well over a hundred hogs at the plantation, with 2 boars set aside from the "killing hogs," possibly for breeding. Nearly 50 cattle joined almost 150 sheep in the fields and barns. No woods hogs were mentioned in Massie's Farm Accounts from the previous several years. All these well-managed animals produced plenty of manure as well. The Pharsalia barn housed several wooden manure beds, multiple manure forks, and plenty of large wagons to haul all that feces out to the fields at plow time.

Yet for all the apparent success of capitalist intensification at the outset of the Civil War, Pharsalia still showed signs of its troubled youth as a traditional Virginia plantation. There was no tobacco in the fields or barns, but the means to return to the old staple were everywhere apparent. Old tobacco plant beds sat in the barn, beside a large tobacco screw. Weeding methods still relied on the old methods more often than not, and there were plenty of hoes alongside the big plows in the sheds and blacksmith shop. The love of autonomy that drove the gentry planter was also evident in the 1862 inventory. Daphne, a Pharsalia slave, ran a home weaving operation, with several wheels and looms at her disposal. Cotton and flax were stored in the lumber house—all so no clothing would have to be bought for the Pharsalia slaves. Nor had Massie wanted to buy leather goods. The newly built lumber house was filled with scraps of skin and hide from various dead Pharsalia animals—including a dog skin valued at a dollar—and sacks of alum salt to aid in the tanning process. If Massie was unwilling to see a dog skin go to waste, he took the same attitude toward old plow irons and other rusted-out metal goods. The blacksmith's shop and other plantation buildings were filled with bits and pieces of tools, metal bars, and assorted pieces of old iron. One can almost sense the exasperation of the tired court officers at having to record the barrel of "tin scraps" they appraised, like the dog skin, at a dollar. Like the new ecological relations in the fields, capitalist farm technology was a recent arrival at Pharsalia and had hardly erased what had come before.

In the end, Pharsalia's embrace of capitalist intensification was never an entirely happy marriage. For more than a decade, new plants, fertilizers, equipment, and ideas had invaded the plantation's ecosystem, transforming it radically. Yet on his deathbed, Massie was still dreaming of completely mastering Pharsalia and still regarding the world beyond its fences with suspicion. The whole search for intensification, or "agricultural improvement," had been built on the understanding that stable agroecosystems meant autonomous ones. Yet in the end, Pharsalia had not attained that independence, sacrificing it for the productivity that capitalist intensification and resource conservation could provide. William Massie and his family never had to, as the planter once grumpily put it, "run off from my house and live in the mountain." [78] Yet the loss of independence came at a cost—he was left trying to manage markets, environments, and people, rather than mastering them. As it approached its final years, Pharsalia was not the secure gentry home place where Massie had hoped to become a self-assured southern aristocrat.

# The Gentry Family and the Fall of Pharsalia, 1861–1889

Pharsalia was in its prime in the years leading up to the Civil War. Capitalist intensification had helped the plantation escape its ecological crisis and achieve a measure of profit and stability. Yet as William Massie's life drew to an end, he still struggled to master its resources in the face of many challengers. The most serious of these threats did not come from outside his fences, as he had always expected. Capitalist intensification's greatest failure in the triangle would be its inability to deliver on the aristocratic ambitions of the Massie family. Products of the Virginia elite, they wanted to assert their status by spending heavily on luxury consumer goods. They also believed that a rural plantation was the proper way to earn the wealth for those purchases and the proper place to display them. While William Massie fought to reinvest his resources in intensive agriculture, his children badgered him for the money, land, and slaves they needed to establish themselves in the southern gentry. Both Massie and his wife, Maria, feared their demands would result in the breakup of Pharsalia, and they tried to keep the plantation intact. They shared their children's ambition, though, and accepted that they would have to provide for it in the end. After her husband's death, Maria Massie tried to manage Pharsalia for profit while still keeping the family's home place secure for the next generation. Her efforts, though, resulted in slowly diminishing returns while occasionally dividing her family. Pharsalia grew old with Maria, and in her final will before her death in 1889, she gave up the battle to keep the plantation intact. Pharsalia died with her.

*Capitalist Intensification and the Southern Family*

In the summer of 1860, just two years before William Massie died, a large group of family members came from across Virginia to stay with him at Pharsalia. As a southern planter-patriarch, the sixty-five-year-old man should have been in the fullness of his glory as his family gathered around him. A lifetime of work managing and developing his property had left him wealthy. Despite the untimely deaths of three of his wives, he still had a crowd of dutiful dependents who now came to pay respects and receive hospitality and inheritances from his generous hand. Rather than being content, though, Massie was seething about the reunion of his extended family in his now crowded mansion home. He groused about the imposition in a series of acrid memorandums supposedly commenting on the weather:

> Aug 4 . . . Burned up without, & devoured substance, body, & soul, with Barbara's [Effinger] cohorts then Goth & Vandal from the Federal City [Hope Massie and friends, then studying in Washington, D.C.], Campbell & elsewhere. The Lynchburgers and Rockinghams I am glad to have, as they have mercy & will not suck at my vitals for all time.
>
> Aug 17 . . . Another Valley suck-gut arrives [probably referring to his wife's relation John Graham Effinger], about noon, from Richmond, and there are now six of that breed of dog here, & how long these Vampires will be quartered on me, my Wife, my negroes, my horses & vehicles smoke houses, poultry yards, Dairy etc. etc., God only knows & to him I devoutly pray for succor— That Prick faced fellow John Graham is a very bad addition to the Vampires.
>
> Aug 18 . . . the Vampires are sucking away and not half full. Thos [Massie's eldest son] and family come this evening, & we have it in full tonight.[1]

Massie's wrath at the idea of feeding his relations a decent dinner seems odd. During the previous three years, he had purchased more land and corresponded at length with his children about his generous plans for their inheritances. Yet his metaphor of vampires sucking the blood from the agricultural resources of his plantation reveals that he was more of a capitalist farmer than just an ill-tempered old man. Massie needed the resources of Pharsalia's carefully managed agricultural ecosystem for profitable production and reinvestment, not redistribution.

Redistribution was what the next generation of Massies and Effingers wanted, though. Massie had six children at this point: a son by his first wife, Thomas James Massie, now forty-three years old, married and living on a nearby farm; a daughter by his second wife, Ellen, now thirty years old and married to Jacob Warwick; and four children by his fourth wife, Maria—Martha Virginia, twenty-five years old and recently married to neighboring farmer Joseph Ligon; seventeen-year-old Hope; twelve-year-old Florence; and six-year-old Bland. Raised among the planter elite, this third generation of Nelson County Massies saw themselves growing up to live the southern gentleman's version of the good life: a big house on a country estate, filled with consumer luxury, slaves working the fields making the money to buy more, and the respect and deference of the surrounding community. Nor were upper-class children patient about their desires: they spent their parents' money with abandon, then demanded land and slaves so they could be independent as well. William Massie had followed this pattern himself. As a teenager, he had run up debts with local store owners while attending Washington College across the Blue Ridge in Staunton.[2] Once out of school, he quickly married a girl from another planter family and forced land and slaves out of his father. He and his young wife then got busy going into debt. The depression of the 1820s shocked him out of some of his aristocratic illusions, though, and he was soon begging his wife "for Gods sake don't spend one cent more than you can help."[3] Massie matured into a frugal manager of his estate, but still bought enough luxury items to live like a gentleman. Like his father before him, he was unable to prevent a love of luxury from creeping into his children. Indeed, as the proud patriarch of a gentry family, he was not entirely willing to do so.

Despite cutting back on his own spending during the 1820s and 1830s, Massie began to run into trouble with his eldest son, Thomas James Massie. While boarded at the New London Academy at the age of twelve, the boy became "extremely inclined to waste money"[4]—a problem that would continue throughout his adolescent and adult life. Yet his father was never able to bring himself to cut him off. Massie did not judge his son solely by his profligacy and his business blunders—Massie's aim was to raise an aristocratic businessman, not just a businessman. For all his failings, Thomas James still seemed to his father "an honorable—high-toned gentleman," earning him the stamp of parental approval: "as such, I feel proud of you." There were other high-toned gentlemen and ladies growing up at Pharsalia, though, and they soon followed their eldest brother's path. After getting married, Ellen and Jacob Warwick quickly racked up several thousand dollars in liabilities. Warwick appealed to his father-in-law to cosign another loan, and when Massie refused, it brought on a quarrel with his daughter and other family members that took several months to heal. Martha got into trouble with excessive spending while at boarding school in Charlottesville. She then lied to her father about the debts, causing him severe embarrassment when he had to clean up the problem.[5]

This culture of upper-class consumerism posed a serious threat to the finances and ecology of capitalist farming. Successful capitalist intensification meant stockpiling resources, holding on to them while the money came in, then reinvesting profits in more purchases to keep up with the market. Runaway spending by planters and their families drained away the income needed to buy new, productive resources. Pressing debts discouraged investments, pushing planters back toward the expedient of extensive, exhausting cultivation. Those who did invest in intensification often found themselves forced to sell land to pay their debts, sacrificing future profits from the improvements they had made. The division of parental estates to provide inheritances for their many children further undermined intensification by breaking up farm infrastructure, pasture and livestock, and crop rotations. Southern capitalist planters were set against themselves. Wanting to improve their farms, they tried to reinvest their meager profits in the hopes of future abundance. Wanting to live well and help their children do the same, they kept spending liberally. The plantation of the capitalist intensifier struggled when asked to be both a highly productive, sustainable agroecosystem and a secure, idyllic gentry home place.

Massie was caught in this contradiction himself. Recognizing the dangers this free-spending culture posed to his estate and his ambitions, he still wanted to make Pharsalia a haven of personal security and abundance, a place where he could spend "the evening of my life comfortable."[6] But his spending, and that of his children, racked up debts that threatened him with having to sell out and emigrate. He responded as good Virginia republicans often did, by thinking he could solve the problem by sealing his children off from the outside world. In a letter to Martha's principal apologizing for her debts, he railed against the influence the society of his home state had on the young, calling eastern Virginia "this land of pride, waste, *indulgence*, indolence & poverty."[7] Perhaps remembering his own experiences, and those of Thomas James and Martha Virginia, Massie fretted about the time the teenage offspring of antebellum southern planters typically spent away at boarding school. At Pharsalia, Massie could control the purse strings and preach the virtues of "economy and close-cutting." Off at school though, his children entered a world where status was measured in fashionable clothes and lavish parties, and, for the boys, horses, gambling, and liquor as well. Massie tried to fight off this culture by keeping his children at home. In response to Martha's troubles in Charlottesville, he and Maria established a small boarding school at Pharsalia for his two youngest daughters and the children of other planters in the neighborhood. Judging from subsequent events, Massie's aim, to "educate this brood with notions of industry and economy,"[8] seems to have been unmet. His own lavish home would have belied his teachings, and his children's materialism grew largely unchecked.

Unable to keep the influence of southern upper-class society at bay, Massie had to face the damage it could do to capitalist intensification. Thomas James Massie proved a failure as a planter. His father gave him an early bequest of slaves and cash, but the young man dissipated it while farming rented land. When Thomas James married, William provided a further inheritance by selling him Red Hill farm on land he owned just across the Tye River. That too proved inadequate to cover the expenses of Thomas James's growing family. As the father climbed out of debt during the late 1840s, his son fell deeper into the red. Throughout the next decade, their personal correspondence was filled with Thomas James's pleas for land, slaves, and money, and his father's admonitions to patience and thrift. Mounting debts then drove Massie's son back into traditional, extensive southern farming. For years, he had followed his father's advice and intensified the agroecology of Red Hill. But the profits had been slow to come in, and his debts kept going up. In 1858, desperate to balance his accounts, Thomas James determined to cash in his improvements, sell off the now valuable farm, and put his slaves to work on rented land in the neighborhood. His father was aghast. "Red Hill," Massie advised his son, "I regard as good landed property, you have improved it, with labor, and I think skill, it's in a condition to make crops, & will if worked with patience, & skill make good returns. To take 15 or 20 likely negroes on that miserable, worn out, hen grass, Old Merchant Thompson place, without as you say fences, fence rail, or building timber, & a scarcity of firewood, seems to me insanity. The negroes would starve, as would you."[9]

Suddenly abandoning a major investment in intensification to work slaves on cheaper land went against everything Massie had been trying to do at Pharsalia. In the long run, he believed, capitalist intensification could reduce more of a planter's debt through regular, abundant crops than could hasty sell-offs of land or slaves. The key was investment, patience, and systematic management of resources, things Massie had grown to pride himself on. In the early 1850s, for instance, he had calculated that his estate provided him with only a thousand dollars in clear profit a year, not much, given its size and large slave force. The problem, he now concluded, was a lack of resources that required greater investment—even if it cut into those profits for the moment. To expand his manuring, he built more barns to house more livestock. Feeling that he had too much land, he refused to farm extensively or sell off the excess. Instead, he waited for his "young negroes [to] grow up so as to clear me of debt."[10] He refused to dissipate his resources by helping Jacob Warwick with his financial problems, informing his son-in-law that he had a long-term plan to make his lands more productive and profitable, that once "broken into, would ruin all."[11] Thomas James, however, had not followed his father into capitalist thinking and was still tempted by quick expedients to retire his debt. His father, after repeatedly chasing quick tobacco profits and considering the temptations of western migration, now insisted on seeing investments through. "I have never taken an inventory of my estate," he lectured his son, " . . . [as] I could see no use in it, having always looked upon my property as sacred, & not as currency with which to pay debts, & bear expenses—my income has been looked to pay debts & current expenses."[12] To a young man facing bankruptcy, he counseled sacrificing profit to make risky long-term investments.

It was not a program Thomas James was willing to embrace. For his part, William Massie remained at heart a plantation patriarch and a fond father, and he responded by caving in. Over the years, he repeatedly compromised his new principles by extending more cash, land, and slaves to cover his son's inability to balance his books. Like his peers, he looked to the day when he could provide landed estates for the next generation of Massies at Pharsalia. Trying to defend himself against Thomas James's repeated requests, he reminded his son of the tens of thousands of dollars he had advanced him. But he then went on to say, "my will & desire is . . . to do you ample justice. . . . This you will see when I am gone." [13] With his other children to be provided for as well, Massie even began longing for the hard years of the 1820s, when he had been "in the prime of life & had a very *small family*." [14] Now, he had to help six children live like aristocrats. For years, he had sacrificed profits by holding on to land he did not have the labor or capital to farm intensively—all to be ready to give farms to his children. He had also hoped to deal with the agroecological consequences of handing on his property by maintaining smaller quarters like Level Green, Tyro, Montebello, and Snug Dale, as separate establishments. But he soon realized that in order to keep his family in the ranks of the plantation gentry, he would have to break up his most profitable property, Pharsalia.

In his final will, Massie divided his landed estate between Maria and his children, while trying to keep Pharsalia intact as best he could. He gave land and cash to his elder children, Thomas James, Ellen Warwick, and Martha (now married to Joseph Ligon), out of other portions of the estate, including Level Green, Snug Dale, and the proceeds from the sale of Montebello. This left Pharsalia and the adjoining Tyro quarter to be divided among his three youngest children, Hope, Florence, and Bland. But Massie was not quite ready to give up on the profits he had hoped to get from the capitalist intensification of Pharsalia by dividing the plantation. In the short run, while the three children were still minors, it remained a single farm under Maria's trusteeship. While relying on his wife to share his values about farming and money, Massie did divide Pharsalia between her portion and the inheritances of Hope, Florence and Bland. For years after Massie's death, his carefully constructed capitalist farm was held together. But the seeds of Pharsalia's division and demise had been sown.

Florence's portion was the poorest of the three, perhaps in anticipation of her getting married to a well-situated planter or businessman (although her first husband, John Tunstall, disappointed in that respect). Her tract was a long, narrow strip on the western edge of Pharsalia, running between Muddy Branch and the Mill Creek from the southern border of the plantation up onto the lower slopes of the Little Priest. It included the long-cultivated, heavily eroded lands of Field Number Two, as well as the erosion-depleted soils on Ned's Hill. Maria maintained direct control until Florence married Tunstall in 1868. Unlike Martha Ligon and the Massie boys, however, Florence left the triangle when she got married. Her part of the estate would hardly have kept her husband there, anyway. Back in 1847, her father had referred to "Field Number Two" at the base of Ned's Hill as being "in the pines," while portions of it cleared for wheat suffered serious gullying during the heavy rains of 1860. Her mother therefore kept managing it as part of Pharsalia while Florence's husband was occupied with his Lynchburg business. For her part, Maria received a similarly narrow strip, but a much richer and more valuable one. Until her death in 1889, William Massie's widow owned the old core of Pharsalia plantation. This included the plantation house and most of the lots and outbuildings, as well as the old orchard. Stretching south of the house, Maria's portion contained the old Front Field (Field Number One), as well as the Cove behind the house. Bland's portion was more generous in land, but lacked the farm infrastructure retained by Maria along with the house and lots. Bland would, in fact, eventually build his own barns and stables at the smaller Tyro farm, much of which he also inherited. Out of Pharsalia, the youngest of the Massie children received most of the eastern fields, including the old meadow on the Spring Run and much of Fields Five (Flat Field) and Six (Tansey Field). For his part, Hope got the northern half of the Flat Field and all of Rambler's Field, to go along with other property in the neighborhood. For more than a decade, however, this division of Pharsalia existed only on paper. Bland was only eight years old at the time of his father's death. Hope soon surrendered control of his portion of the plantation to his mother. Along with Florence's portion, Maria would also keep control of the eastern portion of Pharsalia well into the 1870s.

Yet for all Maria's efforts, Pharsalia could not sustain the ambitions

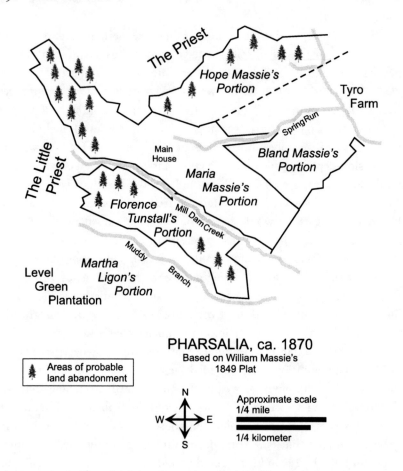

PHARSALIA, ca. 1870
Based on William Massie's
1849 Plat

Areas of probable
land abandonment

N
W ← → E
S

Approximate scale
1/4 mile

1/4 kilometer

the Massie children had for themselves and for their landed inheritances. After William Massie's demise, his failure to save his children from the gentry culture of the Old South—or to save Pharsalia from his children— became clear. Faced with the dangers of the Civil War and the uncertainty of the postwar era, his children fell back on their family's social status for reassurance. As his financial situation deteriorated, Thomas James Massie in particular retreated into nostalgic celebration of his family name. Late in life, he set himself to write a celebratory biography of his grandfather, Maj. Thomas Massie. A like-minded relative, N. H. Massie, encouraged him in the effort, echoing William Massie's own aristocratic sentiments. "We may[,] I fear must[,] continue to be a Republican people," Thomas James was informed, "and yet for all that if one has sprung from a race that can go back for generations, & count nothing but honorable, high tone men and women among his ancestors & forebearers . . . it does have a powerful influence in moulding building up & sustaining that pride of character & name."[15] For the younger Massies, an even more satisfying way to sustain the family name was to keep up aristocratic appearances. Young Florence Massie's social conservatism was as intense as her eldest brother's and rested on her family's material prosperity. Away at school during the Civil War, she wrote Maria about two girls who paid their tuition and board in peaches. "I suppose that shews what kind of girls they are," the fifteen-year-old girl sniffed. "I am very sorry they have come but there always has to be some common girls in schools to give you an example."[16] While visiting various friends during the late 1860s, she peppered her mother with letters praising the lavish dress and expensive entertainments of the people she was socializing with.[17] While at boarding school during the same period, Bland begged money of his mother to keep up with the expensive dress of his classmates. He wound up spending so much money that Maria was forced to go visit her youngest son at school in Staunton and reprimand him.[18]

While they continued to carry themselves like plantation aristocrats, the Massie children found it difficult to succeed at farming in the hard times that followed the war. Wartime death and destruction, the loss of capital and political influence, and increasingly competitive markets combined to break the fortunes, if not the self-image, of many of the Old Dominion's plantation gentry. Their dream of acquiring and enjoying luxury on their own plantations remained undiminished, though, and the distance between ambition and reality weighed heavily on them. Both Thomas James and Hope struggled financially and personally in the postwar world. Thomas James eventually lost his last inheritance from his father—Snug Dale farm—to his creditors, while Hope also lost much of his inheritance after he reached adulthood.[19] He was soon reduced to running a local trade out of his family's mills down by the Tye River. Expecting to be planter-gentlemen like their father, both men grew bitter and isolated as their status declined.[20] Florence's first husband, John Tunstall, also ran into trouble. His generous patriarchal ambition to "expend on the comfort of those around him to the detriment of himself," quickly landed the young couple deep in debt.[21] Martha and her husband,

Joseph Ligon, were also forced to sell off part of their land in the triangle to balance accounts. The Massies' slow descent from the height of the plantation gentry reflected the trend across the region. Planters and their children tried hard to keep farming their ancestral properties. Yet they saw their landholdings and share of the agricultural market diminish.[22] Maria's younger Effinger relations went into business, moving to Richmond and other urban centers. Only Bland was able to re-create a bit of his father's wealth and standing as a rural aristocrat on his inheritance of Tyro farm. As William Massie's children struggled, they grew to dislike and distrust the competitive business of farming for profit. As he slid down toward bankruptcy, Thomas James seemed to feel that business success was an unexplainable stroke of luck. In his brief biography of his grandfather, Major Massie, he explained that "like Midas, everything he touched seemed to have turned to gold so that . . . he [was] found absolutely at a loss what to do with his money."[23] The Major's grandchildren were never so lucky in their own financial affairs.

William Massie had discovered that he could not seal himself off on his plantation and enjoy a masterful independence—and after the Civil War things got even more difficult. Yet in those insecure and disjointed times, his children abandoned the harder lessons he had learned about farming for profit. They preferred to romanticize the antebellum plantation they remembered from happier childhoods—safe, secure, and prosperous.[24] According to Thomas James Massie, his magically prosperous grandfather had achieved the kind of life he vainly dreamed of for himself: "surfeited with success, [he] withdrew from business & spent the remainder of his life living upon his income at Level Green."[25] For the younger generation of Massies and Effingers, the postbellum farm managed by Maria remained "sweet old Pharsalia,"[26] an idyllic retreat from a modern world they could not control.[27] Having moved to the burgeoning railroad center of Roanoke in the 1880s, Maria's nephew John Ott wrote her that his wife "Annie . . . dreamed continually of Nelson, and what a joy it would be to her if her duties would only permit her to go and spend a week or two with you."[28] But the more idealized the landscape of the southern plantation became for the dispirited children of the prewar gentry, the further it drifted from the reality of profitable, sustainable farming. Most of them chose to overlook how difficult it had been to get Pharsalia to keep producing the money that had supported their parents' way of life.

Maria Massie was a little more realistic about the whole problem than the younger generation. As a farmer, she was quite successful under difficult circumstances. Despite a lack of capital, she kept Pharsalia intact and productive until her death in 1889. She maintained the double-cycle and bought new resources when she was able. Better than most of her children and stepchildren, she understood how to manage Pharsalia profitably, and she distrusted their attitudes toward consumer spending and business. Shortly after the war, Thomas James Massie challenged some of the more complex financial arrangements in his father's will. Realizing that providing him with more money would require selling improved land, Maria fought him in court. The extended legal action splintered the family, and she did not speak to her stepson for many years. As she aged and watched her own children struggle financially, Maria also grew distrustful of their abilities. Hoping to preserve some of the estate for her grandchildren, in a succession of codicils to her will Maria gradually excluded Hope, Bland, and her grown daughters from full control of the estate, with uncertain consequences for the family. All the property she retained control over was left in trust to her grandchildren.[29]

Her battles with the land and within her family were difficult for her. Like her late husband, she kept hoping Pharsalia would keep her children in that dying rural gentry. The result of romanticizing the plantation as the setting for the ideal planter's life was to undermine its profitability and break up its agricultural ecosystem. As Florence and Bland approached maturity, William Massie's old division of Pharsalia hung over the plantation. Judging from the way she managed it, Maria may well have concluded that Pharsalia's division was inevitable. Throughout the 1870s and 1880s, she seemed reluctant to spend much to further intensify farming at Pharsalia. After all, any investments she made might soon be broken apart and sold off by her children. Bland handled his portion of the estate with competence, though he did sell tracts he was unable to farm profitably. When Maria died in 1889, the central strip of Pharsalia along with the house went to Martha Ligon, who quickly parted with it. Hope and Florence eventually sold the rest of their landed inheritance, as well. Maria

Massie tried to keep Pharsalia together, but the economics and ecology of capitalist intensification were at war with the ideals and expectations of many members of the southern upper class.

## Pharsalia under Maria Massie

Detailed information about the Pharsalia agroecosystem is scarce for the years after William Massie's death. His widow, Maria, was a precise and engaged financial and farm manager. Yet she apparently never developed her late husband's obsessive habits of record-keeping. William Massie's Farm Accounts peter out quickly after 1860 and end entirely after his death. If Maria kept similar farming records, they have not survived. Some valuable information about Pharsalia's later years can be gleaned from her surviving correspondence, business records, and the agricultural census.[30] But a reconstruction of the story of the plantation's last years contains a good deal of generalization and guesswork. What does emerge from this sparse evidence is that the Civil War and Reconstruction periods were years of inertia for Pharsalia's agricultural ecosystem. The legal restrictions of guardianship and her children's expectations of a landed inheritance made Maria Massie a cautious farmer.[31] While she tried to maintain her late husband's farming system, she was less willing to make risky investments in intensification. In most cases she preferred to defend Pharsalia's existing farm environment, relying on the income generated by the improvements made before the war. This approach gave the plantation a comfortable but declining old age—the security of tested ecological relationships, but the undertow of stagnating productivity. Under Maria, Pharsalia's agroecosystem was not able to produce enough profit to sustain the ambitions of the next generation of Massies.

Maria Massie did share many of her husband's ideas about the nature and business of farming, though. Between 1862 and her own death in 1889, she maintained the double-cycle at Pharsalia. On occasion, she also imported soil additives, equipment, and new crop varieties to keep the plantation's ecology intensive. And while most of her children's landed estates slowly declined around her, she kept Pharsalia largely intact as a profitable farm. Nonetheless, numerous obstacles frustrated further capitalist intensification at the foot of the Priest. Maria's options were limited by her responsibilities to her children as her husband's executrix, by the lack of capital created by the war and emancipation, and by having to sell her crops in competitive and deflated markets.[32] As she grew older, Maria focused her efforts on preserving Pharsalia's value for her children and grandchildren, rather than risking her meager resources on new experiments. Under these pressures, she remained wary about making dramatic changes to the plantation's agricultural ecosystem. While she managed Pharsalia, Maria reduced her financial risk by maintaining the mix of crops and cultivation used during the 1850s. In some ways, her reliance on the now tested ecological adaptations of the new plants, animals, and equipment her husband had brought to Pharsalia was reminiscent of his search for rigid autonomy during the 1830s and 1840s. This caution protected her children's inheritances but did not create the kind of wealth needed to outrun their financial demands.

The Civil War had a mixed impact on the agricultural ecosystem William Massie and the Pharsalia slaves had created. He and Maria did not invest heavily in the plantation during the war years. In fact, there was little to invest with. Sources of capital were cut off as the Confederate government sucked up surplus assets through sales of government securities. Both William and Maria remained suspicious of Confederate bonds, preferring state bank stock. Yet William had already loaned the southern government thirty-five hundred dollars by the time of his death.[33] Biotic resources for intensification were also hard to come by. The national trade in seed and orchard stock was interrupted by the conflict, and the South's supplies of grass seed and fertilizer soon vanished. As it had been during the depression of the early 1840s, Pharsalia was once again thrown back on its own depleted ecological resources.

On the other hand, the wartime economy did reward the double-cycle. William Massie had joined many other Virginia planters in cultivating more tobacco in the years before the war.[34] But as farmers left the fields to fight, and the Confederate government demanded more food to feed them, grain and meat prices skyrocketed. Responding to a war market in which "everything is very dear that is edible," first William and then Maria shifted the focus of farming at Pharsalia back to crops and livestock.[35] The year before William Massie died, there was still hope for a quick peace and the Union naval blockade was not yet effective. He was hopeful enough to send his slaves to cultivate and harvest 48,000 pounds of tobacco at his various plantations in 1861. But the next year he also expanded grain, grass, and livestock production. In 1862, the appraisers of Massie's estate found that the Pharsalia barns held 60,000 pounds of oats, 850 bushels of wheat, 200 barrels of corn, and a full 50 tons of hay. The oat harvest in particular was a huge increase from the yield Massie reported in the agricultural census three years earlier. Several hundred hogs and dozens of cattle, dairy cows, and oxen were housed at Pharsalia and Level Green.[36] Fields of corn, wheat, and oats, and herds of cattle and swine grazing on stubble and even native grasses rewarded the effort by conserving much of the soil structure and nutrients built up by the double-cycle. The urge to clear new grounds at the edge of the plantation for tobacco or to commit established pastures or heavily manured lots to the sot weed was removed. While firm evidence is lacking, from her correspondence it appears that as the war dragged on Maria continued this trend by abandoning tobacco and concentrating entirely on foodstuffs.[37] For a brief moment in the Piedmont, the largest short-term profits could only be found through sustainable crop rotations and animal husbandry.

The Civil War may have led the Massies away from the traditional exhaustive cultivation of the early South. But the conflict threatened capitalist intensification in other ways. Southern conservationists had reversed Virginia's declining agricultural fortunes during the 1850s, but the war dragged many of the region's farmers down once more. Both Union and Confederate armies hit the manuring side of the double-cycle particularly hard. Soldiers requisitioned or stole livestock for draft and food, and pulled down fences and farm buildings for firewood. Planters who had invested labor and capital to expand and care for their livestock herds in the hopes of maintaining soil fertility saw their accomplishments quickly destroyed. Deep in a remote corner of central Virginia, Pharsalia was far enough from the main battlefields to escape much of the devastation. But troops on both sides pillaged the plantation's resources when they did pass by. Maria protested to the Confederate government over depredations committed by the 2nd South Carolina cavalry regiment when it wintered in the neighborhood in early 1863. On the Union side, David Hunter's cavalry took time to make off with sixteen of the Massie's horses as they rode quickly down the Tye Valley the next year.[38]

More threatening than passing cavalry, though, were the growing demands of the Confederacy on plantation resources and produce. The government in Richmond successfully protected the core of central Virginia
from invasion. Yet its leaders looked at the region as a vital breadbasket
and source of manpower. With her husband dead and her adult sons in
the army, slave discipline once again became a worry for Maria, and she
had to fight off attempts to draft her overseers.[39] More ominously, as
the South's food shortage descended into crisis Confederate authorities
grew more aggressive in their efforts to impress livestock and crops to
feed the army.[40] Nelson County's administration soon got into the act as
well, ordering Maria and other planters to feed the wives and widows
of soldiers from the area.[41] In order to keep Pharsalia sustainable and
profitable, she had to keep its resources intact—especially the livestock
herds, precious to her for their manure and to the government for their
work or their meat—if she wanted to ensure the smooth functioning of
the double-cycle. Maria used her nephew John Ott, who worked in the
War Department in Richmond during the conflict, to get leverage with
the government to fend off these demands on Pharsalia's animals and
produce.[42]

Aided by her contacts and social position, Pharsalia's protected location, and high food prices, Maria Massie was able to keep the plantation
intact and profitable during the war years. To be sure, the family's finances took a heavy blow from the South's defeat. The Confederate securities and currency they held became worthless, and the Pharsalia slaves,
one of the bases of William and Maria Massie's fortune, were freed. Yet
Pharsalia's agroecosystem survived the wreck of the South rather well.
Across the rest of eastern Virginia, on the other hand, the physical destruction of the war and the financial devastation of the peace crippled
capitalist agriculture. In 1865, planters and farmers returned from the
front to find their fences and outbuildings torn down, their seed eaten up,
their livestock impressed, their fields overgrown with weeds, and their
slaves gone. In many areas, planters were so starved for capital that they
rented their lands to former slaves as sharecropper farms, while northern
merchants moved in to offer usurious crop liens. By removing the farmers' incentive to protect land values, tenancy accelerated the process of
erosion and exhaustion that the double-cycle had slowed. Furthermore,

many farmers, both black and white, landowner and tenant, were so desperate for food and ready cash that they turned back to corn and tobacco monocultures. This brought back all the agroecological problems of the Revolutionary era.[43] The late nineteenth century proved to be the worst period for destructive soil erosion in the southern Piedmont.[44] Many also made the decision to return to traditional farming because southern markets were flooded with northern produce as early as the fall of 1865. Farmers faced with the large quantities, cheap prices, and high quality of northern crops had few of the ecological or financial resources they would have needed to compete. Even commercial producers retreated into traditional staples—and the colonial economy and ecological destruction they brought with them.[45]

With intensive farming well established at Pharsalia, Maria Massie was able to buck the trend toward sharecropping and extensive cultivation. Freedpeople across the Piedmont resisted the imposition of wage labor, hoping to own their own land or at least to free themselves from daily white supervision by becoming tenant farmers. Many other Nelson County planters knuckled under by breaking up their prewar properties in exchange for shares of the tobacco crop.[46] Despite most of the area's land remaining in the hands of its prewar owners, many of the large plantations in the Tye Valley were dismantled. The region fell into a steep economic decline from which it has never fully recovered. For her part, Maria held on tightly to the new system of free labor and adapted it to her plantation's agroecosystem. She apparently was confident wage workers could support capitalist intensification. Increased labor flexibility was certainly a boon, especially when the family was no longer responsible for maintaining young children and the aged among the plantation hands.[47] In a letter to Maria from the late summer of 1865, her nephew Harvey Effinger recognized the financial advantages to free labor: "I am exceedingly anxious to hear from you since our new system of labor has been introduced. I hope you have been able to make satisfactory arrangements with your best hands, if you can be relieved of all your surplus negroes I have no doubt you will find the new system to work much better than anticipated. Our children will have to learn to do much more than we have been accustomed to do. We have only two young servants & are getting along better than we have ever done."[48]

Flexibility and reduced domestic expenditures were values William Massie might well have endorsed for Pharsalia's profitability, and Maria seems to have shared her husband's sentiments. She hired a number of Pharsalia's slave families to annual work contracts. Others were turned off, left voluntarily, or went to work for her children. Maria then paid a much reduced Pharsalia workforce annual wages, against which she advanced food and other supplies. She kept farming intensively by replacing the lost labor with new equipment, especially in the wheat fields. Maintaining this system for the rest of her life, for the most part, she resisted the temptation to rent out her land. Despite the division in her late husband's will, she fought to keep Pharsalia under her control. Just as slavery had not stopped William Massie from pursuing capitalist intensification, emancipation did not stop his widow from sustaining the agricultural ecology he and his slaves had developed.[49]

Embracing free labor did not mean that Maria and the other Massies were ready to embrace racial equality. Business leaders throughout the area might have seen some of the economic advantages to free labor, but they dreaded the loss of control over black workers. Their response was a surge of vocal, often violent, racism that served to vent their fears and set limits to black Virginians' mobility and opportunity.[50] For her part, Maria became something of a leader in defending the old racial order in the upper Tye Valley. In 1867, Nelson County state senator C. T. Smith spoke in Massie's Mill in favor of accepting Republican demands for black political equality. Outraged, Maria denounced him throughout the neighborhood, and the influence of the Massie name was enough to force a personal apology from Smith.[51] The comings and goings of freedmen and -women challenged the planter's mastery of his (or her) carefully managed domain—particularly in forcing the breakup of plantations into rental farms. Maria saw in emancipation the chance to exert greater control over the role of labor at Pharsalia, not less. Like her husband before her, she wanted to profit from her farm. But she was not ready to allow any further breakdown in white supremacy to cross the plantation's fences.

Maria Massie's conservative adaptation to some of the new realities of race and labor mirrored the outlook of many planters and businessmen across the postbellum South. On the farm, in the factory, and in the countinghouse, there were plenty of wealthy whites eager to push the region's economy past its traditional base of staple crop exports. The prewar planter class's hold on power was broken as merchants and investors in the cities pushed their way into positions of leadership. Reluctantly, the children of the gentry began abandoning farming for business and the professions. In Virginia, "conservative" state politicians established a tax code that favored commerce and industry over agriculture. Entrepreneurs avidly sought northern capital. Yet this new elite joined the descendants of the planter class in idealizing the social order of the antebellum plantation. People like the Massies still hoped to control economic development so that new businesses and new markets would not threaten the rule of a native elite over deferential and dependent black and white laborers.[52]

This reluctance to abandon the old order was reflected in the social snobbery and racial conservatism of the postwar Massies and other members of the elite. Even the most ambitious of Virginia businessmen hung onto old family homes in the countryside. As emblems of their wealth and status, parvenus purchased the plantation homes that gentry bankruptcies had placed on the market.[53] Indeed, many of the Massie descendants deeply regretted the 1890s sell-off of the plantation. Florence Morton, one of Bland Massie's daughters, used money from her husband's invention of ChapStick lip balm to buy back her family's ancestral home in the early 1950s.[54] But, as Maria's postwar management of Pharsalia shows, this conservatism was more than an empty shell. Her caution ruled, and limited, her willingness to embrace the ethics and demands of a capitalist economy and ecology.

Maria was a notably cautious capitalist in her management of the ecology of Pharsalia plantation. To be sure, she struggled to make the farm profitable and saw intensification as the main path to that end. Yet in depressed agricultural markets and with a struggling family, Maria grew averse to risky investments and the loss of ecological and financial security that went along with them. In this, she remained a follower of the region's agricultural press (she subscribed to the old standard for the region, and a favorite of her husband, the Richmond-based *Southern Planter*, throughout her career). After the turmoil of military conquest and emancipation, regional journals lost a bit of the confidence in unending reform they had in the 1840s and 1850s. Unlike the unabashed progressivism that still reigned in the national farm journals, southern conservationists began fretting over how to save some portion of the old world.[55] The investments Maria did make in Pharsalia's intensification during these years went toward maintaining the double-cycle established by her late husband. Once the national plant trade reopened, she began regular purchases of clover seed.[56] The quantities were large enough to indicate that clover had resumed its old role in Pharsalia's crop rotations and livestock husbandry. Maria was probably sending the hired hands out to restore the old meadow between Rambler's and the Flat Field, along with the newer meadow at the eastern edge of Pharsalia. Both were now part of Bland's inheritance but still under her management. She was also probably using clover as a cover crop to retard erosion in the more arable parts of the Cove and the Tansey Field, and as a legume to restore nitrogen levels across the plantation. Maria also continued the habit of buying new wheat seed in an effort to stay ahead of weeds, diseases, and international competition. She seems to have been less aggressive than her husband had been in the late 1840s and early 1850s, though. A Russian variety, Odessa Wheat, appeared along with a strain her husband had used in the 1850s, White Blue Stem, as the only named varieties among her seed purchases. Maria was also cautious in resuming the importation of commercial fertilizer to Pharsalia.[57] Perhaps concerned about high postwar prices, for several years after 1865 she seems to have avoided buying fertilizer. When she did return to this particular strategy of capitalist intensification, she turned back to an old standard, plaster, rather than guano or the newer concoctions appearing on the market.[58]

Pharsalia's postwar owner was a little more ambitious than her late husband when it came to bringing new farm equipment to the plantation, though. Pharsalia was now facing off in the new grain market against northern farmers who had mechanized during the war years. She also had to replace some of the labor lost to emancipation. Within their limited means, Maria and other entrepreneurial Virginia farmers tried to keep up with the latest technology. Most of the new equipment she purchased for Pharsalia went to conserve and more efficiently exploit its always-strained labor, soil, and other biotic resources. A wheat drill in 1866, a newly invented contraption designed to quickly separate cockle seed from grain in 1869, a new mowing machine in 1871, improved threshing machines, and a newly designed hillside plow all made their appearances in Pharsalia's fields under her direction.[59] The seed drill was an excellent example of how investing in farm machinery helped push intensification along. Burying seed grain a few inches under the ground helped stretch seed stock by reducing the losses to the triangle's ever-present heavy rains. William Massie had tried to deal with this problem before the war by ordering his plow hands to turn the soil over the broadcast-sown grain. The plantation's reduced postwar workforce made investment in a mechanical solution more attractive. Evenly spacing plants also helped reduce competition for water, light, and soil nutrients. The purchase of specialized plows and mechanical threshers indicated that, like her husband before her, Maria remained most concerned with conserving Pharsalia's existing soil resources. She wanted to keep them from leaking off the plantation and hoped to block outside organisms from competing for them as well. In the end, Maria seems to have seen Pharsalia's grain fields in much the same way her late husband had throughout the antebellum era. She hoped they would become part of a stable, self-sustaining crop and resource cycle managed to conserve soil structure and fertility. She and her employees were investing to conserve and still defending the double-cycle as the long-term road to stable yields.

Maria was apparently unwilling or unable to make the kind of investments necessary to keep grain farming highly profitable, though. The technology and crop varieties she and her workers used after the war remained well behind the capitalist intensification of wheat cultivation elsewhere in the country. In 1879, the workforce on Maria's portion of the estate harvested twelve hundred bushels of wheat on seventy planted acres, a yield of just over seventeen bushels to the acre. This was a competitive yield when measured against national averages, but it remained well behind what the best capitalized farmers were getting on midwestern and western lands. Steadily decreasing prices for Virginia grain reinforced this problem. Railroads connected the South with larger markets while steel plows and mechanical threshers drove out onto the central plains of the United States. The old autonomous double-cycle delivered a security slowly eroded by diminishing commercial returns.[60]

Maria responded by looking for ways to shift to other, more profitable crops. Yet like her late husband during the difficult years of the 1830s and early 1840s, she was reluctant to venture beyond the borders of Pharsalia to find them. Instead, she refocused her attention on produce her husband and the Pharsalia slaves had tried to make profitable during the 1840s—orchard crops and hog meat. Improved rail transport after the Civil War opened the possibility of shipping fresh apples long distances to market. Maria and her neighbors had a stroke of good luck when merchants up and down the eastern seaboard began taking notice of the old apple orchards at the foot of the Blue Ridge. Buyers were particularly interested in those that produced the Albemarle Pippin, an old graft of a New York apple onto wild Virginia crabapple stock widely popular in the Tye Valley.[61] Maria responded by sending her workers out to restore the orchards in front of Pharsalia and behind in the Cove, planting new ones in parts of Rambler's Field and the old Flat Field, and shipping fresh apples to market. With Pippins in high demand, aggressive merchants were prepared to risk buying fresh apples direct from local store owners or even from farmers. Maria's husband had struggled to make brandy for a saturated regional tavern market, but her Pharsalia apples entered the market with a competitive edge. Her neighborhood reputation as an arborist grew along with her profits, and she began getting letters asking for advice on technique.[62]

Maria also looked for profit in another area in which she and the Pharsalia workers had long experience—hog-rearing and ham sales. By the late 1860s, she and her employees were back working to improve the quality and care of the plantation's herd of swine. In this effort they were building on the long struggle of her husband and his slaves to intensify hog husbandry on the plantation. Little specific evidence about pasturing, penning, breeding, and the like is available for postwar Pharsalia. However, Maria did maintain a large herd of valuable (and presumably well-kept) animals at Pharsalia throughout the postwar years, and she sold salted hams to regional merchants and private buyers. Under her supervision, the Massie ham made a comeback in Lynchburg and Richmond markets, providing her with a little more revenue.[63]

These ventures helped keep the aging plantation mildly profitable. Yet they also reflected the creeping conservatism in Maria's thinking that would slow capitalist intensification at Pharsalia after the Civil War. In the cases of both apples and hams, Maria's efforts rested on the old ecological relationships of the plantation. The apple trees in front of the house and behind it in the Cove had been planted in William Massie's youth. These half-century-old trees became the basis of the plantation's apple production after the war. The importance of relying on the older orchard was revealed by the 1880 agricultural census. The Pharsalia orchard owned by Maria was more than three and a half times as productive per tree, and its apples worth twice as much per unit, as the newer orchards that Maria had planted on Bland's portion of the plantation.[64] The age of the older orchards was matched by the detailed knowledge Maria and her workers had of their ecology. When her own knowledge of the interaction between the fruit trees, the physical environment, and techniques failed her, she could fall back on the recollections of her former slaves or, better yet, on the incredibly detailed orchard books her late husband had kept. She did not have to gamble the family's struggling estate on importing new techniques or new trees, and then facing the spread of dread orchard diseases like apple-cedar and quince-apple rust. Instead, she was able to force the risk of the new trade in fresh apples onto aggressive shippers like the Baltimore merchant who came to buy Pharsalia's crop off the trees in 1867.[65] In such a competitive market, however, the advantages of local adaptation and ecological stability were short lived. More and more planters in the western Piedmont expanded apple production as their orchards matured and their experience grew, driving prices steadily down. Like fruit produce across Virginia, the value of Pharsalia's orchard products declined by a third in the decade between the 1870 and 1880 censuses, and it would dip even further over the next decade.[66]

Like the turn to fresh apples, Maria's push into ham production also reflected a growing ecological and fiscal conservatism. William Massie, his overseers, and his slaves had spent much of the antebellum era occupied with a slow, independent intensification of hog husbandry at Pharsalia. Stock had been brought in from the ridges and old fields to the hog lot to feast on clover. Winter housing protected the best animals while close culls slowly improved the overall quality of the herd. The Pharsalia slaves steadily developed their skills as butchers over the years as well. The Massie ham had been a known brand on the best tables in central Virginia well before the war. As a result, Maria was able to build on a long tradition of local experience and adaptation when she redoubled efforts at hog-rearing and meat preservation after 1865. Yet like her husband before her, Maria seems to have seen the intensification of hog-rearing as something that could be done solely with Pharsalia's own resources. Maria's advice on butchering and salting techniques went out from Pharsalia, but there is little evidence she made a similar effort to bring new techniques in.[67]

Exploiting the long-standing market for high-quality Virginia hams with a minimum of investment or ecological risk brought some profit to the estate. As with the apple orchards, though, the absence of aggressive investment in intensification meant steadily diminishing profits. Armed with reformed fence laws,[68] other Virginia hog farmers began improving their herds. Entrepreneurs started mass-producing cured hams in Smithfield and other towns. Even then, they did not keep up with the intensification and mechanization of cattle-rearing, slaughter, and shipping elsewhere. The Virginia ham remained a regional delicacy. After a brief price spike during the food shortages after the war, prices for Virginia pork began a slow slide down for the rest of the nineteenth century.[69] Indeed, the market for the Massie ham reflected the postbellum South's particular strain of cultural conservatism. Many of the Massies' customers appear to have come from family connections and friends among the region's gentry, who saw Pharsalia's "luxurious" hams as a connection with the life of the old plantation.[70] For her part, Maria slowly lowered the number of hogs on her portion of Pharsalia during the 1870s, as this narrow market in nostalgia inevitably contracted.

The limited growth potential of the market for high-quality Virginia hams was just one manifestation of the restrictions postwar conservatism placed on the region.[71] Maria's farm strategies led to a steady drag on Pharsalia's productivity and commercial potential. Her ability to maintain her family as old-style gentry grew steadily weaker as a result. To be sure, she kept both serious debt and ecological problems at arm's length by minimizing risk. Yet the overall value of the plantation declined after the war. Drawing again on the agricultural census, the estimated value of Pharsalia and the other Massie farms went down much faster than the general deflation of postbellum America.[72] This decline is not surprising, given the way that Maria's postwar management of Pharsalia duplicated her late husband's unsuccessful ecological retrenchment during the late 1830s and early 1840s—right down to the emphasis on the plantation's apple trees and hogs. William Massie had temporarily escaped the commercial and ecological failure of traditional intensification by investing in new crop varieties and fertilizers. The generous crop markets of the 1850s rewarded his investments and further emboldened him as a capitalist intensifier. Postwar markets, in contrast, offered Maria little encouragement, and she was loath to tamper with the plantation's proven ecological relationships.

If anything, Pharsalia's agricultural environment drifted even further back into the past. Information about the old problems of defending the ecological boundaries of Pharsalia is particularly hard to come by after the war. A few clues, though, suggest that the plantation was once again being threatened by some of the old invaders—and some new ones, as well. A series of wet summers reportedly brought damaging wheat rust back to the Tye River region during the war years. Only a run of severe droughts in the area eased the problem later in the decade.[73] At the same time cockle seems to have caused serious trouble for Tye River grain farmers during the late 1860s. Rather than importing new varieties or fertilizers to help the grain compete, though, Maria's response was to buy machinery to remove the cockle seed from the final harvest. In 1869, local entrepreneur A. B. Cabell thought it worth his while to obtain a license to manufacture a newly designed cockle machine for Nelson County's remaining grain farmers. Maria purchased a competing model the same year.[74] Other species also competed with cereal grain for soil resources. Maria's late 1860s wheat fields were still infested with volunteer rye, a problem her husband had faced decades before.[75] Several fruit fungi—particularly cedar-apple rust—were also causing considerable damage to commercial orchards across Virginia.[76] Although Maria's records include no mention of fruit tree diseases, it is unlikely that Pharsalia's apple trees escaped unscathed. Some of the steep decline in the value of Pharsalia's orchard products may have been the result of these new scourges, and not just poor prices. By the 1880s, granary weevils, a problem never mentioned by William Massie, were infesting Maria's wheat.[77] The impact of these problems on Pharsalia's ecological sustainability and profitability are impossible to nail down for the postwar period. These few leads indicate, however, that outside invasion of the plantation's agroecosystem continued to create problems of competition for crop plants. The caution and frugality of Maria's farming suggest that some of the ecological problems that had struck Pharsalia during the 1840s had reappeared.

Wheat produced by the double-cycle slowly declined in quantity and price,[78] and hams and apples also brought less and less for the effort. Maria and her children responded by turning back to another old expedient—tobacco. Between 1870 and 1880, Maria, Hope, and Bland more than doubled tobacco cultivation at Pharsalia. They did so despite a crash in prices that saw Virginia dark tobacco lose more than half its market value during the decade.[79] This approach was unsustainable, of course, both ecologically and financially. As always, tobacco brought high commercial returns per acre when compared with cereal grains. But its demands on labor and soils remained as heavy as always. Worse, Pharsalia's red clay loams could not support the most popular new variety, bright tobacco, which grew best on the sandier soils of the southside and central North Carolina.[80] Turning Pharsalia back into a tobacco plantation would never have generated the profits needed to make up for the loss of ecological sustainability. Nor would it have kept the Massie estate competitive with intensifying farms elsewhere in the United States. As during Pharsalia's adolescence, pursuing traditional strategies slowed down the loss of ecological resources and minimized financial risk. It did little, however, to ensure the plantation's long-term sustainability—especially as its division among the Massie heirs gathered speed in the 1870s.

## Pharsalia at the End

If John Ott's wife, Annie, had been able to get away from Roanoke and visit Maria Massie at Pharsalia in 1879, what would she have found at the foot of the Priest? One suspects that when Annie Ott dreamed of Pharsalia, the Massie place represented to her a comfortable security that she, like so many of her generation of white Virginians, nostalgically identified with the antebellum plantation. As she faced upheaval in every aspect of her life and society, Annie Ott probably saw her Massie relations and their old plantation as a haven. In many ways the reality of Maria Massie's Pharsalia would have met her expectations. John Ott had left Richmond after the Civil War to set up legal practice in a rapidly growing railroad town. It was a move that separated his wife from the circle of family relations with which southerners had been used to living. To Annie Ott, the triangle would have seemed a welcome throwback to the old days. Florence and her second husband, lawyer John Horsely, lived in Lynchburg, and Ellen Warwick had followed her husband, but otherwise the Massie family had stayed together through the upheavals of war and reconstruction. Aunt Maria still lived in the plantation house at Pharsalia, and several of her children lived on adjoining farms. Martha Ligon and her husband were in the Major's old house at Level Green, while Hope, married to Annie's in-law Laura Effinger, was running the family's mills. Bland, now twenty-six years old and married to Eliza Sneed for three years, had taken over management of his inheritance and was living at Tyro farm. Thomas James Massie had died two years earlier, removing some of the dissension in the family. Pharsalia and the surrounding neighborhood was still the territory of the Massie and Effinger families. A family gathering around the matriarch's table would have offered a vision of security to someone uprooted by the South's broken past and uncertain future.

John Ott had dragged his wife to the bustle and noise of Roanoke in order to keep his family wealthy. It was a sound move financially, but one that showed how many white Virginians had been forced to give up on the hope of finding prosperity on the land. The South's agricultural sector was devastated, and the national depression of the 1870s was driving farmers down even further. To reach Pharsalia, Annie Ott would have had to take the train from Lynchburg up to the depot at Arrington. It would not have been a promising journey into a pastoral past. Virginia journalist Orra Langhorne made the same train trip at about the same time, and her description of rural Amherst and Nelson Counties was a gloomy one: "The ride from Lynchburg to Charlottesville is, for the most part, through a desolate region. . . . At long intervals, an old fashioned farm house with the mud-daubed, wood chimnied, windowless cabins, once occupied by the slaves [but] now deserted and in ruins, came into view, and gave the impression of a God-forsaken land, unloved by nature, uncherished by man."[81] For people in the postwar South, trips from their growing urban centers into the desolate countryside were similarly depressing—many chose, like John Ott, to migrate in the other direction to escape. Yet once Annie Ott had gotten into a carriage at the depot and ridden up the road along the Tye River, an oasis of relative prosperity would have appeared when she got her first good look at the triangle. In that summer of 1879, the scene presented by Pharsalia's fields would probably have fulfilled many of the dreams she had of it.[82]

Despite Maria's struggles, the Massie plantation's environment had not changed much in twenty years. As in 1859, most of the fields were still being managed in the double-cycle. Other planters and farmers in the area had dealt with the hard times of the Civil War and Reconstruction by returning to extensive cultivation or subsistence farming. Yet the signs of the problems that sort of farming created—abandoned old fields and run-down, empty farm houses—were not present on Maria's and Bland's land at the foot of the Priest. Most of the problem areas of the old plantation—especially the heavily eroded soils of Ned's Hill, Field Number Two, and Rambler's Field—had been either abandoned or replanted in apple trees. Annie Ott may not have been a farmer, but she could have seen the evidence of stable and fertile soils on the rest of the plantation. The two large, seeded meadows tilled and maintained by the Pharsalia slaves before the war were almost certainly still there, while Bland had added more clover hayfields at Tyro. These nearly thirty acres of permanent pasture helped support a respectable population of improved livestock, including more than eighty cattle, forty sheep, and dozens of high-quality hogs. When penned in the winter, these animals would have fed on the more than seventy tons of clover hay that were then growing in the meadows and the fallowed ground in the plantation's main fields.

Alongside those hayfields, nearly two hundred acres of corn, over a hundred of wheat, and nearly a hundred of oats were growing. The wheat, almost ready for harvest, would have looked particularly good in that summer. Pharsalia's grain crop might not have been as abundant as on the best northern or midwestern farms, but it would certainly have looked good compared to what Annie Ott had seen on the way from Roanoke. Compared with the surrounding waste of eroded, exhausted land and deserted farms, Pharsalia's crop fields revealed how hard Maria had struggled to keep up the crop rotations, the clover plantings, and especially the manuring of the plantation's long-cultivated red clays. More importantly for Annie Ott, the sight of productive fields meant the Massie lands were reliably bringing in a healthy income, providing Maria and her children with a kind of assurance missing in her own life. With depression and defeat hanging so heavily over the rural Piedmont, Pharsalia seemed defiant, the embodiment of that earlier hope for prosperity and landed independence.

Arriving at the old house, Mrs. Ott would have found it well preserved and still a very comfortable gentry home place. Its white residents and black servants were no doubt reduced in number from William Massie's heyday, but it was still the gathering place for a host of family and friends. It was surrounded by barns, smokehouses, and many other functional outbuildings, as well as the old plantation garden. As she sat down in the parlor with Maria, or at the dinner table with her relations, Annie Ott would have seen the material abundance left over from the antebellum era—expensive furniture, dishes and cutlery, large beds with soft linen. To someone who wanted to find an idealized Old South, Pharsalia would have provided it in 1879: a productive farm providing material prosperity to a close-knit, upper-class white family.

If she had wanted to look critically, though, Ott would certainly have noticed some important ways Pharsalia was no longer an antebellum plantation. The most important difference from 1859 would have been the absence of slavery. Yet even here the past would have been powerfully present. Although many of the Massie slaves had left the triangle after emancipation, a large core group had stayed to work as farm laborers for Maria and her children. Men like Marshall Johnson, Paul Mead, and their families had cultivated the plantation's fields as slaves and kept working for the Massies as freedpeople. Like their former owners, the black residents of the triangle valued the support and assurance offered by having relatives close by. Once freed, of course, they were unwilling to accept too many of the old trappings of slavery. But even with free labor, and despite Maria's well-known positions on racial politics, relations between black and white in the triangle still took on the shapes of the past, defined by old work routines developed in Tandy's time and connections to generations of family. Ironically, the fact that the Massies' former slaves had abandoned or taken away the old cabins around Pharsalia may well have supported Annie Ott's idealistic nostalgia for the plantation. Pharsalia's old black populations was present just enough to maintain the productivity of the plantation and the aristocratic air of the Massie home. But their freedom relieved Maria and her children of much of the burden of the frustrating search for mastery over slave labor that had caused William Massie such difficulty—and brought on the old South's destruction.

At the same time, though, other flaws in the Massies' attempt to keep their pre–Civil War plantation alive would have been apparent. Annie Ott's window onto the problems would certainly have been her familiarity with the family. Even as she joined the thick Massie-Effinger network in the triangle, gathering at Pharsalia to renew their ties, she would have remembered the family's divisions and difficulties. In turn, those problems were reflected in the triangle's agricultural environment. Hope Massie's personal troubles were being reflected in his financial predicament. As he struggled to make a living from milling in a remote mountain community, he farmed what was left of his patrimony in expedient but destructive ways. While his mother still practiced the double-cycle, Hope had drifted back into traditional Virginia farming, growing tobacco and corn, but no hay, on his 350 acres down by the Tye River. He had already exhausted and abandoned 25 of those acres in 1879, with the prospect of more to come. Martha and her husband were also struggling to keep their heads above water at Level Green. Not that Maria or Bland could claim to be immune from the temptation of extensive farming. They still had households to support, and grain prices were heading steadily downward. By 1879, the Massies' aggressive investments in capitalist intensification had largely come to an end. Maria's purchases of new equipment seem to have stopped, and her income was going to cover expenses and hold off debt. The assessed value of Pharsalia's farm equipment had gone down by more than two-thirds since the 1870 census—well ahead of the rate of deflation. On her ride up to the main house, Annie Ott might well have noticed the tobacco growing on newly cleared grounds on both Maria's and Bland's properties. The ratio of improved land to woodland at Pharsalia had jumped from just over 40 percent in 1870 to more than 60 percent a decade later, as Maria had sent her workers to clear some of the marginal land she had abandoned after the war.[83] The Massies were beset by the problems facing southern agriculture in the 1870s, and their difficulties were apparent around the edges of the vision of the country gentry's landscape Annie Ott so desperately wanted to see.

The contradictions within the southern gentry's goal of prosperity and independence through commercial farming were threatening the unity of the Massie family, and through it the agricultural environment of Pharsalia. For all the friends, family, and guests that came to Maria's home, she occupied the old house largely alone. Ellen and Florence had left the neighborhood, while Martha, Hope, and Bland had left Pharsalia to establish their own homes. The grand prewar gathering of the Massie and Effinger clans that had grated on William Massie had been replaced by a family straining against the centralization of their father's old estate. Their longing for landed independence, and the prosperity they hoped would come with it, was tugging against the profitable agricultural ecosystem at Pharsalia—and their emotional ties to their childhood home. If Annie Ott had visited the plantation in 1879, she would have had to shut out thoughts about the future of the family in order to enjoy her plantation idyll. Among her Massie relations, she probably identified with Maria more than her own peers for two reasons. Maria was a link to the past, but it was also clearly her will that was holding together the old plantation that Annie loved so much.

Maria Massie died in 1889 at the age of seventy-five, her commitment to holding Pharsalia together apparently broken along with her health. At the time, crop prices in Virginia were stumbling toward historic lows. Wheat, after holding on at just over a dollar a bushel during most of the 1870s, had dipped down below eighty cents in 1887. Tobacco had lost nearly half its value since the early 1870s.[84] The agricultural census data from 1890 for Nelson County is unavailable, but the farming equipment listed in Maria's probate inventory suggests that little had changed in the agricultural system at Pharsalia since Annie Ott's imaginary visit of ten years before.[85] The choice made by several of her children to become planters seemed more and more dubious. The old plantation, the double-cycle, and its specialties in apples and hams, were all proving unable to support multiple families of southern gentry. Nor were the Massies willing, or able, to invest in intensification under the stringent terms and with seemingly little hope of reward. In her will, Maria acknowledged the inevitability of Pharsalia's breakup under the pressure of her descendants' financial struggles and expectations. Maria apparently feared that farming in the triangle was a dead end that would leave little for subsequent generations. After jealously guarding Pharsalia for her children for more than a quarter century, she reversed the tendency in her previous wills and put few restrictions on her children's authority as executors, leaving them free to sell the property.[86]

Her daughter Martha Ligon, who received the old core of Pharsalia in trust for her daughter, sold the house and the attendant land to a man named James Bentz in 1893. She sold off large chunks of Level Green up through 1909, as well. Her descendants managed to keep the house in the family, but its role as a working farm steadily diminished. Frances Horsely held on to her portion of the estate until 1908, but probably to little economic purpose. Field Number Two and much of Ned's Hill are covered with mature forest today. Despite his relative success as a farmer, Bland also wound up selling off a fair amount of his landed inheritance after 1900.[87] By the 1890s, Pharsalia no longer existed as the coherent agricultural ecosystem first created by William Massie and his slaves back in the 1810s and 1820s.

William Massie's children sold off most of Pharsalia at the end of the nineteenth century because they needed an income and did not think the old plantation could turn the kind of profits they wanted. Yet we should not interpret their unwillingness or inability to make farming in the triangle sustainable as evidence of an excess of capitalist principles. Massie's children certainly wanted to make money, and they wanted to spend it, and they hoped to do both by farming the red clays at the foot of the Priest. But they wanted more from the land than just money, and none of the family's attempts to manage Pharsalia's agricultural ecology had been able to bear all their demands for long. More important to the Massies, their ancestral plantation was the place where they hoped they could live as southern aristocrats—not just wealthy, but independent and masterful as well. But commercial farming grew more competitive after the Civil War, and they needed to divide their father's land in order to find their own autonomy. Suddenly, the investments their father had made in intensifying Pharsalia's ecology seemed very risky. In that sense, Thomas James, Ellen, Martha, Hope, Florence, and Bland were their father's children. His own embrace of capitalist intensification had always been conditional. Massie wanted to be a southern planter—to survey his land and chattels from a big house, a man in control of his surroundings, independent and respected. In the end, he imagined he would be buried in the family graveyard, having handed his land and his status on to his children. He needed to profit from his fields to secure his legacy, though. When extensive farming and ecological autonomy both failed to provide the necessary income, he turned to risky, aggressive investments. For just over a decade at the end of his life, Massie had broken with the political and agricultural traditions of his society. He had tried to think of Pharsalia as capital to be invested, as a collection of resources to be conserved. His reward for his efforts at capitalist intensification was better productivity, higher profits, and greater sustainability than the plantation had ever had. But it was not enough for him, for his wife, or for his descendants. Pharsalia's life as a Massie plantation came to an end when it could not deliver on an impossible set of demands.

EPILOGUE    Mourning Pharsalia

In the mid-1930s, the Virginia Writers' Project, an offshoot of the Works Progress Administration, undertook the Virginia Historical Inventory (VHI). The VHI sent fieldworkers across the Old Dominion to write up descriptions of the state's surviving eighteenth- and nineteenth-century structures. In Nelson County, Massie Thacker of Arrington was hired to complete the survey in the western part of the county, including the triangle at the foot of the Priest. In the summer of 1936, Thacker went to Tyro to speak with Florence Morton, one of Bland Massie's daughters, and Mrs. M. E. Massie, Hope's daughter, to get information about Pharsalia. The old plantation house, then in the possession of E. P. Parson, who had bought it from James Bentz, was still in good repair. With Florence Morton as her main informant, Thacker wrote a quick sketch of the appearance and condition of the Massie estate.[1]

Judging from Thacker's report, Pharsalia was still a jewel in the eyes of the Massie family. Florence and John Morton had returned to the area a few years before, buying back much of her father's Tyro farm. They continued to admire the big house up the road, though. Thacker clearly adopted Florence Morton's perspective and presented Pharsalia, William Massie's pre–Civil War gentry home place, as a home that had once united natural beauty with gracious living. The VHI surveyor adored the setting of the house "located on a high ridge which extends down from the lofty peaks of the Blue Ridge." She also admired the "many beautiful" ornamental flagstone walks that William Massie's slaves had built around the house nearly a century before. Florence Morton also drew Thacker's attention to the "signs of very high class workmanship" that survived inside the house, "despite the many repairs," especially the ornate mantles above the various fireplaces. Mentally, Florence Morton may already have been restoring the house she and her husband would buy sixteen years later. Thacker praised the Pharsalia house as being "in a perfect state of preservation" despite "the use of much paint" in the interior.[2]

Thacker's description of the old plantation also revealed the way the Massies still separated their ideal of the gentry home place from the business of commercial farming that went on there. When explaining the "historical significance" of the plantation, Thacker recounted William Massie's career as a progressive planter and petty industrialist. Yet in the memory of his descendants, his capitalist outlook on agriculture and the environment had been reduced to a personal eccentricity. He "had a strong mind for experiments," Thacker reported, a quirk that "went to the extent of trying to raise cranberries on this farm . . . which was not very successful." The grandchildren of William and Maria Massie preferred to remember their grandfather as "Mars Billy." He was the patriarch who built the great mansion of the neighborhood to house their family—before the upheaval of the Civil War and the breakup of the plantation.[3] Like other romantic Virginians of the early twentieth century, they thought of Pharsalia as a genteel refuge from an unstable world, rather than an aggressive enterprise struggling to master that world.[4] Capitalist intensification floundered in the South because the region's farmers did not believe they could have the peace and security of rural life while investing heavily in reformed agriculture.

### The Problem of Southern Agriculture

So why, precisely, did southern farmers not take the remedy prescribed by the region's conservationists? Judging from the story of Pharsalia plantation, we should be cautious before accepting the reformers' view and blaming the region's cultivators for being obstinate and ignorant. There were few places in the nineteenth-century South where agricultural reform was pursued as aggressively as at Pharsalia. Yet for all the Massies' efforts at intensifying the plantation's agricultural ecosystem, the place never quite met their goals. Europeans came to the South in the hopes that agriculture would provide them with both independence and prosperity. Secure on their own property, white men like Maj. Thomas Massie and his son William believed they could rule over their dependents and defy the demands of the outside world. With no one able to make claim on them, they reasoned, they could accumulate wealth by confidently selling crops grown by the labor they controlled and live the good life of material abundance. Southern farmers appreciated the Bible's memorial of King Solomon's reign—"every man under his vine and under his fig tree"[5]— for how it summed up their own goals: possessive individualism. But the ecological realities of farming the southern landscape drove a wedge between the possession and the individualism.

As they cultivated the southern landscape, men like the Massies found themselves risking much of what they had hoped to gain. Like so many other southern farmers, they wound up making some reasonable, but ultimately self-defeating, calculations of the risks agricultural reform posed for their dream of being both comfortable and independent. Those risks appeared at a number of levels—the most basic being the economics of intensification. Their first serious attempts to wring higher yields from less land—plowing, the three-field system, penning livestock, and the like— rewarded them with diminishing labor returns and profits. Just working harder only promised a slow slide into debt and bankruptcy. Extensive farming on cheap, fertile soils under mature frontier forests reversed that equation, encouraging thousands to head over the mountains to the west. Many southern farmers who were too poor to buy frontier property saw a way they might at least save their independence. They retreated onto unclaimed land in the mountains, swamps, and pine forests, accepting poverty in exchange for autonomy. Fear of working too hard for too little return was hardly the sum of the problem, though. Like the Massies, many planters and farmers wanted to enjoy their wealth surrounded by the security of property and family, and they were prepared to attempt intensification to avoid emigration. Besides, those who escaped to the frontier only postponed a reckoning. After the Civil War, their descendants once more faced the old southern problems of soil erosion and exhaustion. They then wound up returning to the southern conservationists for guidance.

Those who remained on their old farms struggled to make intensification work economically and financially, however. The early southern conservationists first advised their neighbors to restore and conserve their soils by abandoning tobacco in favor of clover and hard grain–based crop rotations. Adapting a system of ecological relationships developed in northern Europe to the climate and soils of the South was fraught with dangers, though. One experiment after another struggled in warm humid weather and acidic, easily eroded soils. Farmers like the Massies who tried to adopt the double-cycle kept sneaking back to hack down second-growth forest and plant tobacco in order to get a quick income. Watching them butt heads against the environment and lose, their more cautious neighbors nurtured a contempt for "book farming." Southern farmers did not resist "scientific" agriculture just because they resented being lectured by their wealthier and more educated neighbors. Rather, they understood that anyone who thought creating new agroecological systems was a simple, manageable, and instantly profitable process was a fool.

When the double-cycle did not provide stable yields and high profits, southern intensifiers fell back on their belief that personal independence would solve any problem that presented itself. Southern farm reformers preached conservation because they believed that even farmers on worn-out land had enough resources to prosper, if only they could just hold on to them. Yet as William Massie found out during the 1830s and 1840s, it was impossible to seal off even a large plantation from the outside world. A host of competitors invaded his fields, attacking his crops and stealing water, light, and nutrients from them. Massie could draw out clever schemes to recycle soil resources and scour his plantation for every scrap of fertility in every little microenvironment. But the rust spores, briars, cheatgrass, and cockle ignored his fences. Again, he found himself facing the old trap. He could grow tobacco and corn and watch his land decline and his wealth disappear, or he could give up and emigrate before his creditors took whatever the weeds had left.

By the 1840s, the leading southern reformers were offering a counterintuitive way out of the problem—capitalist intensification. Bring in more outside resources, they told farmers, get quick increases in productivity and beat down the problems of ecological adaptation with continual import and experimentation. Practice soil conservation even more aggressively, they went on, and achieve the highest long-term productivity. Then sit back and watch the profits roll in, they promised. Plenty of farmers reasoned that this approach was a little like beating your head against a brick wall, then concluding the answer was to get a running start. Even during the 1850s, William Massie had trouble adapting all his imports to the environment at the foot of the Priest and struggled to control his resources against a host of competitors—some natural, some human. Yet those who did adopt capitalist farming found a surprising degree of environmental and economic success at midcentury. But Massie and his descendants discovered investing in intensification set their farming against both their materialism and their love of personal autonomy. If capital was the base of successful agriculture, then consumerism sucked resources away from the fields. If patient, large-scale investment was the path to profit, then the constant need to break farm resources into smaller, inheritable chunks for the children undermined every program. Trying to preserve her family's place in the southern aristocracy, Maria Massie drifted back into a more conservative, less profitable system of cultivation. Farms like Pharsalia were broken apart or passed away, and the Piedmont forests closed in around the old homes.

In the end, agricultural reformers were unable to fill the southern countryside with a class of prosperous, property-owning family farmers. But as long as their fellow southerners kept dreaming of the good life on the land, they kept trying to find ways to make the agricultural ecology work. When the Virginia conservation movement rose again out of the wreck of the Civil War during the late nineteenth and early twentieth century, it revived the program of capitalist intensification. It took on an even more ethereal tone than before, though, often pursued as an avocation by wealthy men playing the planter-gentleman. The emblematic figure of progressive farm reform in the early twentieth-century Tye Valley was prodigal son Thomas Fortune Ryan. Born in Nelson County, Ryan abandoned a depressed and declining rural Virginia to make his fortune on Wall Street. Having made millions in the market, he retired to the neighborhood in 1901. He bought Oak Ridge plantation, formerly owned by one of the county's wealthiest families, and set himself up as a member of the landed gentry. He then invested his enormous wealth in restoring Oak Ridge's soils and experimenting with new crops and cultivation techniques. At the same time, he added on to the mansion, built tennis courts and a golf course, stables and riding paths, ornamental gardens, and a fox-hunting course for friends and members of the western Piedmont elite. To help encourage the development of truck farming along the old Orange & Alexandria rail line, he built a scale replica of London's Crystal Palace as a showpiece greenhouse.[6] To tenants and smallholders struggling to wring rent and tax money out of the kind of eroded clay soils Hugh Hammond Bennett found in the Piedmont in 1905, Ryan's Oak Ridge must have seemed rather unreal.

Southerners in the federal agricultural bureaucracy were perceptive enough to realize that the gentleman improver was not a workable way of saving the rural South. Most southern farmers were averse to risk because they did not have several million dollars in the bank to cover up for the mistakes they might make experimenting with the ecological relationships on their farms. The next generation of southern conserva-tionists tried to use the government's power to supply their need for eco-logical adaptation and capital. Men like Hugh Hammond Bennett framed their farm programs as educational, but their most successful efforts took on the ecological risks of capitalist intensification—regional experiment stations, local demonstration farms, county extension agents, the Soil Conservation Service's farm-level soil surveys and free soil testing, land grant college agricultural research, and so on. They all provided farmers with detailed knowledge of how to adapt new resources and techniques to their unique farm environments, making it safer to intensify. Since farmers also lacked the capital to invest, the Department of Agriculture poured cheap credit into the rural South, lessening even further the risk of investing. Yet all these programs also failed to bridge the gap between conservationists and the mass of southern farmers. As Maria Massie and her children discovered, if land was just capital, the market valued it for the profit it generated, not any social or psychological rewards it brought to its owners. Southern conservationists created a more stable and prof-itable regional agriculture, but at the cost of denying the old promise of possessive individualism to most southerners.

Many people in the modern South were still frustrated with the results of capitalist intensification, no matter what the profit. The Massies, in particular, refused to give up on living the good life on the old plantation. Florence Morton convinced her husband to buy back Pharsalia and the land still attached to the house in 1951. Whatever Massie Thacker and Florence Morton might have thought of William Massie's experiments with cranberries, John Morton clearly thought progressive farming was an appropriate part of restoring a gentry home place. He revived apple production during the 1950s, replanting the older trees and clearing forested old fields for new orchards. His daughter, Perkins Morton Flippin, continued this work, expanding into commercial apple production. She then partnered with another orchard-owning family in the neighborhood to form Flippin-Seaman, a produce company with a large warehouse on State Route 56 near Tyro. Mrs. Flippin's son, Bill, has turned his grandfather's hobby into a business, continuing the fruit company while expanding into prize breeding cattle and perennial garden plants. A few of William Massie's descendants once again earn their keep by farming in the triangle.

Their farming business trades on southerners' nostalgia for their rural past, as well. In the 1960s, Perkins Flippin founded a store, the Farm Basket, near Lynchburg to sell Pharsalia produce. The venture, now run by her daughters, has expanded over the years into a restaurant serving home-cooked meals, a garden shop providing plants and cuttings from Pharsalia, and a gift and craft store selling Virginia specialty products. Bill Flippin actively participates in the agritourism boom, as well, hosting several pick-your-own apple days and an apple butter festival at Pharsalia each fall.[7] For the moment, at least, the family has found a way to profit from the dream of possessive individualism in the countryside—but their revival of Pharsalia depends on the fact that the heavy majority of southerners can only appreciate that dream, rather than live it.

*Pharsalia Today*

In 2005, I went to Pharsalia to take photographs for this book. I was accompanied around the plantation by Beth Goodwin, a descendant of Hope Massie who lives on the old family land at Tyro and who is also a passionate local and family historian. Mrs. Goodwin introduced me to Perkins Flippin, shortly before William Massie's great-granddaughter passed away at an advanced age, as well as other generations of the family still living at the old plantation. For the next couple of hours, she and I toured the house and the surrounding fields, taking pictures and talking about our shared interest in the Massie family and Pharsalia.

As an environmental historian, I was intent on looking past the modern landscape of the triangle, hoping to peel it away to see the agricultural ecosystem managed by William Massie before the Civil War. The house still sits at the foot of the mountain, overlooking the bench running down toward the Tye River. Well preserved by Bentz, Parsons, and the Mortons, it is the main reminder of the antebellum plantation. Most of the old outbuildings and the lots surrounding it are gone, and the old garden has been reduced to a small patch just behind the house. One can still identify the landforms, of course, but the Piedmont forest has closed in over the last hundred years. Field Number Two is now a stand of mature hardwoods, although some of the western end has been cleared for apple trees. Ned's Hill has not been cultivated for many years, either, although some brush and pine still grow, a wide track has been hacked out across the top of the hill for some power lines. Both Muddy Branch and the Mill Dam Creek now run clear, except in the worst downpours. Some of the land in the Cove is still cleared for a small pasture and a few older apple trees, but the upper reaches of the hollow have been abandoned to the forest creeping down the slopes of the Priest. The northern stretches of Rambler's Field have also been left to the trees. The old Spring Run has been dammed up to make a large irrigation pond for the fields of garden plants on the southern side of the antebellum field. There is still a little evidence remaining of the farming and conservation work done at the old plantation. Nelson County Road 666 runs past the old plantation house, apparently following the path of the road the Massies' slaves built between Level Green, Pharsalia, and Tyro. As one stands in front of the house and looks south and east down toward the Tye, some of the field divisions seem to follow the antebellum fence lines, especially between Field Number 2, the Front Field, and the Flat Field—although the original live fences William Massie's slaves planted have doubtless long since been torn out. Evidence of his attempts to manage the streams that crossed the plantation is largely absent, too, abandoned as unnecessary or washed away by the Hurricane Camille floods. Some of the old flood levees are still visible on the land just across the Tye River that Massie got from

Nancy Coffey, now overgrown with trees but still protecting some bottomland pasture. The agricultural environment of the early nineteenth-century tobacco and wheat plantation no longer exists, apart from a few echoes running across the modern landscape.

Mrs. Goodwin's perspective on the landscape of Pharsalia was quite different from my own, and the stories she told much less final. With her relatives still living in the old house and farming the land, the plantation's past was alive in more ways than just the few fence lines and piles of rocks I had noticed. Portraits of William and Maria Massie and Florence and John Morton hang in the house, declaring the family's continuity across the nineteenth and twentieth centuries. From the small pile of stones in the front yard where visiting ladies used to step off their carriages to the modern property lines and the uses made of the remaining antebellum buildings, the Massies' landscape is full of stories that bind the past and present far beyond being able to mentally trace old fields on modern topography. At the old Tyro mill where Hope Massie's fortunes declined after the Civil War, or at Snug Dale farm where Thomas James Massie dreamed of his grandfather's financial success, the landscape also tells the story of the family's struggles. The Massies' struggle to find independence on the land keeps Pharsalia alive, despite what an environmental historian might say about the life and death of agricultural ecosystems.

When I first moved to the South, I was surprised at how crowded the countryside was. Growing up in Kansas in the 1970s, I was used to a landscape of aggressively capitalist farms: quarter-sections of improved varieties of corn and wheat harvested by sixty thousand dollar combines and marked by small, strangely lettered roadside signs telling what insecticides to spray on each field. The tiny ranch homes were scattered miles apart—everyone had moved to town, including most of the farmers themselves. When I drove down southern back roads, on the other hand, they were lined with houses, often fronting the few acres of family land descendants still clung to while working industrial jobs. Many southerners still look to the land as a place to find comfort free from markets, creditors, and bosses. That tenacious desire to be independent brought the Massies to the triangle and became the founding purpose for Pharsalia. Across the nineteenth and twentieth centuries, southern conservationists tried to force it out of Tidewater sand and Piedmont clay, hot summers, and pounding rains—but with limited success. Like the history of the southern landscape, the life story of Pharsalia's agricultural ecosystem tells of an unsuccessful battle to reconcile the southern environment, the marketplace, and the search for personal independence. While the Massies' nineteenth-century plantation failed, the agricultural revival of the family and of the Pharsalia name suggests that southerners are not yet ready to accept defeat.

# NOTES

*Introduction. The Soils of Old Virginia*

1. Quoted in Cook, "Hugh Hammond Bennett."
2. For a description of this incident, see Worster, *Dust Bowl*, 213.
3. Bennett and Pryor, *This Land We Defend*, 45, 31.
4. Ibid., 51–52.
5. Quoted in Jackson, *New Roots for Agriculture*, 40.
6. Ibid., 45.
7. Bennett, "Lectures on Soil Erosion."
8. Madison, "An Address Delivered before the Agricultural Society of Albemarle," *Farmers' Register* 7 (1837): 412–22.
9. Bennett, "Thomas Jefferson."
10. See, for instance, Craven, *Soil Exhaustion*, 86–91, 105–6.
11. Levin, "Women in Soil Science"; Hall, "Early Erosion-Control Practices" and "Soil Erosion and Agriculture." Another SCS historian, Angus McDonald, cited Hall and gave considerable credit to the Virginians in his larger pamphlet "Early American Soil Conservationists," USDA Misc. Publ. 449 (Washington, D.C.: Government Printing Office, 1941).
12. Craven, *Soil Exhaustion*, 20–29.
13. For a brief discussion of Gray's governmental career, see Lehman, *Public Values, Private Lands*, 9–17; Gray, *History of Agriculture*, 85–87, 446–48, 800–802.
14. Craven, *Soil Exhaustion*, 122, 161; Gray, *History of Agriculture*, 801.
15. For a sampling of this sizable literature, see Kathleen Bruce, "Virginia Agricultural Decline to 1860"; Craven, *Edmund Ruffin*; Fields, "Agricultural Population of Virginia"; Genovese, *Political Economy of Slavery*; Rubin, "Limits of

Agricultural Progress"; Earle, *Evolution of a Tidewater Settlement System* and "Myth of the Southern Soil Miner"; Mathew, *Edmund Ruffin and the Crisis of Slavery*; Allmendinger, *Ruffin*; Kirby, *Poquosin*; Ruffin, *Nature's Management*; Silver, *New Face on the Countryside*; David Hardin, "Alterations They Have Made"; Stoll, *Larding the Lean Earth*; McEwan, *Thomas Jefferson, Farmer*; Shalhope, *John Taylor of Caroline*.

16. For support of the Craven thesis, see Kathleen Bruce, "Virginia Agricultural Decline to 1860," and Fields, "Agricultural Population of Virginia." For scholars blaming reformers for erosion problems, see Earle, "Myth of the Southern Soil Miner," and Earle and Hoffman, "Genteel Erosion." Steven Stoll's *Larding the Lean Earth* avoids taking a clear stand on the cause of agricultural reform's perceived failure in the South.

17. For intellectual biographies of prominent reformers, see Shalhope, *John Taylor of Caroline*, or Faust's chapter on Ruffin in *Sacred Circle*.

18. For a basic introduction to agroecology, see, for example, Altieri, *Agroecology*; Tivy, *Agricultural Ecology*; or Gliessman, Engles, and Krieger, *Agroecology*.

19. Recent historical works by agroecological scientists include Garrity and Agustin, "Historical Land Use Evolution," and Santos Perez and Remmers, "Landscape in Transition."

20. Refsell, "Massies of Virginia," 8–16. Many of the Massie papers are also available on microfilm in *Records of Ante-bellum Southern Plantations*. Prominent use of the Massie papers was made by Phillips in *Life and Labor in the Old South*, 238–49, 310–13. See also Genovese, *Roll, Jordan, Roll*, 453. At the time this book was published, noted southern historian Randolph Campbell was also working with the Massie papers.

21. "Two Volumes of Farm Accounts, 1817–1844 and 1845–1862," William Massie Papers, 1766–1890, Special Collections, Perkins Library.

22. "Priest Wilderness." For the geology of the soils that would make up Pharsalia, see Ogg and Baker, "Pedogenesis and Origin." See also Mooney, *Soil Survey*.

23. The most spectacular of these floods occurred in August 1969, when the remnants of Hurricane Camille passed over the ridge. The resulting downpour dumped nearly thirty inches of rain in Nelson County in just a few hours, tore out mountain forests, stripped stream valleys of soils, and killed 117 people. Numerous works have been written on the causes and impact of soil erosion on the southeastern Piedmont. See in particular, Hall, "Soil Erosion and Agriculture," and Trimble, *Man-Induced Soil Erosion*.

24. For work on the chestnut and the blight, see Forest, Bebee, and Cook, *American Chestnut*. For an accessible historical and environmental study of the cove forests of the southern mountains, see the work of Chris Bolgiano, particularly, *The Appalachian Forest*.

25. The history of the Monacan tribe is best covered by Hantmann in "Between Powhatan and Quirank." For a study of the Monacan community at Bear Mountain, see Houck, *Indian Island in Amherst County*.

26. For the career of Parson Rose in the Pharsalia region, see Rose, *Diary of Robert Rose*. For more on Rose's life, see Seaman, *Tuckahoes and Cohees*, 195–201. For a study of the practice of slash-and-burn farming in Virginia, see Silver, *New Face on the Countryside*, 105–10.

27. There is notable controversy on this point. Several scholars have argued that "long fallowing"—the practice of abandoning land to forest succession for a period of twenty to fifty years and then reclearing it once soil structure and nutrient levels had been restored made for a sustainable agroecology. Recent work, both ecological and historical, suggests that such arrangements rarely worked over the long term. See in particular David Hardin, "Alterations They Have Made," 133–45. For more on Piedmont succession patterns in Virginia, see Foster Hill, "Succession or Continuity?" Plentiful research on the North Carolina Piedmont is also informative on many broader issues.

28. For details on the history of the Rose and Massie families and their relationship to the property at the foot of the Priest, see Refsell, "Massies of Virginia."

29. For the economics of frontier cultivation, see Boserup, *Conditions of Agricultural Growth*, 70–76, and David O. Percy, "Embarrassment of Riches." For specific work on the resource and labor economics of frontier agriculture in the Chesapeake region, see in particular Carr, Menard, and Walsh, *Robert Cole's World*.

30. For discussions of the politics of outmigration from Virginia, see Fischer and Kelly, *Bound Away*, and Philyaw, *Virginia's Western Visions*.

31. For definitions of intensification and sustainability, see Matson et al., "Agricultural Intensification and Ecosystem Properties," and Kates et al., "Sustainability Science." The classic study of the economics of intensification is Boserup, *Conditions of Agricultural Growth*.

32. Madison, "An Address Delivered before the Agricultural Society of Albemarle."

33. The struggles of gentry farmers to pass their operations on to many children has been described by Allmendinger, *Ruffin*, esp. 57–105.

*Chapter One. Property Lines and Power before Pharsalia, 1738–1796*

1. For the classic study of the frontier mythology of free land, see Henry Nash Smith, *Virgin Land*, esp. 151–64; see also Frederick Jackson Turner, "Significance of the Frontier." The most influential critics of the free land idea are Paul Wallace Gates, in essays such as "Role of the Land Speculator" and "Tenants of the Log Cabin" (in *Landlord and Tenant*, 13–71), and Thomas Perkins Abernethy, *Western Lands*.

2. These grants frequently came in exchange for gentry support in the House of Burgesses. For a general discussion of the role of land speculation in early Virginia, see Billings, Tate, and Selby, *Colonial Virginia*, 40–41, 134–35, 209–11. For an excellent case study in Virginia land policy, see Rawson, "Anglo-American Settlement."

3. An excellent study of the intersection between the land and political system in early Virginia is Hughes, *Surveyors and Statesmen*. For a good case study, see McCleskey, "Rich Lands, Poor Prospects."

4. Marmon, *Lee Marmon Manuscript*, 75–76. See also Rose, *Diary of Robert Rose*. For specific land grants, see Virginia Land Patents, 16:379; 15:450; 22:179, in Virginia Patents and Grants. Virginia's western frontier was organized as Henrico County as early as 1634. As the Piedmont was settled, new counties were carved out of the original. Hence, the land that became Pharsalia plantation lay sequentially in a number of county jurisdictions: Henrico to 1728; Goochland County from 1728 until 1745; Albemarle County between 1745 and 1765; Amherst County between 1765 and 1807; and finally Nelson County thereafter.

5. For a brief look at migration onto Virginia's Piedmont frontier in the eighteenth century, see Fischer and Kelly, *Bound Away*, 94–101. For studies of the role of land speculators in westward migration, see Gates, "Role of the Land Speculator," and Land, "Land Speculator."

6. For settlement and speculation on the Tye River frontier, see Marmon, *Lee Marmon Manuscript*, and Seaman, *Tuckahoes and Cohees*, esp. pt. 2. For more on Dr. William Cabell, see Anna Marie Mitchell, "Dr. William Cabell."

7. For a case study of the complexities of the Virginia land system, see McCleskey, "Strange Career of Ned Tarr." For a general study of the imposition of the square-grid survey system, see Linklater, *Measuring America*.

8. McCleskey, "Strange Career of Ned Tarr."

9. For a discussion of the opportunities and challenges in using the trees noted as corner markers in early surveys to analyze presettlement forest ecology, see

Mitchell, Hofstra, and Connor, "Reconstructing the Colonial Environment,"
167–90.

10. As a patronage plum, county surveyor positions were handed out to older
members of the gentry like William Mayo. Given that Mayo died the same year
the Rose grant was recorded, Peter Jefferson was almost certainly surveying the
parson's lines. For more on Peter Jefferson's career, see Ron Bailey, "Surveyor for
the King."

11. For the fondness of frontier settlers for clearings and old fields, see Jordan
and Kaups, *American Backwoods Frontier*, esp. 94–105. For more on shifting
cultivation on the frontier, see Otto, *Southern Frontiers*, 13–15, 20–23.

12. See Nelson, "Agroecologies of a Southern Community," esp. chap. 2.

13. See Nelson, "Planters and Hill People."

14. For a brief discussion of the origins and impact of the open range in the
South, see Otto, *Southern Frontiers*, 15–17, and Jordan and Kaups, *American
Backwoods Frontier*, 119–23.

15. For a general look at woods-burning in the early South, see Silver, *New Face
on the Countryside*, 59–64, 181–82. For broader studies of the phenomenon, see
Pyne, *Fire and America*, esp. 123–60, and Kuhlken, "Settin' the Woods on Fire."

16. The classic piece of theorizing on the ecological impact of commonly held
land is Garrett Hardin, "Tragedy of the Commons." But the results of agricultural
settlement and the commons grazing that went with it were not uniformly "tragic"
for forests on the Piedmont frontier. Once the plants of the forest understory had
been eliminated by initial fires, subsequent blazes burned at a much lower level,
allowing youthful pine and mixed pine-hardwood forests to survive with a degree
of stability. As farms and plantations grew in size and number, settlers worked
harder to keep fires away from their valuable fences and crops, allowing hardwood stands to reestablish themselves in farm neighborhoods. Animals driven
into the high mountains during the heat of the Virginia summer also created and
maintained the Appalachian balds so popular with mountain ramblers.

17. Ginseng was popular in traditional Chinese medicine. Many frontier settlers
were able to gain access to credit or ready cash by collecting the wild root from
the forests for sale to merchants working the China trade out of Philadelphia. See
Carlson, "America's Botanical Drug Connection."

18. Dill, "Sectional Conflict in Colonial Virginia."

19. Bliss, "Rise of Tenancy in Virginia."

20. Virginia State Property Tax Rolls for Amherst County (1787); Seaman,
*Tuckahoes and Cohees*, 342–44. For data on the slaveholdings of the Rose heirs,
see Virginia State Property Tax Rolls for Amherst County (1787).

238 NOTES TO CHAPTER ONE

21. For an ecological consideration of frontier settlement, see Green, "Agricultural Colonization." For more specifics on this kind of agriculture, see Primack, "Land Clearing," and for its ecological benefits, see Kirby, *Poquosin*, chap. 3.

22. For tenants as potential soil abusers, see Walsh, "Land, Landlord, and Leaseholder," and a study of more recent issues, Harbaugh, "Twentieth-Century Tenancy and Soil Conservation." There is considerable debate on the nature and causes of erosion in the Chesapeake. Through studies of Chesapeake Bay sediment cores, Grace Brush conclusively proved that erosion rates spiked during the Revolutionary Era. See Brush, "Geology and Paleoecology of the Chesapeake Bay." Several scholars, including David Percy and Carville Earle, have argued from this that the introduction of plow agriculture and high farming caused heightened erosion rates in the region. See David O. Percy, "Ax or Plow?" and Earle, "Myth of the Southern Soil Miner," esp. 194–200, and Earle and Hoffman, "Genteel Erosion." I argue, in contrast, that traditional hoe agriculture was quite capable of causing destructive erosion. The increased sedimentation rates described by Brush may be better attributed to a rapid increase in the Piedmont population in the years after the Revolution. This migration pushed cultivation onto the hillsides of the region, areas most vulnerable to damaging erosion. See Nelson, "Agroecologies of a Southern Community," esp. chap. 2. For various kinds of support for this notion, see Wennersten, "Soil Miners Redux," and David Hardin, "Alterations They Have Made," esp. chaps. 4, 6–7.

23. Erosion rates are determined by a combination of factors, including soil type, rainfall rates and intensity, and topography. Pharsalia would be particularly hard hit by the latter two, with frequent heavy rains and several steeply sloped fields.

24. "Remarks on the Agriculture of Nelson and Amherst—No. 1," *Farmers' Register* 5 (1837): 652.

25. For some classic studies of old field succession in the southern Piedmont, see Keever, "Causes of Succession," and Borman, "Factors."

26. For crop progressions, see Earle, "Myth of the Southern Soil Miner," 196.

27. Nelson, "Then the Poor Planter." For a study on soil fertility issues in tobacco cultivation in Virginia, see Sharrer, "Farming, Disease, and Change in the Chesapeake Ecosystem."

28. William Cabell Commonplace Books, vol. 8, 24 October 1780.

29. Seaman, *Tuckahoes and Cohees*, 342–44. For data on the slaveholdings of the Rose heirs, see Virginia State Property Tax Rolls for Amherst County (1787).

30. Virginia Land Office Grants, 37:595–603, in Virginia Patents and Grants.

31. For the ecological effects of deforestation in the early South, see Silver, *New Face on the Countryside*, 171–85.

32. For a discussion of consumer spending habits and their impact on gentry finance, see Land, "Economic Behavior," and Carr and Walsh, "Standard of Living."

33. For studies of the role of social "deference" in traditional Virginia politics and society, see Sydnor, *American Revolutionaries in the Making*, and Isaac, *Transformation of Virginia*, esp. 76–78. For the importance of stable family lineages for claiming deference, see David Jordan, "Political Stability."

34. On the development of ornamental gardens in the region, see Yentsch and Reveal, "Chesapeake Gardens and Botanical Frontiers," and C. Allan Brown, "Eighteenth-Century Virginia Plantation Gardens."

35. Seaman, *Tuckahoes and Cohees*, 314–24. For a detailed study of the Cabell family's use of the plantation house to display its status in the region, see Heck, "Palladian Architecture."

36. Yentsch and Reveal, "Chesapeake Gardens and Botanical Features," 253–54, 266–70.

37. William Cabell Rives, "Speech before the Agricultural Society of Albemarle," reprinted in *Southern Planter* 2 (1842): 277.

38. For the cult of the family graveyard in antebellum Virginia, see Cashin, "Landscape and Memory."

39. Garland, *Life of John Randolph*, quoted in Fischer and Kelly, *Bound Away*, 204.

40. For the best analysis of the economic calculations surrounding this problem, see Carr and Menard, "Land, Labor, and Economies of Scale." For a general study of the geographic mobility of slave owners in their attempt to extract the maximum return on their slaves' labor, see Oakes, *Ruling Race*, esp. chap. 3. For Virginia, see Fischer and Kelly, *Bound Away*, esp. chap. 3.

41. See Cashin, "Landscape and Memory," 480–81, for a discussion of Virginians' perception of their landscape's "ugliness."

42. "Remarks on the Agriculture of Nelson and Amherst—No. 1," *Farmers' Register* 5 (1837): 652.

43. For discussions of the spread of plow cultivation in the post-Revolutionary Chesapeake, see David O. Percy, "Ax or Plow?"; Miller, "Transforming a 'Splendid and Delightsome Land' "; and Zirkle, "To Plow or Not To Plow."

44. For antebellum recollections of the three-field system in late eighteenth-century Virginia, see T. B. A., "Farming Poor Lands," *Farmers' Register* 2 (1834):

612–14, and "Fencemore," "The Policy of the Law of Enclosures Defended," *Farmers' Register* 3 (1835): 47–49.

45. See Brush, "Geology and Paleoecology of the Chesapeake Bay," and Miller, "Transforming a 'Splendid and Delightsome Land.'" See also Trimble, *Man-Induced Soil Erosion*.

46. For the movement of slaves in and out of Virginia, see Fischer and Kelly, *Bound Away*, 100–101, chap. 3. For the debt crisis in the years after the Revolution, see Mann, *Republic of Debtors*, and Kierner, "The Dark and Dense Cloud."

47. Edmund Ruffin, "On the Causes of the Long-Continued Decline, and the Great Depression of Agriculture in Virginia, No. 2," *Farmers' Register* 5 (1837): 726.

48. "On the Lands and Farming of Amherst," *Farmers' Register* 5 (1837): 460.

49. Fischer and Kelly, *Bound Away*, esp. 202–6.

50. "Remarks on the Agriculture of Nelson and Amherst—No. 1," *Farmers' Register* 5 (1837): 651.

51. Amherst County Deed Books, Book H, p. 29; see also Seaman, *Tuckahoes and Cohees*, 308.

52. "On the Lands and Farming of Amherst," 460.

53. "A Glance at the Farming of Albemarle," *Farmers' Register* 2 (1834): 233–34.

54. Refsell, "Massies of Virginia," 23–25, 55–57.


*Chapter Two. Independence and the Birth of Pharsalia, 1796–1830*

1. William Byrd II to the Earl of Orrery, 5 July 1726, reprinted in "Virginia Council Journals."

2. For some discussion of the link between the fear of indebtedness and Revolutionary sentiment in Virginia, see Holton, *Forced Founders*, esp. chaps. 2–4, and Ragsdale, *Planter's Republic*.

3. Refsell, "Massies of Virginia," 20–22.

4. Ibid., 23–24. See also Robert D. Mitchell, "Content and Context," for the influence of gentry culture on the Frederick County region.

5. Jefferson, *Notes on the State of Virginia*, 164–65.

6. William H. Cabell to Joseph Carrington Cabell, 17 August 1825, Cabell Deposit, Special Collections Department, Alderman Library, University of Virginia, Charlottesville.

7. William Ballard Preston, "Address of Wm. Ballard Preston before the Vir-

ginia State Agricultural Society at Its Second Annual Exhibition," reprinted in *Southern Planter* 14 (1854): 357.

8. For the perception of declension brought on by outmigration, see Fischer and Kelly, *Bound Away*, 202–5. See also Sutton, "Nostalgia, Pessimism, and Malaise," and Kierner, "The Dark and Dense Cloud." A longer case study of aristocratic decline is Hamilton, *Making and Unmaking*, esp. chap. 4.

9. Refsell, "Massies of Virginia," 24–27.

10. Major Thomas Massie to ?, 30 September 1808, Massie Family Papers.

11. Peggy Bradfute to Sarah Steptoe Massie, 27 December 1816, Massie Family Papers.

12. Refsell, "Massies of Virginia," 23.

13. Ibid., 27–29.

14. William Massie to Thomas James Massie, 6 March 1852, *Records of Antebellum Southern Plantations*. All citations to Massie letters come from this collection, unless otherwise noted.

15. "On the Lands and Farming of Amherst," 460.

16. For the agricultural obsessions of the Revolutionary generation in Virginia, see Craven, *Soil Exhaustion*, chap. 3, esp. 86–90. More generally, see Andrews, "Agriculture in Virginia, 1789–1820"; Cabell, "Some Fragments"; and Cabell, *Early History*. For work on the Albemarle Agricultural Society, see Charles W. Turner, "Virginia State Agricultural Societies," and True, "Early Days of the Albemarle Agricultural Society."

17. Stoll, *Larding the Lean Earth*, 38.

18. Madison, "An Address Delivered before the Agricultural Society of Albemarle," 418. All subsequent Madison quotations in this chapter are to this work.

19. Virginia agricultural conservation has been studied by numerous scholars. Classic treatments include Craven, *Soil Exhaustion*, esp. chaps. 3–4, and Kathleen Bruce, "Virginia Agricultural Decline to 1860." See also Gray, *History of Agriculture*, chap. 38. More recent works have been critical of the success of reform movements. See in particular Mathew, *Edmund Ruffin and the Crisis of Slavery*.

20. John Taylor, *Arator*. For closer analysis of Taylor's political ideas and focus on personal independence, see, among many others, Shalhope, *John Taylor of Caroline*, and Bushman, "A Poet, a Planter."

21. John Taylor, *Arator*, 67.

22. Ibid., 86.

23. Ibid., 73.

24. There is considerable work on the influence of English agricultural reform-

ers worldwide. See, for instance, the older work of Loehr, "Influence of English Agriculture," and "Arthur Young and American Agriculture." More recently, see Stoll, *Larding the Lean Earth*, 49–63. For classic works on the development of high farming in England, see Kerridge, *Agricultural Revolution*, and Chambers and Mingay, *Agricultural Revolution*.

25. John Taylor, *Arator*, 68, 126.

26. Ibid., 39.

27. Ibid., 157.

28. For the switch to wheat farming in early national Virginia, see Gill, "Wheat Culture in Colonial Virginia" and "Cereal Grains in Colonial Virginia"; and Klingaman, "Significance of Grain."

29. Otto, *Southern Frontiers*, 14–17. See also Laing, "Cattle in Seventeenth-Century Virginia." Massie mentioned his slaves taking cattle into the mountains in the summer of 1819 and was still noting the slaughter of "wild hogs" in his Farm Account Books as late as 1840.

30. Massie generally recorded the annual number of hogs slaughtered and the total weight of the pork meat preserved, enabling a rough calculation of average animal weights. Ten "sandy-hill hogs" were slaughtered in January 1845, at an average weight of only ninety pounds. William Massie, Farm Accounts, vol. 2, William Massie Papers, 1766–1890, Special Collections, Perkins Library.

31. John Taylor, *Arator*, 161.

32. Edmund Ruffin, "First Views Which Led to Marling in Prince George County," *Farmers' Register* 7 (1839): 659–67, reprinted in Ruffin, *Incidents of My Life*, 191.

33. Ruffin, *Incidents of My Life*, 193.

34. Ibid., 190, 192.

35. Ibid., 203.

36. Ibid., 193.

37. John Taylor, *Arator*, 309. For Thomas Massie's problems with consumer spending, see Refsell, "Massies of Virginia," 22–23.

38. The Massie family's papers are one of the great collections of plantation records surviving from the old South. Spread over various archives, they include accounts, business and personal correspondence, slave registers, and farming memoranda. The bulk of the collection was generated by William Massie and survives primarily at the Center for American History at the University of Texas. This collection has been published in microfilm in *Records of Ante-bellum Southern Plantations*. Smaller collections of his papers are housed at the Swem Library at the College of William and Mary and at the Perkins Library at Duke Univer-

sity, which holds the vital Farm Accounts. Refsell's "Massies of Virginia" is a three-volume dissertation comprised mainly of transcriptions of selected Massie documents.

39. Much of the information on the development of the field structure at Pharsalia comes from a list William Massie put together in 1832, "Cleared Land at Pharsalia," Oversize Papers, 1770–1854, *Records of Ante-bellum Southern Plantations*.

40. Most of the information regarding farming at Pharsalia has been drawn from William Massie's two volumes of Farm Accounts, housed in the Special Collections department of the Perkins Library at Duke University, Durham, N.C. Given that most of the appropriate dates are included in the text, in the interests of space this information will not be footnoted unless a direct quote is included. The dates covered are vol. 1, 1817–44, and vol. 2, 1845–62.

41. "Cleared Land at Pharsalia."

42. Major Thomas Massie to William Massie, Deed of Sale, 25 March 1816, Massie Family Papers; "Cleared Land at Pharsalia."

43. "Cleared Land at Pharsalia."

44. Major Thomas Massie to William Massie, Deed of Sale, 25 March 1816, Massie Family Papers; "Cleared Land at Pharsalia."

45. Thomas Massie to William Massie, 31 December 1814, and William Massie to Sarah Steptoe Massie, 15 September 1815, Massie Family Papers.

46. William Massie to Sarah Steptoe Massie, 15 September 1815, Massie Family Papers.

47. Ibid.

48. Ibid.

49. William Massie to Sarah Steptoe Massie, 9 September 1824, Massie Family Papers.

50. The 1820s saw the severest agricultural depression Virginia was to suffer before the end of the Civil War. The proximate cause of this collapse was the end of the Napoleonic Wars in Europe, which reduced the continent's demand for foodstuffs, particularly flour. Virginia farmers were thrown back onto tobacco for a cash income, but also on depleted soils to grow the sot weed. Thousands of planters went bankrupt, while many more left the state for the cotton frontier to the southwest. For Virginia farm prices during this period, see Peterson, *Historical Study of Prices*.

51. In his Farm Accounts, Massie frequently recorded the number of hogs slaughtered at various plantations, as well as the total weight of pork preserved. The "slaughter weights" mentioned here are calculated from those numbers.

52. William Massie recorded his debts in his "Yearly Summary and Balances," *Records of Ante-bellum Southern Plantations.*

53. "Cleared Land at Pharsalia."

54. William Massie Collection, negative photostat vol. 8, Plats of Land, 1766–1840 and undated, *Records of Ante-bellum Southern Plantations.*

55. For the role of gypsum as a fertilizer in early national Virginia, see Rosser H. Taylor, "Sale and Application of Commercial Fertilizers"; Craven, *Soil Exhaustion*, 94–97; and Crothers, "Agricultural Improvement."

56. William Massie, Farm Accounts, vol. 1, 1831.

57. Pharsalia in the 1820s most closely resembled an infield-outfield system. The term is drawn from agricultural practice on the Celtic fringes of early modern Britain. Welsh, Scottish, and some Irish farmers maintained high levels of fertility on intensively cultivated plots near their houses, while reserving larger tracts of less fertile mountainside and waste for livestock grazing and occasional cropping.

*Chapter Three. Pharsalia's Ecological Crisis, 1828–1848*

1. Peterson, *Historical Study of Prices.*

2. William Massie received Level Green plantation and Montebello, the quarter in the Blue Ridge above Crabtree Falls, as well as additional lands along the Tye River, in the estate settlement. By the late 1840s, he had established two additional quarters, Tyro and Snug Dale, from those lands and others he had purchased. Judging from his records, though, Massie managed his farms separately, rarely exchanging equipment, slaves, or other resources between them. Pharsalia remained essentially independent throughout this period, probably because Massie was already planning to hand down complete plantations to his children.

3. William Massie, Farm Accounts, vol. 1, 1842.

4. William Massie, "Yearly Summary and Balances," 1840.

5. The tobacco grown by Virginia colonists was *Nicotiana tabacum*, obtained from the Spanish West Indies by John Rolfe. It was a close relative of the native variety, *Nicotiana rustica*, but more palatable to European consumers. Cultivation methods were similar, and Rolfe and other colonists doubtless received instruction from their native neighbors. The maize varieties they planted were almost certainly entirely native.

6. Knowledge of the craft of tobacco farming was one of the marks of excellence among gentlemen of colonial Virginia. See T. H. Breen's discussion of the intense pride planters took in their reputations as skilled tobacco growers in *Tobacco Culture*, 61–65.

7. Ibid., 72.

8. For discussions of hemp agriculture in Virginia, see the work of Herndon, "Hemp in Colonial Virginia" and "War-Inspired Industry." For a quick survey of the early nineteenth-century hemp boomlet, see Gray, *History of Agriculture*, 821–22.

9. See Herndon, "Hemp in Colonial Virginia" and "A War-Inspired Industry," for discussion of hemp cultivation in the eighteenth-century Shenandoah Valley.

10. See, for instance, Reuben Cash to William Massie, 11 January 1829; Daniel Brown to William Massie, February 1829; William Massie to Joseph Hines, 12 June 1829; John Thompson to William Massie, 9 June 1829.

11. See, for instance, Reuben Cash to William Massie, 19 August 1832, William Massie Collection, Special Collections, Swem Library, College of William and Mary, Williamsburg, Va.

12. William Massie, Farm Accounts, vol. 1, 1828, 1831.

13. Vlume and Co. to William Massie, 16 August 1830, 28 October 1830.

14. Peterson, *Historical Study of Prices*, 101; "Amherst Tillage," *Farmers' Register* 3 (1835): 104.

15. Pharsalia's low tobacco yields must be inferred from Massie's actions. Massie pooled tobacco yields from Pharsalia, Level Green, Tyro, and Montebello together in his records. The fact that tobacco was unique in being treated this way offers further evidence that Massie could not envision the crop fitting into the systems he hoped to establish on each farm. Peterson, *Historical Study of Prices*, 101.

16. Peterson, *Historical Study of Prices*, 101.

17. John Jones to William Massie, 20 September 1847.

18. William Massie, Farm Accounts, vol. 2, 1847.

19. For a brief discussion of wheat rust in the early United States and Virginia, see Sharrer, "Farming, Disease, and Change in the Chesapeake Ecosystem," 307–9, and Gray, *History of Agriculture*, 819.

20. William Massie, Farm Accounts, vol. 2, 1847.

21. See Bidwell and Falconer, *History of Agriculture*, 93–94, for a short history of stem rust in early America.

22. William Massie to Lewis Webb, 2 June 1842.

23. John Taylor, *Arator*, 223; Craven, *Soil Exhaustion*, 145, 156; Gray, *History of Agriculture*, 819.

24. William Massie, Weather Memoranda, 4 August 1850, 25 August 1846, *Records of Ante-bellum Southern Plantations*.

25. For instance, William Massie, Weather Memoranda, 29 August 1843, 18 August 1848.

26. Ibid., 1 August 1853.

27. Ibid., 23 June 1841.

28. Ibid., 8 June 1858.

29. Craven, *Soil Exhaustion*, 145, 156; Gray, *History of Agriculture*, 819. For the life cycle and hosts of stem rust, see Martin and Salmon, "Rusts of Wheat, Oats, Barley, Rye."

30. Rye prices generally fluctuated between fifty and seventy cents a bushel in these years, while oats typically fetched less than forty cents. Only in the lowest points of the depression of the 1840s did wheat slip below ninety cents. Peterson, *Historical Study of Prices*, 72, 76–78.

31. William Massie, Wheat Record, 1845.

32. For a general discussion of weed biology, see Radosevich and Holt, *Weed Ecology*, esp. 20–26.

33. For a basic discussion of briar characteristics, see Muenscher, *Weeds*, 160. For the role weeds played in taking light, water, and nutrients from crop plants, see Radosevich and Holt, *Weed Ecology*, 97–116, and Zimdahl, *Weed-Crop Competition*.

34. Muenscher, *Weeds*, 201–2.

35. For the adoption of row cultivation in the post-Revolutionary Chesapeake, see Earle, "Myth of the Southern Soil Miner," 198–200, and Earle and Hoffman, "Genteel Erosion," 287–91.

36. William Massie to the *Southern Planter*, 2 June 1842, reprinted in the *Southern Planter* 2 (1842): 160.

37. William Massie, Weather Memoranda, 1 June 1845, 12 June 1846, 26 June 1841.

38. William Massie, Farm Accounts, vol. 1, 1828, 1829.

39. Ibid., 1830.

40. William Massie to the *Southern Planter*, 2 June 1842.

41. William Massie, Farm Accounts, vol. 1, 1844.

42. Ibid., 1831.

43. Ibid., vol. 2, 1845.

44. The Cove wheat field was one of ten the slaves planted at Pharsalia in 1845.

45. "Inventory and Appraisement of William Massie's Estate," 1862, *Records of Ante-bellum Southern Plantations*.

46. For the selection of seed stocks in the nineteenth century, see Bidwell and Falconer, *History of Agriculture*, 95.

47. In 1838, he bought half a bushel of Baltimore spring wheat and planted it in old clearings at Pharsalia. In 1843, he planted one and a half bushels of red wheat in the Cow Lot.

48. William Massie to the *Southern Planter*, 2 June 1842.

49. William Massie, Farm Accounts, vol. 1, 1831.

50. Ibid., vol. 1, 1842.

51. Ibid., vol. 2, 1847.

52. Ibid., vol. 1, 1844.

53. Ibid., 1837.

54. William Massie, Pharsalia Orchard Book, *Records of Ante-bellum Southern Plantations*. See also, for instance, William Massie to Peter Wills and Co., 24 June 1839, 26 June 1839.

55. John Jones to William Massie, 29 October 1849; R. M. Burton to William Massie, 20 June 1850.

56. Slaughter weights of hogs at Pharsalia made little obvious progress during these years, fluctuating between 130 and 150 pounds per animal. Massie only provided gross figures for pork production in his notes. Given the activity expended on the hogs, and Massie's interest in marketing his hams, it seems probable that intensive effort was expended on some portion of the herd to prepare it for market. Certainly, keeping animal weights constant during a severalfold increase in the size of the herd indicates considerable success in intensification.

57. The best price records begin in 1807, when bacon was consistently selling at more than ten cents a pound on the Virginia market. These prices crashed after the Panic of 1819. Despite inflation and slowly improving breeding and care, prices would only reach those levels again during brief periods of prosperity in the 1830s and 1850s. Peterson, *Historical Study of Prices*, 95–96.

58. William Massie, Farm Accounts, vol. 1, 1842.

59. Refsell, "Massies of Virginia," 500.

60. See Gouger, "Northern Neck of Virginia"; Gagliardo, "Germans and Farming"; and Wayland, *German Element*, 188–95.


*Chapter Four. Capitalism and Conservation at Pharsalia, 1848–1862*

1. This retreat from commercial farming in agriculturally marginal environments has been commented on in a number of works. See, for instance, Salstrom, *Appalachia's Path to Dependency*, chaps. 1–3, esp. 8–19, and Kirby, *Poquosin*, chaps. 3–4.

2. William Massie to John Thompson, 12 February 1850.

3. Fletcher, *Letters of Elijah Fletcher*, 183.

4. Ruffin had attacked banking in the pages of his *Farmer's Register* during the last years of its existence. Its successor, the *Southern Planter* out of Richmond,

deliberately avoided politics. By the end of the antebellum era, in fact, there was a noticeable correlation between farm conservationists and Whiggish politics. See, for instance, Crofts, *Old Southampton*.

5. "Portrait of an Anti-book Farmer," *Southern Planter* 20 (1860): 700.

6. "Sketches of the Habits and Manners of Old Times in Virginia," *Farmers' Register* 5 (1838): 579.

7. Probate data are drawn from my dissertation, "Agroecologies of a Southern Community." See "Appendix: Statistical Tables," tables 4.1–4.6.

8. The basic system of tobacco cultivation in Virginia predated the spread of slavery in the late seventeenth century, nor did the importation of large numbers of West Africans disrupt it. The emergence of capitalist intensification at midcentury did not result from any change in the system, nor did emancipation seriously derail developments already under way. The classic contemporary analysis of the negative impact of slavery on intensification in the South is in the work of Frederick Law Olmsted. See, for instance, Olmsted, *Cotton Kingdom*.

9. "A MERCHANT," "Proper Disposition of Farming Capital," *Southern Planter* 3 (1843): 222.

10. Annual Report of the Commissioner of Patents for the Year 1843, U.S. Patent Office, 1844. For the local success of multicole rye, see Tarleton Pleasants to William Massie, 2 July 1848, and Seventh Census of the United States (1850), Manuscript Schedules for Agriculture, Nelson County, Va.

11. Massie's Wheat Record leaves off in 1850. Calculations of later yields were compiled from the Farm Account Books, vol. 2.

12. For grass seed prices, see Peterson, *Historical Study of Prices*, 103.

13. For a survey of the guano craze in antebellum American agriculture, see Stoll, *Larding the Lean Earth*, 187–94.

14. William Massie, Weather Memoranda, 8 June 1858.

15. Ibid., 26 July 1853.

16. William Massie, Farm Accounts, vol. 2, 1854.

17. A view best expressed by William Cronon in *Changes in the Land*, esp. chap. 8.

18. "Report on the State of Agriculture in Prince George," *Farmers' Register* 1 (1833): 233–4.

19. The best piece discussing the difficulties of adapting the English and northern genetic stocks that supported the double-cycle to the South is Rubin, "Limits of Agricultural Progress."

20. "The Science of Agriculture," *Southern Planter* 3 (1843): 227.

21. "Pasturage vs. Tillage," *Southern Planter* 3 (1843): 97.

22. "Agricultural Aphorisms, No. 5," *Southern Planter* 3 (1843): 216.

23. For a discussion of the role of fencing in timber shortages, see Herndon, "Significance of the Forest." The fence law issue was discussed extensively in Ruffin's *Farmers' Register* (albeit entirely supporting the change). See Ruffin, *Nature's Management*, chap. 4, for a selection of opinion. For a summary of Ruffin's position, see Kirby, *Poquosin*, 76–78.

24. Peterson, *Historical Study of Prices*, 103.

25. William Massie, Weather Memoranda, 25 August 1852.

26. For plow technology at Pharsalia, see "Inventory and Appraisement of William Massie's Estate," 1862.

27. For 1859 crop year production at Pharsalia, see Eighth Census of the United States (1860), Manuscript Schedules for Agriculture, Nelson County, Va.

28. Edward Hubbard to William Massie, 21 February 1851.

29. William Massie, Farm Accounts, vol. 2, 1860.

30. William Massie to the President and Directors of the James River and Kanawha Co., 6 September 1850; William Massie to C. C. Flanagan, 17 February, 1860.

31. Massie began keeping this record in 1841, as his debts deepened in the depression that followed the Panic of 1837, and continued doing so until his health failed. The records are reproduced in *Records of Ante-bellum Southern Plantations*.

32. For discussions of the guano craze in the South, see Weymouth Jordan, "Peruvian Guano Gospel," and Rosser H. Taylor, "Sale and Application of Commercial Fertilizers."

33. William Massie to the Editors and Proprietors of the *American Farmer* 28 December 1855.

34. For the politics and diplomacy of the guano trade, see Skaggs, *Great Guano Rush*.

35. Massie to *American Farmer*, 28 December 1855. See also "The Guano Convention," *Southern Planter* 16 (1856), 178–181. "Editor's Introduction," and "Report to the Virginia Agricultural Society," *Southern Planter* 16 (1856): 80–90.

36. See Fussell, *Crop Nutrition*, and Rossiter, *Emergence of Agricultural Science*, for a discussion of the slow development of soil chemistry in the United States. For the problems of soil chemistry in the South, see Stoll, *Larding the Lean Earth*, 150–55.

37. Massie to *American Farmer*, 28 December 1855.

38. William Massie, Farm Accounts, vol. 2, 1852.

39. Ibid. See also "The Inspection Laws," *Southern Planter* 16 (1856): 81.

40. Benjamin Hallowell, "The Mode of Using Guano," *Southern Planter* 14 (1854): 299. See also "Random Thoughts on the Use of Guano," *Southern Planter* 16 (1856): 255–56.

41. See, for instance, "Improving Land from Its Own Resources," *Southern Planter* 16 (1856): 352–56.

42. See, in particular, Genovese, *Political Economy of the Cotton South*, and Mathew, *Edmund Ruffin and the Crisis of Slavery*.

43. William Massie to Jacob Warwick, 26 February 1851.

44. This view has been most recently expressed by Mart Stewart in "Re-greening the South," 249–50.

45. Roberts, "African-Virginian Extended Kin," 47–52.

46. William Massie, "General Memorandum," 31 December 1836, *Records of Ante-bellum Southern Plantations*.

47. William Massie, Farm Accounts, vol. 1, 1836; William Massie, "Memoranda Concerning Misbehavior and Punishment of Slaves," 1 June 1839, 22 September 1839, 1839–41, *Records of Ante-bellum Southern Plantations*.

48. William Massie, Farm Accounts, vol. 1, 1844; William Massie, "Memoranda Concerning Misbehavior and Punishment of Slaves"; William Massie, Weather Memoranda, 30 March 1860.

49. Massie did embrace the illusions of paternalism enough to try to use his overseers to buffer him from the harsh realities of race slavery. When writing to another planter regarding Munroe, Massie complained that the overseer had "always been too savage and cruel to my negroes." Yet in the end what mattered was productivity. Munroe had kept people working and produced good crops, so Massie backed him in both deed and word. When Munroe sought another position in 1850, the planter recommended him "as an overseer . . . the best I ever had." Massie to Cocke, 26 June 1850.

50. William Massie to Matthias Law, 21 April 1847.

51. William Massie, Weather Memoranda, 6 March 1847.

52. William Massie to David Graham, 1 January, 1850.

53. William Massie to Alexander Rives, 22 December 1851.

54. William Massie, "Deposition in the Turner Runaway Negro Case, 1853," *Records of Ante-bellum Southern Plantations*. For Massie's battles over Pollard, see Refsell, "Massies of Virginia," 685, and Charles Scott to William Massie, 8 June 1852.

55. John Ott to Maria Massie, 25 July 1864.

56. Refsell, "Massies of Virginia," 1095; John Ott to Colonel A. L. Rives, 20 July 1864.

57. Philander, "Enormous Losses Caused by the Fence Law of Virginia," *Farmers' Register* 1 (1833), 633.

58. Quote on Virginia's low grounds from R. N., "On Draining: Addressed to Young Farmers," *Farmers' Register* 1 (1833), 388.

59. Tye River and Blue Ridge Turnpike Company Accounts, William Massie Papers, 1747–1919, Center for American History.

60. Suum Cique, "On the Law of Enclosures," *Farmers' Register* 1 (1833), 398.

61. For a general discussion of the debate over fence- and drainage-law reform in antebellum Virginia, see Kirby, *Poquosin*, 76–78, and Ruffin, *Nature's Management*, chaps. 4, 7.

62. P. W. Harper, "Necessity for a Law to Permit Draining in Virginia," *Farmers' Register* 1 (1833), 519.

63. R. N., "On Draining," 386–87.

64. William Massie to Chiswell Dabney, 2 February 1853.

65. William Massie, Weather Memoranda, 23 April 1853.

66. Ibid.

67. Ibid., 8–10 November 1841.

68. Ibid., 22 April 1847. For a more general discussion, see Nelson, "Planters and Hill People."

69. Crop Memoranda, 30 April 1836.

70. William Massie to John Thompson, 12 February 1850.

71. Pollard in fact referred to another Nelson County family, the Fitzpatricks, as the suspected trespassers. However, since no Fitzpatricks seem to have lived near his property, while it was surrounded by Fitzgerald tenants and landowners, it seems very probable that from a distance he simply confused the names.

72. Richard Pollard to William Massie, 27 August 1850.

73. William Massie and Nelson Munroe, Memorandum of Contract, 26 June 1844. For a more extensive discussion of Massie's problems with the Coffey Gang and other mountain residents, see Nelson, "Adventures of 'The Coffey Gang.'"

74. William Massie to Alexander Fitzpatrick, 11 April 1841, William Massie Papers, Special Collections, Swem Library.

75. William Massie to Charles Davenport, 3 April 1842.

76. "Inventory and Appraisement of William Massie's Estate," 1862.

77. Eighth Census of the United States (1860), Manuscript Schedules for Agriculture, Nelson County, Va.

78. William Massie to Elizabeth Effinger, 29 March 1842.

*Chapter Five. The Gentry Family and the Fall of Pharsalia, 1861–1889*

1. William Massie, Weather Memoranda, 4–18 August 1860.

2. For instance, Major Thomas Massie to William Massie, 10 October 1811. Washington College was renamed Washington and Lee University after the death of Robert E. Lee, its president.

3. William Massie to Sarah Massie, 22 July 1824.

4. William Massie to Nicholas Cobbs, 3 January 1829.

5. William Massie to Thomas James Massie, 6 March 1852; Refsell, "Massies of Virginia," 613; William Massie to John R. Jones, 19 February 1850; Jacob Warwick to William Massie, 25 February 1851.

6. William Massie to James Heath, 14 October 1841.

7. William Massie to John R. Jones, 19 February 1850.

8. William Massie to Daniel Brown, 27 February 1851.

9. William Massie to Thomas James Massie, 14 December 1858.

10. Ibid.

11. William Massie to Jacob Warwick, 26 February 1851.

12. William Massie to Thomas James Massie, 14 December 1858.

13. Ibid.

14. William Massie to Jacob Warwick, 26 February 1851.

15. N. H. Massie to Thomas James Massie, 31 January 1876, quoted in Refsell, "Massies of Virginia," 1199. Unless otherwise noted, quotations in this chapter are from Refsell, "Massies of Virginia."

16. Florence Massie to Maria Massie, 23 February 1863.

17. Florence Massie to Maria Massie, 24 May 1867, Florence Massie Tunstall to Maria Massie, 11 January 1869. Maria Massie's postwar correspondence was not included in the microfilm edition of the Massie Papers.

18. Margaret Effinger to Maria Massie, 14 May 1869; Bland Massie to Maria Massie, 31 October 1870.

19. Hope Massie, Memorandum of Contract with Lobban and Wood, 28 June 1868; Executrix of William Massie v. Hope Massie et al., 3 June 1874.

20. Hope struggled with alcohol abuse throughout his adult life, and his mother eventually turned control of his share of the inheritance to his son Effinger Massie. See M. M. Jurey to Maria Massie, 29 January 1877, and Bland Massie to Maria Massie, 12 May 1886. Thomas James made his home at Snug Dale after the war; he continued going deeper into debt, eventually losing the farm to his creditors. Thacker, "Survey Report: Snug Dale."

21. Florence Massie Tunstall to Maria Massie, 30 August 1870.

22. See Townes, "Effect of Emancipation," esp. 412. Townes argued against

the view of C. Vann Woodward that the plantation system of landholding and agriculture was quickly and comprehensively destroyed by the end of slavery. She did acknowledge, however, that while absolute numbers of large landholders remained close to constant in Nelson after the war, their relative numbers and proportional landholdings declined. Pharsalia's last years seem to reinforce that general picture.

23. Thomas James Massie, "Historical Account."

24. John Burdick has written on the economic and philosophical dilemmas of the postwar gentry in "From Virtue to Fitness." In this study of the Hubard family of nearby Buckingham County (who also owned a plantation just down the Tye from Pharsalia), Burdick describes their struggle to embrace liberal capitalist values. Even family members who accepted the economic realities of the late nineteenth century and got out of farming held onto the old plantation homes as the only suitable place to display the wealth they acquired from business and the professions.

25. Thomas James Massie, "Historical Account."

26. Massie Tunstall to Maria Massie, 19 January 1889. See also M. W. Baskerville to Maria Massie, undated.

27. See Cardwell, "Plantation House," and Titus, "Groaning Tables." Thomas Nelson Page's postbellum romanticization of Old Virginia is again the best example of the broader popularity of the idealization of the prewar plantation landscape. For analysis, see in particular MacKethan, "Thomas Nelson Page."

28. John Ott to Maria Massie, 1 August 1889.

29. See Refsell, "Massies of Virginia," 1047. For the sudden blizzard of problems between Maria and her children over William Massie's will, see also, for instance, Maria Massie, "Notice," 25 October 1862; Robert Whitehead to Maria Massie, 2 November 1862, 3 April 1863, 12 August 1863; Thomas James Massie to Maria Massie, 2 July 1863, 9 July 1863; Maria Massie to Robert Whitehead, 27 January 1864; Jacob Warwick to Maria Massie, 6 September 1864; and Maria Massie to Joseph Ligon, 30 November 1865.

30. Maria's records are spotty compared with those of her late husband, but still sizable. A large body of family and business correspondence, some brief account books, and a book of accounts with servants (farm laborers) survive in the Massie papers at the Center for American History. Unfortunately, no detailed information on her farming routine comparable to William Massie's Farm Accounts appears to have been kept.

31. For some details of Maria's guardianship and executorship and the limitations it placed on her manipulation of the estate, see George Stevens to Maria Massie, 30 April 1863.

32. For a quick survey of the postbellum agricultural depression in Virginia, see Kerr-Ritchie, *Freedpeople in the Tobacco South*, 125–38.

33. Inventory of William Massie's Estate, 25 August 1862.

34. Robert, *Tobacco Kingdom*, 151–57; Peterson, *Historical Study of Prices*, 101.

35. W. and W. S. Peters to Maria Massie, 2 February 1864.

36. Inventory of William Massie's Estate, 25 August 1862.

37. Potatoes were in particular demand in the last years of the war, and Pharsalia's garden seems to have been expanded to meet that market.

38. Maria Massie to Colonel Hampton, 29 April 1863; Maria Massie to "Nelson County," 12 August 1864. For a case study of wartime destruction in central Virginia, see Sutherland, "Introduction to War."

39. Maria Massie to James Seddon, Secretary of War, 14 May 1864.

40. See, for example, Floyd Whitehead to Maria Massie, 25 November 1863. For a more general discussion, see Zornow, "Aid for the Indigent Families."

41. William Cabell to Maria Massie, 29 November 1864; Cabell to Massie, 14 December 1864.

42. John Ott to Maria Massie, 28 April 1864; James Cobbs to Maria Massie, 24 June 1864.

43. Siegel, *Roots of Southern Distinctiveness*, 163–66.

44. Trimble, *Man-Induced Soil Erosion*.

45. James Cobbs to Maria Massie, 26 September 1865; John Ott to Maria Massie, 1 May 1877.

46. Morgan, *Emancipation in Virginia's Tobacco Belt*, 190. Interestingly, James Irwin reports that for the Virginia Piedmont as a whole, wage labor had come to predominate over sharecropping. Certainly the 1870 and 1880 agricultural and population censuses suggest that many of Maria's neighbors were following the example she set at Pharsalia in insisting on wage labor. See Irwin, "Farmers and Laborers."

47. See Morgan, *Emancipation in Virginia's Tobacco Belt*, chaps. 11–12, esp. 205–9.

48. M. Harvey Effinger to Maria Massie, 11 August 1865.

49. See Maria Massie, "Book of Accounts with Servants," William Massie Papers, 1747–1919, Center for American History. See also Roberts, "African-Virginian Extended Kin," 67–73. For rental of Tyro plantation, see Philip Nelson to Maria Massie, 29 October 1866. For broader discussions of free labor and progressive agriculture, see Kerr-Ritchie, *Freedpeople in the Tobacco South*, 101–17.

50. For discussions of racial violence in the postwar Piedmont, see Lynda Mor-

gan, *Emancipation in Virginia's Tobacco Belt*, 154–55, 168–70, and Tripp, *Yankee Town, Southern City*, 224–49.

51. C. T. Smith to Maria Massie, 7 September 1867.

52. Pulley, *Old Virginia Restored*, esp. chaps. 1–2, and Moger, *Virginia*, esp. chap. 6. For case studies in the conservative social vision of postwar Virginia capitalists, see Peter Thomas, "Matthew Fontaine Maury," and Lindgren, "First and Foremost a Virginian."

53. See Burdick, "From Virtue to Fitness."

54. Bland Massie's daughter Florence married Lynchburger John Morton, who had purchased the formula for ChapStick lip balm. Working out of their kitchen, Florence and her husband built up the Morton Manufacturing Company, which manufactured ChapStick, until they sold the formula to A. H. Robbins Co. in 1963. In 1952, the Mortons used their lip balm profits to buy back Pharsalia. Their daughter, Perkins Morton Flippin, occupied the house until her death in late 2004. See Refsell, "Massies of Virginia," 44.

55. Harvey and Williams to Maria Massie, 13 January 1869; R. A. Brock to Maria Massie, 7 February 1881.

56. James Cobbs to Maria Massie, 28 September 1865; C. W. Price to Maria Massie, 8 March 1867; Allison and Addison to Maria Massie, 17 February 1871; Harvey Effinger to Maria Massie, 7 February 1871.

57. John Mead to Maria Massie, 8 September 1866; Miles and Marshall to Maria Massie, 4 October 1866; John Ott to Maria Massie, 16 October 1871.

58. Robert Jamieson to Maria Massie, 7 April 1873; Acree and Shatton to Maria Massie, 25 November 1878. For a general discussion of the fertilizer market of the period, see Sheridan, "Chemical Fertilizers in Southern Agriculture."

59. B. H. Harris to R. A. Marshall (overseer at Pharsalia), 4 August 1866; C. D. Rice to Maria Massie, 19 June 1871; James Cobbs to Bland Massie, 5 August 1872.

60. For "modern" methods of wheat cultivation nationwide after the war, see Fite, *Farmer's Frontier, 1865–1900*, esp. chaps. 5–6.

61. The Albemarle Pippin was first planted near Massie's Mill in 1814. See Pollard, *Under the Blue Ledge*.

62. Tyree Dollins to Maria Massie, 20 November 1872.

63. John Graham Effinger to Maria Massie, 10 April, 1868; John Ott to Maria Massie, 30 January 1878.

64. Tenth Census of the United States (1880), Manuscript Schedules for Agriculture, Nelson County, Va.

65. A. H. Armistead to Maria Massie, 6 September 1867.

66. Tenth Census of the United States (1880), Manuscript Schedules for Agriculture, Nelson County, Va.; Peterson, *Historical Study of Prices*, 177–78.

67. William Rose to Maria Massie, 22 November 1866.

68. For a brief discussion of postbellum fence law reform in Virginia, see Kirby, *Poquosin*, 178.

69. Peterson, *Historical Study of Prices*, 95–96, 190–91.

70. John Graham Effinger to Maria Massie, 10 April 1868; John Ott to Maria Massie, 30 January 1878.

71. Some limited case studies suggest that many Virginia businessmen were forced to abandon their economic conservatism in favor of a more open approach by the turn of the century. See, for instance, Simms, "Phillip Alexander Bruce"; Moger, "Industrial and Urban Progress"; and Renda, "Advent of Agricultural Progressivism."

72. Maria's portion of Pharsalia was assessed at fifteen thousand dollars in 1880, barely 60 percent of its value ten years earlier. In contrast, national consumer prices retained almost 80 percent of their value over the same period. Economic History Association, "What Is Its Relative Value in U.S. Dollars?"

73. Kerr-Ritchie, *Freedpeople in the Tobacco South*, 97; Burdick, "From Virtue to Fitness," 20.

74. A. B. Cabell to Maria Massie, 13 July 1869; J. J. Hite to Maria Massie, 29 July 1869.

75. Harvey and Williams to Maria Massie, 29 October 1867.

76. Sharrer, *Kind of Fate*, 127.

77. Lee, Taylor, and Sneed to Maria Massie 9 March 1885.

78. Ninth and Tenth Censuses of the United States (1870 and 1880), Manuscript Schedules for Agriculture, Nelson County, Va.

79. Ibid.; Peterson, *Historical Study of Prices*, 101.

80. Sharrer, *Kind of Fate*, 67–69; Robert, *Tobacco Kingdom*, 49–50. See also Tilley, *Bright-Tobacco Industry*, 13–18.

81. Langhorne, *Southern Sketches*, 4–5.

82. Unless otherwise noted, all information in this section is taken from the Tenth Census of the United States (1880), Manuscript Schedules for Agriculture, Nelson County, Va.

83. Bland and Maria had sold some land in the area during the 1870s, but not nearly enough to account for such a shift.

84. Peterson, *Historical Study of Prices*.

85. For a transcription of the probate inventory of Maria's estate, see Refsell, "Massies of Virginia," 1226–38.

86. "Will of Maria C. Massie," Florence Massie Morton Papers (private collection), transcribed in Refsell, "Massies of Virginia," 1221–25, entered in Nelson County Will Book N, 311–16. In her first will, Maria placed Martha Ligon's share in trust with a family friend, presumably to protect it from John Ligon's debts. A subsequent codicil placed Hope's inheritance under the management of his son Effinger Massie. Only Bland retained his mother's confidence.

87. Nelson County Deed Book 26, 172. See also Nelson County Index to Deeds, Index of Grantors H–K, 475, L–Z 17, 98, 100–101, for other Massie family land sales.

## Epilogue. Mourning Pharsalia

1. Thacker, "Survey Report: Tyro #2." Given that Thacker did not list Doctor Parson under her "sources of information," she may not have been able to arrange a visit to the house and relied entirely on Florence Morton's knowledge of it.

2. Ibid.

3. Ibid.

4. Virginians of the early twentieth century carried on the postbellum idealization of pre–Civil War plantation life. This romanticism took the form of preserving and restoring old plantation homes like Pharsalia and decorating them in the colonial revival style. See Rasmussen and Tilton, *Old Virginia*, chaps. 4–5, and Pulley, *Old Virginia Restored*, esp. chaps. 1–2.

5. 1 Kings 4:25 (AV).

6. Oak Ridge Estate, "Oak Ridge History, Page 2."

7. http://www.thefarmbasket.com/; http://shop.storesense.com/farm/Page.bok ?file=nelson.htm (accessed 9 February 2006).

# BIBLIOGRAPHY

*Primary Sources*

MANUSCRIPT COLLECTIONS
Cabell, William. Commonplace Books. Virginia Historical Society, Richmond.
Cabell Deposit. Special Collections Department. Alderman Library, University of
  Virginia, Charlottesville.
Massie Family. Papers. 1767–1993. Virginia Historical Society, Richmond.
Massie, William. Papers. Special Collections. Swem Library, College of William
  and Mary, Williamsburg, Va.
————. Papers, 1747–1919. Center for American History. University of Texas,
  Austin.
————. Papers, 1766–1890. Special Collections. Perkins Library, Duke Univer-
  sity, Durham, N.C.

MICROFILM COLLECTIONS
*Records of Ante-bellum Southern Plantations from the Revolution through the
  Civil War.* Ed. Kenneth Stampp. Series G: Selections from the Center for Amer-
  ican History, University of Texas at Austin, Part 2: William Massie Collection.
  Bethesda, Md.: University Publications of America, 1987.

GOVERNMENT RECORDS
Amherst County (Va.) Deed Books [microfilm]. Library of Virginia, Richmond.
Nelson County (Va.) Deed Books [microfilm]. Library of Virginia, Richmond.
Nelson County (Va.) Will Books [microfilm]. Library of Virginia, Richmond.
Seventh Census of the United States (1850). Manuscript Schedules for Agriculture.
  Nelson County, Va.
Eighth Census of the United States (1860). Manuscript Schedules for Agriculture.
  Nelson County, Va.

Ninth Census of the United States (1870). Manuscript Schedules for Agriculture. Nelson County, Va.

Tenth Census of the United States (1880). Manuscript Schedules for Agriculture. Nelson County, Va.

Virginia Patents and Grants [microfilm]. Library of Virginia, Richmond.

Virginia Property Tax Rolls for Amherst County (1787) [microfilm]. Library of Virginia, Richmond.

PERIODICALS

*American Farmer.* Baltimore. 1819–61.

*Farmers' Register.* Shellbanks, Va. 1833–42.

*Southern Planter.* Richmond. 1841–61.

PUBLISHED

Byrd, William, II, to the Earl of Orrery, 5 July 1726. Reprinted in "Virginia Council Journals." *Virginia Magazine of History and Biography* 32 (1924): 27.

Davis, Bailey Fulton. *The Deeds of Amherst County, Virginia, 1761–1807, and Albemarle County, Virginia, 1748–1763.* Easley, S.C.: Southern Historical Press, 1979.

Fletcher, Elijah. *Letters.* Ed. Martha von Briesen. Charlottesville: University of Virginia Press, 1965.

Jefferson, Thomas. *Notes on the State of Virginia.* Chapel Hill: University of North Carolina Press for the Institute of Early American History and Culture, 1982.

Langhorne, Orra. *Southern Sketches from Virginia, 1881–1900.* Charlottesville: University of Virginia Press, 1964.

Lederer, John. *The Discoveries of John Lederer.* Ed. William Cumming. Charlottesville: University of Virginia Press, 1958.

Massie, Thomas James. "Historical Account." Typescript copy in the Nelson County (Va.) Historical Society Collections. Nelson Memorial Library, Lovingston, Va.

Refsell, Oliver M. "The Massies of Virginia: A Documentary History of a Planter Family in 3 Volumes." Ph.D. diss., University of Texas, 1959.

Rose, Robert. *The Diary of Robert Rose: A View of Virginia by a Scottish Colonial Parson, 1746–1751.* Ed. Ralph Emmett Fall. Verona, Va.: McClure Press, 1977.

Ruffin, Edmund. *Incidents of My Life.* Ed David F. Allmendinger Jr. Charlottesville: Published for the Virginia Historical Society by the University of Virginia Press, 1990.

———. *Nature's Management: Writings on Landscape and Reform, 1822–1859.* Ed. Jack Temple Kirby. Athens: University of Georgia Press, 2000.

Taylor, John. *Arator, Being a Series of Agricultural Essays, Practical and Political: In Sixty-four Numbers.* Petersburg, Va.: Whitworth and Yancey, 1818.


*Secondary Sources*

Abernethy, Thomas Perkins. *Three Virginia Frontiers.* Baton Rouge: Louisiana State University Press, 1940.

———. *Western Lands and the American Revolution.* New York: Appleton-Century, 1937.

Agustin, Patricio. "Historical Land Use Evolution in a Tropical Acid Upland Agroecosystem." *Agriculture, Ecosystems, and Environment* 53 (1995): 83–95.

Albert, Peter Joseph. "The Protean Institution: The Geography, Economy, and Ideology of Slavery in Post-Revolutionary Virginia." Ph.D. diss., University of Maryland, 1976.

Allmendinger, David F., Jr.. *Ruffin: Family and Reform in the Old South.* New York: Oxford University Press, 1990.

Altieri, Miguel. *Agroecology: The Scientific Basis of Alternative Agriculture.* Boulder, Colo.: Westview Press, 1987.

Anderson, Ralph V. "Labor Utilization and Productivity, Diversification and Self-Sufficiency, Southern Plantations, 1800–1840." Ph.D. diss., University of North Carolina, 1974.

Andrews, Archie D. "Agriculture in Virginia, 1789–1820." Master's thesis, University of Virginia, 1950.

Appleby, Joyce. "The Changing Prospect of the Family Farm in the Early National Period." *Working Papers from the Regional Economic History Research Center* 4: 3 (1981): 1 25.

———. "Commercial Farming and the 'Agrarian Myth' in the Early Republic." *Journal of American History* 68 (1982): 833–49.

Armstrong, Thomas F. "Urban Vision in Virginia: A Comparative Study of Antebellum Fredericksburg, Lynchburg, Staunton." Ph.D. diss., University of Virginia, 1974.

Bailey, Fred Arthur. "Thomas Nelson Page and the Patrician Cult of the Old South." *International Social Science Review* 72 (1997): 110–21.

Bailey, Joseph Cannon. *Seaman A. Knapp: Schoolmaster of American Agriculture.* New York: Columbia University Press, 1945.

Bailey, Ron. "A Surveyor for the King." *Colonial Williamsburg* (Summer 2001). http://www.history.org/foundation/journal/Summer01/Surveyor.cfm (accessed 23 November 2005).

Belmore, Margaret. "Major Thomas Massie, a Gentleman of the Old South." Master's thesis, University of Virginia, 1932.

Bennett, Hugh Hammond. "Lectures on Soil Erosion: Its Extent and Meaning and Necessary Measures of Control." http://www.nrcs.usda.gov/about/history/speeches/19321104.html (accessed 13 November 2005).

———. *Soil Conservation.* New York: McGraw-Hill, 1939.

———. "Thomas Jefferson: Soil Conservationist." USDA Misc. Publ. 548. Washington, D.C.: Government Printing Office, 1944.

Bennett, Hugh Hammond, and William Clayton Pryor. *This Land We Defend.* New York: Longmans, Green, 1942.

Bidwell, Percy, and John Falconer. *History of Agriculture in the Northern United States, 1620–1860.* New York: Peter Smith, 1941.

Billings, Warren, Thad Tate, and John Selby. *Colonial Virginia: A History.* White Plains, N.Y.: KTO Press, 1986.

Bliss, Willard. "The Rise of Tenancy in Virginia." *Virginia Magazine of History and Biography* 58, no. 4 (October 1950): 427–41.

Bolgiano, Chris. *The Appalachian Forest: A Search for Roots and Renewal.* Mechanicsburg, Pa.: Stackpole Books, 1998.

Bonner, James C. "Advancing Trends in Southern Agriculture." *Agricultural History* 21 (1947): 449–59.

Borman, F. H. "Factors Determining the Role of Loblolly Pine and Sweetgum in Early Old-Field Succession in the Piedmont of North Carolina." *Ecological Monographs* 23 (1953): 339–58.

Boserup, Ester. *The Conditions of Agricultural Growth: The Economics of Agrarian Change under Population Pressure.* Chicago: Aldine, 1965.

Botkin, Daniel. *Discordant Harmonies: A New Ecology for the Twenty-first Century.* New York: Oxford University Press, 1992.

Botkin, Daniel, John E. Estes, Margriet F. Caswell, and Angelo A. Orio. *Changing the Global Environment: Perspectives on Human Involvement.* Boston: Academic Press, 1989.

Botkin, Daniel, and Edward A. Keller. *Environmental Science: Earth as a Living Planet.* 3rd ed. New York: John Wiley and Sons, 2000.

Botkin, Daniel, David Quammen, John McPhee, Stephen Jay Gould, Lynn Margulis, et al. *Forces of Change: A New View of Nature.* Washington, D.C.: National Geographic Society, 2000.

Braun, Emma L. *The Deciduous Forests of Eastern North America*. New York: Hafner Publishing, 1964.

Breen, T. H. *Tobacco Culture: The Mentality of the Great Tidewater Planters on the Eve of the Revolution*. Princeton, N.J.: Princeton University Press, 1985.

Brewer, Holly. "Entailing Aristocracy in Colonial Virginia: 'Ancient Feudal Restraints' and Revolutionary Reform." *William and Mary Quarterly* 3rd ser., 54 (1997): 307–46.

Brink, Wellington. *Big Hugh: The Father of Soil Conservation*. New York: MacMillan, 1951.

Brooks, Daniel. "Historical Ecology: A New Approach to Studying the Evolution of Ecological Associations." *Annals of the Missouri Botanical Garden* 72 (1985): 660–80.

Brown, Alexander. *The Cabells and Their Kin: A Memorial Volume of History and Genealogy*. Richmond.: Garrett and Massie, 1895.

Brown, C. Allan. "Eighteenth-Century Virginia Plantation Gardens: Translating an Ancient Idyll." In *Regional Garden Design in the United States*, ed. Therese O'Malley and Marc Treib, 125–62. Washington, D.C.: Dumbarton Oaks Research Library and Collection, 1995.

Bruce, Kathleen. "Virginia Agricultural Decline to 1860: A Fallacy." *Agricultural History* 6 (1932): 3–13.

Bruce, Philip A. *Institutional History of Virginia in the Seventeenth Century*. 2 vols. Boston: G. P. Putnam, 1910.

Brummer, E. C. "Diversity, Stability, and Sustainable American Agriculture." *Agronomy Journal* 90 (1998): 1–2.

Buckley, Thomas E. "The Declension of Virginia, 1776–1860: An Historiographical Perspective." In possession of the author.

Buol, S. W., F. D. Hole, and R. J. McCracken. *Soil Genesis and Classification*. Ames: Iowa State University Press, 1973.

Burdick, John. "From Virtue to Fitness: The Accommodation of a Planter Family to Postbellum Virginia." *Virginia Magazine of History and Biography* 93 (1985): 14–35.

Brush, Grace S. "Geology and Paleoecology of the Chesapeake Bay: A Long-Term Monitoring Tool for Management." *Journal of the Washington Academy of Sciences* 76, no. 3 (1986): 146–60.

Bushman, Richard. "A Poet, a Planter, and a Nation of Farmers." *Journal of the Early Republic* 19 (1999): 1–14.

———. *The Refinement of America: Persons, Houses, Cities*. New York: Alfred Knopf, 1992.

Bushnell, David I. "The Five Monacan Tribes of Virginia." *Smithsonian Collections* 82, no. 12 (1930).

Cabell, Nathaniel Francis. *Early History of Agriculture in Virginia*. Washington, D.C.: [n.p.], 1915.

———. "Some Fragments of an Intended Report on the Post Revolutionary History of Agriculture in Virginia." Ed. Earl G. Swem. *William and Mary Quarterly* 26: 3 (1918): 145–68.

Cadenasso, Mary, Steward Pickett, and Kathleen Weavers. "An Interdisciplinary and Synthetic Approach to Ecological Boundaries." *BioScience* 53 (2003): 717–22.

Cardwell, Guy. "The Plantation House: An Analogical Image." *Southern Literary Journal* 2 (1969): 3–21.

Carlson, Alvar W. "America's Botanical Drug Connection to the Orient." *Economic Botany* 40 (1986): 229–51.

Carr, Francis F. "The *Southern Planter*, 1841 to 1861." Master's thesis, University of Richmond, 1971.

Carr, Lois Green, and Russell Menard. "Land, Labor, and Economies of Scale in Early Maryland: Some Limits to Growth in the Chesapeake System of Husbandry." *Journal of Economic History* 49 (1989): 407–18.

Carr, Lois Green, Russell R. Menard, and Lorena S. Walsh. *Robert Cole's World: Agriculture and Society in Early Maryland*. Chapel Hill: University of North Carolina Press for the Institute of Early American History and Culture, 1991.

Carr, Lois Green, Philip Morgan, and Jean Russo, eds. *Colonial Chesapeake Society*. Chapel Hill: University of North Carolina Press for the Institute of Early American History and Culture, 1988. 99–132.

Carr, Lois Green, and Lorena Walsh. "The Standard of Living in the Colonial Chesapeake." *William and Mary Quarterly*, 3rd ser., 45 (1988): 135–59.

Carter, M. R. "Editorial: Researching the Agroecosystem/Environmental Interface." *Agriculture, Ecosystems, and Environment* 83 (2001): 4.

Cashin, Joan. *A Family Venture: Men and Women on the Southern Frontier*. New York: Oxford University Press, 1991.

———. "Landscape and Memory in Antebellum Virginia." *Virginia Magazine of History and Biography* 102 (1994): 477–500.

Chambers, J. D., and G. E. Mingay. *The Agricultural Revolution, 1750–1880*. London: B. T. Batsford, 1966.

Chaplin, Joyce. *An Anxious Pursuit: Agricultural Innovation and Modernity in the Lower South, 1730–1815*. Chapel Hill: University of North Carolina Press for the Institute of Early American History and Culture, 1993.

Chapman, J. L., and M. J. Reiss. *Ecology: Principles and Applications.* Cambridge: Cambridge University Press, 1992.

Chernov, A. V. *The Nature of Soil Acidity.* Madison, Wisc.: Soil Science Society of America, 1964.

Clark, Christopher. *The Roots of Rural Capitalism: Western Massachusetts, 1780–1860.* Ithaca, N.Y.: Cornell University Press, 1990.

Clark, Thomas D. *The Greening of the South.* Lexington: University Press of Kentucky, 1984.

Clarkson, John. "The Origins of the Batteau." In *The James River Batteau Festival: 1991,* 12–13. Lynchburg, Va.: Progress Printing.

Clemens, Paul G. E. *The Atlantic Economy and Colonial Maryland's Eastern Shore: From Tobacco to Grain.* Ithaca, N.Y.: Cornell University Press, 1980.

Collins, W. W., and C. O. Qualset, *Biodiversity in Agroecosystems.* Boca Raton, Fla.: CRC Press, 1998.

Cook, Maurice. "Hugh Hammond Bennett: The Father of Soil Conservation." http://www.soil.ncsu.edu/about/century/hugh.html (accessed 2 September 2005).

Comp, T. Allan. "Grain and Flour in Eastern Virginia, 1800–1860." Ph.D. diss., University of Delaware, 1978.

Conklin, Harold. *Hanunóo Agriculture: A Report on an Integral System of Shifting Cultivation in the Philippines.* Rome: Food and Agriculture Organization of the United Nations, 1957.

Cowdrey, Albert. *This Land, This South: An Environmental History.* Lexington: University Press of Kentucky, 1983.

Craven, Avery O. *Edmund Ruffin, Southerner: A Study in Secession.* Baton Rouge: Louisiana State University Press, 1966.

———. "John Taylor and Southern Agriculture." *Journal of Southern History* 4 (1938): 137–47.

———. *Soil Exhaustion as a Factor in the Agricultural History of Virginia and Maryland, 1606–1860.* 1926; Gloucester, Mass.: Peter Smith, 1965.

Crofts, Daniel. *Old Southampton: Politics and Society in a Virginia County, 1834–1869.* Charlottesville: University of Virginia Press, 1992.

Cronon, William. *Changes in the Land: Indians, Colonists, and the Ecology of New England.* 1983; New York: Hill and Wang, 2003.

Crosby, Alfred. *The Columbian Exchange: Biological and Cultural Consequences of 1492.* Westport, Conn.: Greenwood Press, 1972.

———. "Virgin Soil Epidemics as a Factor in the Aboriginal Depopulation in America." *William and Mary Quarterly* 3rd ser., 33 (1976): 289–99.

Crothers, A. Glenn. "Agricultural Improvement and Technological Innovation in a Slave Society: The Case of Early National Northern Virginia." *Agricultural History* 75 (2001): 135–67.

Curtin, Philip D., Grace S. Brush, and George W. Fisher, eds. *Discovering the Chesapeake: The History of an Ecosystem*. Baltimore: Johns Hopkins University Press, 2001.

Dabney, Virginius. *Virginia: The New Dominion*. Garden City, N.Y.: Doubleday, 1971.

Davis, Jackson. "Seaman A. Knapp, Pioneer in Southern Agriculture." Papers of Jackson Davis, 1910–1947, Special Collections Library, Alderman Library, University of Virginia. http://etext.lib.virginia.edu/etcbin/browse-mixed-new.chris?id=DavKnap&data=/texts/english/davis&tag=public (accessed 18 March 2005).

Day, Gordon. "The Indian as an Ecological Factor in the Northeastern Forest." *Ecology* 34 (1953): 329–46.

Demaree, Albert Lowther. *The American Agricultural Press, 1819–1860*. New York: Columbia University Press, 1941.

Dill, Alonzo. "Sectional Conflict in Colonial Virginia." *Virginia Magazine of History and Biography* 87 (1979): 300–315.

Dilsaver, Lary M., and Craig E. Colten, eds. *The American Environment: Interpretations of Past Geographies*. Lanham, Md.: Rowman and Littlefield, 1992.

Doran, Michael F. *Atlas of County Boundary Changes in Virginia, 1634–1895*. Athens: University of Georgia Press, 1985.

Dowdey, Clifford. *The Golden Age, a Climate for Greatness: Virginia, 1732–1775*. Boston: Little, Brown, 1970.

Drell, Bernard. "John Taylor of Caroline and the Preservation of an Old Social Order." *Virginia Magazine of History and Biography* 46 (1938): 285–98.

Dunaway, Wilma A. *The First American Frontier: Transition to Capitalism in Southern Appalachia, 1700–1860*. Chapel Hill: University of North Carolina, 1996.

Dunlap, Riley E., ed. "Ecology and the Social Sciences." *American Behavioral Scientist* 24 (1980): 3–151.

Earle, Carville V. *The Evolution of a Tidewater Settlement System: All Hallow's Parish, Maryland, 1650–1783*. Chicago: Department of Geography, University of Chicago, 1975.

———. "The Myth of the Southern Soil Miner: Macrohistory, Agricultural Innovation, and Environmental Change." In *The Ends of the Earth: Perspectives on Modern Environmental History,* ed. Donald Worster, 175–210. New York: Cambridge University Press, 1988.

Earle, Carville V., and Ronald Hoffman, "Genteel Erosion: The Ecological Consequences of Agrarian Reform in the Chesapeake, 1730–1840." In *Discovering the Chesapeake,* ed. Curtin, Brush, and Fisher, 279–303.

Economic History Association. "What Is Its Relative Value in U.S. Dollars?" http://www.eh.net/hmit/compare/ (accessed 31 December 2004).

Egloff, Keith. "Colonial Plantation Hoes of Tidewater Virginia." Virginia Research Center for Archaeology Research Report Series, No. 1. Richmond: Virginia Historic Landmarks Commission, 1980.

Elton, Charles. *The Ecology of Invasions by Animals and Plants.* London: Methuen, 1958.

*Encyclopedia of Southern Culture.* Ed. Charles Reagan Wilson and William Ferris. 4 vols. Chapel Hill: University of North Carolina Press, 1989.

Evans, Emory. "Planter Indebtedness and the Coming of the Revolution in Virginia." *William and Mary Quarterly* 3rd ser., 19 (1962): 511–33.

Faust, Drew Gilpin. "The Rhetoric and Ritual of Agriculture in Antebellum South Carolina." *Journal of Southern History* 45 (1979): 541–68.

———. *A Sacred Circle: The Dilemma of the Intellectual in the Old South, 1840–1860.* Philadelphia: University of Pennsylvania Press, 1977.

Fields, Emmett B. "The Agricultural Population of Virginia, 1850–1860." Ph.D. diss., Vanderbilt University, 1953.

Fischer, David Hackett, and James Kelly. *Bound Away: Virginia and the Westward Movement.* Charlottesville: University of Virginia Press, 2000.

Fite, Gilbert. *The Farmer's Frontier, 1865–1900.* New York: Holt, Rinehart and Winston, 1966.

Forest, Herman, Charles Bebee, and Richard Cook. *The American Chestnut: A Bibliography.* Beltsville, Md.: National Agricultural Library, 1990.

Foster Hill, Jane. "Succession or Continuity? The First Hundred Years of a Forest in the Virginia Piedmont." Master's thesis, George Washington University, 1976.

Freer, Ruskin S. "Flora of the Central Virginia Blue Ridge." *Castanea* 23 (1958): 96–104.

———. "Notes on the Occurrence of Some Unusual Plants in the Virginia Blue Ridge." *Bartonia* 11 (1933): 15.

Fussell, G. E. *Crop Nutrition: Science and Practice before Liebig.* Lawrence, Kans.: Coronado, 1970.

————. *Jethro Tull: His Influence on Mechanized Agriculture*. Reading, Berkshire: Osprey, 1973.

Gagliardo, John. "Germans and Farming in Colonial Pennsylvania." *Pennsylvania Magazine of History and Biography* 83 (1959): 192–218.

Garland, Hugh. *The Life of John Randolph of Roanoke*. New York: Greenwood, 1969.

Garrity, Dennis, and Patricio Agustin. "Historical Land Use Evolution in a Tropical Acid Upland Agroecosystem." *Agriculture, Ecosystems, and Environment* 53 (1995): 83–95.

Gates, Paul Wallace. *The Farmer's Age: Agriculture, 1815–1860*. New York: Holt, Rinehart and Winston, 1960.

————. *Landlord and Tenant on the Prairie Frontier: Studies in American Land Policy*. Ithaca, N.Y.: Cornell University Press, 1973.

Genovese, Eugene. *The Political Economy of Slavery: Studies in the Economy and Society of the Slave South*. New York: Vintage Books, 1967.

————. *Roll, Jordan, Roll: The World the Slaves Made*. New York: Pantheon Books, 1974.

Gill, Harold. "Cereal Grains in Colonial Virginia." Foundation Research Report No. 72. Williamsburg, Va.: Colonial Williamsburg Foundation, 1974.

————. "Tobacco Culture in Colonial Virginia: A Preliminary Report." Williamsburg, Va.: Colonial Williamsburg Foundation, 1972.

————. "Wheat Culture in Colonial Virginia." *Agricultural History* 52 (1978): 380–93.

Gilliam, Sarah K. *Virginia's People: A Study of the Growth and Distribution of the Population of Virginia from 1607 to 1943*. Richmond: Virginia State Planning Board, 1944.

Gliessman, Steven, Eric Engles, and Robin Krieger. *Agroecology: Ecological Processes in Sustainable Agriculture*. Boca Raton, Fla.: Lewis Publishers, 2000.

————. *Agroecosystem Sustainability: Developing Practical Strategies*. Boca Raton, Fla.: CRC Press, 2001.

Goldfield, David R. *Urban Growth in an Age of Sectionalism: Virginia, 1847–1861*. Baton Rouge: Louisiana State University Press, 1977.

Gouger, James. "The Northern Neck of Virginia: A Tidewater Grain-Farming Region in the Antebellum South." *West Georgia College Studies in the Social Sciences* 16 (1977): 73–90.

Gray, Lewis Cecil. *History of Agriculture in the Southern States to 1860*. Washington, D.C.: Carnegie Institute, 1933.

Green, Stanton. "The Agricultural Colonization of Temperate Forest Habitats: An Ecological Model." In *The Frontier: Comparative Studies*, ed. William W.

Savage Jr. and Stephen I. Thompson, 2:69–103. Norman: University of Oklahoma Press, 1980.

Greenberg, Michael S. "Gentleman Slaveholders: The Social Outlook of Virginia's Planter Class." Ph.D. diss., Rutgers University, 1972.

Greene, Jack P. "Independence, Improvement, and Authority: Toward a Framework for Understanding the Histories of the Southern Backcountry during the Era of the American Revolution." In *An Uncivil War: The Southern Backcountry during the American Revolution*, ed. Ronald Hoffman and Thad Tate, 3–36. Charlottesville: University of Virginia Press, 1985.

———. *Pursuits of Happiness: The Social Development of Early Modern British Colonies and the Formation of American Culture*. Chapel Hill: University of North Carolina Press, 1988.

Gross, Leo. "Dairy Cattle and Climate in the Southern United States." Ph.D. diss., University of Maryland, 1963.

Gupton, Oscar, and Fred Swope. *Trees and Shrubs of Virginia*. Charlottesville: University of Virginia Press, 1981.

Hahn, Stephen. *The Roots of Southern Populism: Yeoman Farmers and the Transformation of the Georgia Upcountry, 1850–1890*. New York: Oxford University Press, 1983.

Hall, Arthur. "Early Erosion-Control Practices in Virginia." USDA Misc. Publ. 256. Washington, D.C.: Government Printing Office, 1937.

———. "Soil Erosion and Agriculture in the Southern Piedmont." Ph.D. diss., Duke University, 1948.

Hallock, Judith Lee. "The Agricultural Apostle and His Bible: Edmund Ruffin and the *Farmers' Register*." *Southern Studies* 3 (1984): 205–15.

Hamilton, Phillip. *The Making and Unmaking of a Revolutionary Family: The Tuckers of Virginia, 1752–1830*. Charlottesville: University of Virginia Press, 2003.

Hantmann, Jeffrey. "Between Powhatan and Quirank: Reconstructing Monacan Culture and History in the Context of Jamestown." *American Anthropologist* 92 (1990): 676–90.

Happ, Stafford C., Gordon Rittenhouse, and G. C. Dobson. "Some Principles of Accelerated Stream and Valley Sedimentation." *USDA Technical Bulletin*, No. 633, 1939.

Harbaugh, William. "Twentieth-Century Tenancy and Soil Conservation: Some Comparisons and Questions." *Agricultural History* 66 (1992): 95–119.

Hardacre, Val. *Woodland Nuggets of Gold: The Story of American Ginseng Cultivation*. New York: Vantage Press, 1968.

Hardesty, Donald. *Ecological Anthropology*. New York: Wiley, 1977.

Hardin, David. " 'Alterations They Have Made at This Day': Environment, Agriculture, and Landscape Change in Essex County, Virginia, 1600–1782." Ph.D. diss., University of Maryland, 1995.

———. "Laws of Nature: Wildlife Management Legislation in Colonial Virginia." In *The American Environment: Interpretation of Past Geographies*, ed. Lary Dilsaver and Craig Colten, 137–62. Lanham, Md.: Rowman and Littlefield, 1992.

Hardin, Garrett. "The Tragedy of the Commons." *Science* 156 (1968): 1243–48.

Harrar, Ellwood S., and J. George Harrar. *A Guide to Southern Trees*. New York: McGraw-Hill, 1946.

Harris, Marvin. *Cannibals and Kings: The Origins of Cultures*. New York: Random House, 1977.

Hasse, Larry. "Watermills in the South: Rural Institutions Working against Modernism." *Agricultural History* 58 (1984): 280–95.

Hays, Samuel. *Conservation and the Gospel of Efficiency: The Progressive Conservation Movement, 1890–1920*. Cambridge, Mass.: Harvard University Press, 1959.

Headlee, Sue. *The Political Economy of the Family Farm: The Agrarian Roots of American Capitalism*. New York: Praeger, 1990.

Heck, Marlene. "Palladian Architecture and Social Change in Post-Revolutionary Virginia." Ph.D. diss., University of Pennsylvania, 1988.

Hendrickson, B. H., and A. P. Barnett. "Runoff and Erosion Control Studies on Cecil Soil in the Southern Piedmont." *USDA Technical Bulletin*, No. 1281 (1963).

Henretta, James. "Families and Farms: *Mentalité* in Pre-industrial America." *William and Mary Quarterly*, 3rd ser., 35 (1978): 3–33.

Herndon, G. Melvin. "Agricultural Reform in Antebellum Virginia: William Galt, Jr., a Case Study." *Agricultural History* 52 (1978): 394–406.

———. "Hemp in Colonial Virginia." *Agricultural History* 37 (1963): 86–93.

———. "Indian Agriculture in the Southern Colonies." *North Carolina Historical Review* 44 (1967): 283–97.

———. "The Significance of the Forest to the Tobacco Plantation Economy in Antebellum Virginia." *Plantation Society* 1, no. 3 (October 1981): 430–39.

———. "A War-Inspired Industry: The Manufacture of Hemp in Virginia during the Revolution." *Virginia Magazine of History and Biography* 74 (1966): 301–11.

Hilliard, Sam B. *Hog Meat and Hoecake: Food Supply of the Old South, 1840–1860*. Carbondale: Southern Illinois University Press, 1972.

Hite, James C., and Ellen J. Hall. "The Reactionary Development of Economic Thought in Antebellum Virginia." *Virginia Magazine of History and Biography* 80 (1972): 476–88.

Holland, Lorraine Eve. "Rise and Fall of the Ante-bellum Virginia Aristocracy: A Generational Analysis." Ph.D. diss., University of California, Irvine, 1980.

Holton, Woody. *Forced Founders: Indians, Debtors, Slaves, and the Making of the American Revolution in Virginia.* Chapel Hill: University of North Carolina Press for the Institute of Early American History and Culture, 1999.

Houck, Peter. *Indian Island in Amherst County.* Lynchburg, Va.: Progress Printing, 1984.

Hudson, Charles E. *The Southeastern Indians.* Knoxville: University of Tennessee Press, 1976.

Hughes, Sara S. *Surveyors and Statesmen: Land Measuring in Colonial Virginia.* Richmond: Virginia Surveyors Foundation and the Virginia Association of Surveyors, 1979.

Hunt, George T. *The Wars of the Iroquois: A Study in Intertribal Trade Relations.* Madison: University of Wisconsin Press, 1960.

Irwin, James. "Exploring the Affinity of Wheat and Slavery in the Virginia Piedmont." *Explorations in Economic History* 25 (1988): 295–322.

———. "Farmers and Laborers: A Note on Black Occupations in the Postbellum South." *Agricultural History* 64 (1960): 53–60.

Isaac, Rhys. *The Transformation of Virginia, 1740–1790.* Chapel Hill: University of North Carolina Press for the Institute of Early American History and Culture, 1982.

Jackson, Wes. "Natural Systems Agriculture: A Truly Radical Alternative." *Agriculture, Ecosystems, and Environment* 88 (2002): 111–17.

———. *New Roots for Agriculture.* Lincoln: University of Nebraska Press, 1980.

Jacobs, Wilbur S. "The Great Despoliation: Environmental Themes in American Frontier History." *Pacific Historical Review* 47 (1978): 1–26.

Jones, E. L. "Creative Disruptions in American Agriculture, 1690–1820." *Agricultural History* 48 (1974): 510–28.

Jordan, David. "Political Stability and the Emergence of a Native Elite in Maryland." In *Chesapeake in the Seventeenth Century,* ed. Tate and Ammerman, 243–73.

Jordan, Terry, and Matti Kaups. *The American Backwoods Frontier: An Ethnic and Ecological Interpretation.* Baltimore: Johns Hopkins University Press, 1989.

Jordan, Weymouth T. "The Peruvian Guano Gospel in the Old South." *Agricultural History* 24 (1950): 211–21.

Kates, Robert, William C. Clark, Robert Corell, J. Michael Hall, Hans Joachim Schellnhuber, Bert Bolin, Nancy M. Dickson, et al. "Sustainability Science." *Science* 292 (2001): 641–42.

Keever, Catherine. "Causes of Succession on Old Fields of the Piedmont, North Carolina." *Ecological Monographs* 20 (1950): 229–50.

Kerridge, Eric. *The Agricultural Revolution.* New York: Augustus Kelley, 1968.

Kerr-Ritchie, Jeffrey. *Freedpeople in the Tobacco South: Virginia, 1860–1890.* Chapel Hill: University of North Carolina Press, 1999.

Kierner, Cynthia. " 'The Dark and Dense Cloud Perpetually Lowering Over Us': Gender and the Decline of the Gentry in Post-Revolutionary Virginia." *Journal of the Early Republic* 20 (2000): 185–217.

King, J. Crawford. "The Closing of the Southern Range: An Exploratory Study." *Journal of Southern History* 48 (1982): 53–70.

Kirby, Jack Temple. *Poquosin: A Study of Rural Landscape and Society.* Chapel Hill: University of North Carolina Press, 1995.

———. "Virginia's Environmental History: A Prospectus." *Virginia Magazine of History and Biography* 99 (1991): 449–88.

Klingaman, David C. "The Significance of Grain in the Development of the Tobacco Colonies." *Journal of Economic History* 29 (1969): 268–78.

Kricher, John, and Gordon Morrison. *Peterson's Field Guides: Eastern Forests.* Boston: Houghton-Mifflin, 1988.

Kuhlken, Robert. "Settin' the Woods on Fire: Rural Incendiarism as Protest." *Geographical Review* 89 (1999): 343–63.

Kulikoff, Allan. *The Agrarian Origins of American Capitalism.* Charlottesville: University of Virginia Press, 1992.

———. *Tobacco and Slaves: The Development of Southern Cultures in the Chesapeake, 1680–1800.* Chapel Hill: University of North Carolina Press for the Institute of Early American History and Culture, 1986.

Laing, Wesley. "Cattle in Early Virginia." Ph.D. diss., University of Virginia, 1952.

———. "Cattle in Seventeenth-Century Virginia." *Virginia Magazine of History and Biography* 67 (1959): 143–63.

Land, Aubrey. "Economic Behavior in a Planting Society: The Eighteenth-Century Chesapeake." *Journal of Southern History* 33 (September 1967): 469–85.

———. "A Land Speculator in the Opening of Western Maryland." *Maryland Historical Magazine* 48 (1953): 191–203.

Laurance, William, Thomas Lovejoy, and Heraldo Vasconcelos. "Ecosystem Decay of Amazonian Forest Fragments: A 22-Year Investigation." *Conservation Biology* 16 (2002): 605–18.

Lehman, Tim. *Public Values, Private Lands: Farmland Preservation Policy, 1933–1985.* Chapel Hill: University of North Carolina Press, 1995.

Levin, Maxine. "Women in Soil Science." http://www.awss.org/articles/histwomensoil.html (accessed 18 March 2005).

Lewis, Jan. *The Pursuit of Happiness: Family and Values in Jefferson's Virginia.* New York: Cambridge University Press, 1983.

Liddle, William. "Virtue and Liberty: An Inquiry into the Role of the Agrarian Myth in the Rhetoric of the American Revolutionary Era." *South Atlantic Quarterly* 77 (1978): 15–38.

Lindgren, James. " 'First and Foremost a Virginian': Joseph Bryan and the New South Economy." *Virginia Magazine of History and Biography* 96 (1988): 157–80.

Linklater, Arlo. *Measuring America: How an Untamed Wilderness Shaped the United States and Fulfilled the Promise of Democracy.* New York: Walker, 2002.

Loehr, Rodney. "Arthur Young and American Agriculture." *Agricultural History* 3 (1969): 43–56.

———. "Influence of English Agriculture on American Agriculture, 1775–1825." *Agricultural History* 11 (1937): 3–15.

Loomis, R. S., and D. J. Connor. *Crop Ecology: Productivity and Management in Agricultural Systems.* Cambridge: Cambridge University Press, 1992.

Low, W. A. "The Farmer in Post-Revolutionary Virginia, 1783–1789." *Agricultural History* 25 (1951): 122–27.

Lowdermilk, W. C. "Acceleration of Erosion above Geologic Norms." *Transactions of the American Geophysical Union* 15, pt. 2 (1934): 505–9.

Lowerey, Charles D. "James Barbour, a Progressive Farmer of Antebellum Virginia." In *America: The Middle Period: Essays in Honor of Bernard Mayo*, ed. John Boles, 168–87. Charlottesville: University of Virginia Press, 1973.

Lowrance, Richard, Benjamin R. Stinner, and Garfield J. House, eds. *Agricultural Ecosystems: Unifying Concepts.* London: John Wiley and Sons, 1984.

Lukesic, Craig. "Soils and Settlement Location in 18th-Century Colonial Tidewater Virginia." *Historical Archaeology* 24 (1990): 1–17.

MacArthur, R. H., and E. O. Wilson. *The Theory of Island Biogeography.* Princeton, N.J.: Princeton University Press, 1967.

MacKethan, Lucinda. "Thomas Nelson Page: The Plantation as Arcady." *Virginia Quarterly Review* 54 (1978): 314–32.

MacPherson, C. B. *The Political Theory of Possessive Individualism: Hobbes to Locke.* Oxford: Clarendon Press, 1962.

Mann, Bruce. *Republic of Debtors: Bankruptcy in the Age of American Independence.* Cambridge, Mass.: Harvard University Press, 2002.

Marmon, Lee. *The Lee Marmon Manuscript.* Comp. Catherine H. C. Seaman. Sweet Briar, Va.: Sweet Briar College Printing Press, 1989.

Martin, John, and S. C. Salmon. "The Rusts of Wheat, Oats, Barley, Rye." In *Plant Diseases: The Yearbook of Agriculture, 1953,* 329–32. Washington, D.C.: U.S. Department of Agriculture, 1953.

Marx, Leo. *The Machine in the Garden: Technology and the Pastoral Ideal in America.* New York: Oxford University Press, 1964.

Massey, Arthur K. *Virginia Flora.* Blacksburg, Va.: Virginia Polytechnic Institute and State University, 1961.

Mathew, William M. *Edmund Ruffin and the Crisis of Slavery in the Old South: The Failure of Agricultural Reform.* Athens: University of Georgia Press, 1988.

———. "Edmund Ruffin and the Demise of the *Farmers' Register.*" *Virginia Magazine of History and Biography* 94 (1986): 3–24.

Matson, P. A., W. J. Parton, A. G. Power, M. Swift. "Agricultural Intensification and Ecosystem Properties." *Science* 277 (1977): 504–9.

Maunder, Elwood, ed. *Voices from the South: Recollections of Four Foresters.* Santa Cruz, Calif.: Forest History Society, 1977.

Maxwell, Hu. "The Use and Abuse of Forests by the Virginia Indians." *William and Mary Quarterly* 19 (1910): 73–103.

McClelland, Peter D. *Sowing Modernity: America's First Agricultural Revolution.* Ithaca, N.Y.: Cornell University Press, 1997.

McCleskey, N. Turk. "Across the First Divide: Frontiers of Settlement and Culture in Augusta County, Virginia, 1738–1770." Ph.D. diss., College of William and Mary, 1990.

———. "Processing the Past: A User's Guide to Locating Early Property Lines." In possession of author.

———. "Rich Lands, Poor Prospects: Real Estate and the Formation of a Social Elite in Augusta County, Virginia, 1738–1770." *Virginia Magazine of History and Biography* 98, no. 3 (July 1990): 449–86.

———. "The Strange Career of Ned Tarr: Freedom and Patriarchy on the Virginia Frontier." In possession of author.

McCoy, Drew R. *The Elusive Republic: Political Economy in Jeffersonian America.* Chapel Hill: University of North Carolina Press for the Institute of Early American History and Culture, 1980.

McCusker, John, and Russell Menard. *The Economy of British America, 1607–1789.* Chapel Hill: University of North Carolina Press for the Institute of Early American History and Culture, 1985.

McEwan, Barbara. *Thomas Jefferson, Farmer.* Jefferson, N.C.: McFarland Publishers, 1991.

McLeroy, Sherrie S., and William McLeroy. *More Passages: A New History of Amherst County.* Lynchburg, Va.: Peddler Press, 1995.

McWhiney, Grady. *Cracker Culture: Celtic Ways in the Old South.* University: University of Alabama Press, 1988.

Meinig, D. W. *The Shaping of America: A Geographical Perspective on 500 Years of History.* Vol. 1, *Atlantic America, 1492–1800.* New Haven, Conn.: Yale University Press, 1986.

———. *The Shaping of America: A Geographical Perspective on 500 Years of History.* Vol. 2, *Continental America, 1800–1867.* New Haven, Conn.: Yale University Press, 1993.

Menard, Russell. "The Tobacco Industry in the Chesapeake Colonies, 1617–1730: An Interpretation." *Research in Economic History* 5 (1980): 109–77.

Merchant, Carolyn. *Ecological Revolutions: Nature, Gender, and Science in New England.* Chapel Hill: University of North Carolina Press, 1989.

Miller, Henry M. "Transforming a 'Splendid and Delightsome Land': Colonists and Ecological Change in the Chesapeake." *Journal of the Washington Academy of Sciences* 76 (1986): 173–87.

Mitchell, Anna Marie. "Dr. William Cabell: The Pioneer and Founder." Master's thesis, University of Virginia, 1939.

Mitchell, Robert D. *Commercialism and Frontier: Perspectives on the Early Shenandoah Valley.* Charlottesville: University of Virginia Press, 1977.

———. "Content and Context: Tidewater Characteristics in the Early Shenandoah Valley." *Maryland Historian* 5 (1974): 79–92.

Mitchell, Robert D., Warren R. Hofstra, and Edward F. Connor. "Reconstructing the Colonial Environment of the Upper Chesapeake Watershed." In *Discovering the Chesapeake,* ed. Curtin, Brush, and Fisher, 167–90.

Moger, Allen W. "Industrial and Urban Progress in Virginia, 1880–1900." *Virginia Magazine of History and Biography* 66 (1958): 307–36.

———. *Virginia: Bourbonism to Byrd, 1870–1925.* Charlottesville: University of Virginia Press, 1968.

Mooney, Charles N. *Soil Survey of the Albemarle Area, Virginia.* Washington, D.C.: Government Printing Office, 1902.

Morgan, Lynda J. *Emancipation in Virginia's Tobacco Belt, 1850–1870.* Athens: University of Georgia Press, 1992.

Morrison, A. J. "Note on the Organization of Virginia Agriculture." *William and Mary Quarterly* 26: 3 (1918): 171–72.

Morton, Richard Lee. *Colonial Virginia: Westward Expansion and Prelude to Revolution, 1710–1763.* Chapel Hill: University of North Carolina Press, 1960.

Muenscher, Walter. *Weeds.* Ithaca, N.Y.: Cornell University Press, 1980.

Murcia, C. "Edge Effects in Fragmented Forests: Implications for Conservation." *Trends in Ecology and Evolution* 10 (1995): 58–62.

Neft, Audubon H. "The Native Trees of Albemarle County." Master's thesis, University of Virginia, 1927.

*Nelson County, Virginia: Heritage, 1807–2000.* Summersville, Va.: S. E. Grose, 2001.

Nelson, Lynn A. "The Adventures of 'The Coffey Gang': Re-thinking the Struggle for Land and Autonomy in Early Nineteenth-Century Appalachia." Paper delivered before the Shenandoah Valley Regional Studies Seminar, James Madison University, Harrisonburg, Va., March 2003.

———. "The Agroecologies of a Southern Community: Virginia's Tye River Valley, 1730–1860." Ph.D. diss., College of William and Mary, 1998.

———. " 'Equal Capacity for the Work of Improvement': Early Capitalist Agroecologies in the Middle James River Valley of Virginia, 1820–1860." Paper presented at the American Society for Environmental History Convention, Baltimore, March 1997.

———. "The Pilot Who Braved the Storm: William Massie and the Agrarian Economy of the Tye River Valley, 1830–1860." In *After the Backcountry: Rural Life in the Great Valley of Virginia, 1800–1900,* ed. Kenneth E. Koons and Warren R. Hofstra, 265–73. Knoxville: University of Tennessee Press, 2000.

———. "Planters and Hill People: Competing Agroecologies in Virginia's Blue Ridge Mountains." Paper delivered at the American Society for Environmental History Convention, Las Vegas, Nev., 1994.

———. " 'Then the Poor Planter Hath Greatly the Disadvantage': Tobacco Inspection, Soil Exhaustion, and Formation of a Planter Elite in York County, Virginia, 1700–1760." *Locus* 6:2 (Spring 1994): 19–34.

Noe, Kenneth W. *Southwest Virginia's Railroad: Modernization and the Sectional Crisis.* Urbana: University of Illinois Press, 1994.

Oakes, James. *The Ruling Race: A History of American Slaveholders.* New York: Random House, 1982.

Oak Ridge Estate. "Oak Ridge History, Page 2." http://www.oakridgeestate.com/ oakridgeestate/history2.htm (page discontinued).

Odum, Eugene P. *Fundamentals of Ecology*. 3rd ed. Philadelphia: Saunders, 1971.

Ogg, C. M., and J. C. Baker. "Pedogenesis and Origin of Deeply Weathered Soils Formed in Alluvial Fans of the Virginia Blue Ridge." *Soil Science Society of America Journal* 63 (1999): 601–6.

Ohno, Tsutomu, and M. Susan Erich. "Effect of Wood Ash Application on Soil pH and Soil Test Nutrient Levels." *Agriculture, Ecosystems, and Environment* 32 (1990): 223–39.

Olmsted, Frederick Law. *The Cotton Kingdom: A Traveller's Observations of Cotton and Slavery in the American Slave States*. Ed. Arthur M. Schlesinger. New York: Alfred Knopf, 1953.

Opie, John. *Nature's Nation: An Environmental History of the United States*. Orlando, Fla.: Harcourt-Brace, 1998.

Otto, John Solomon. *The Southern Frontiers, 1607–1860: The Agricultural Evolution of the Colonial and Antebellum South*. New York: Greenwood Press, 1989.

Owlsey, Frank. *Plain Folk of the Old South*. Baton Rouge: Louisiana State University Press, 1949.

Papenfuse, Edward C. "Planter Behavior and Economic Opportunity in a Staple Economy." *Agricultural History* 46 (1972): 297–311.

Penn, Sydney. "Agricultural Organization in Ante-bellum Virginia." Master's thesis, University of Virginia, 1935.

Percy, Alfred. *The Amherst County Story: A Virginia Saga*. Madison Heights, Va.: Percy Press, 1961.

Percy, David O. "Ax or Plow?: Significant Culture Landscape Alteration Rates in the Maryland and Virginia Tidewater." *Agricultural History* 66 (1992): 66–74.

———. "An Embarrassment of Riches: Colonial Soil Cultivation Practices." *Associates NAL Today* 2 (1977): 4–11.

Peterson, Arthur G. "Flour and Grist Milling in Virginia: A Brief History." *Virginia Magazine of History and Biography* 43 (1935): 97–108.

———. *Historical Study of Prices Received by Producers of Farm Products in Virginia, 1801–1927*. Blacksburg: Virginia Agricultural Experiment Station, 1929.

Phillips, Ulrich B. *Life and Labor in the Old South*. Boston: Little, Brown, 1939.

Philyaw, L. Scott. *Virginia's Western Visions: Political and Cultural Expansion on an Early American Frontier*. Knoxville: University of Tennessee Press, 2004.

Pollard, Oliver. *Under the Blue Ledge: Nelson County, Virginia*. Richmond: Dietz Press, 1997.

Powers, Laura. *Ecological Principles of Agriculture*. Albany, N.Y.: Thomson Delmar Learning, 2000.

"Priest Wilderness." http://www.fs.fed.us/r8/gwj/recreation/wilderness/priest. shtml (accessed 11 November 2005).

Primack, Martin. "Land Clearing under Nineteenth-Century Techniques." *Journal of Economic History* 22 (1962): 448–71.

Pryor, Elizabeth. *Agricultural Implements Used by Middle-Class Farmers in the Colonial Chesapeake*. National Colonial Farm Research Report, No. 16, Accokeek, Md.: Accokeek Foundation, 1984.

———. *Forage Crops in the Colonial Chesapeake*. Accokeek, Md.: Accokeek Foundation, 1983.

Pulley, Raymond. *Old Virginia Restored: An Interpretation of the Progressive Impulse, 1870–1930*. Charlottesville: University of Virginia Press, 1968.

Pyne, Stephen. *Fire and America: A Cultural History of Wildland and Rural Fire*. Princeton, N.J.: Princeton University Press, 1982.

Radosevich, Steven, and Jodie Holt. *Weed Ecology: Implications for Management*. New York: John Wiley and Sons, 1984.

Ragsdale, Bruce. *A Planter's Republic: The Search for Economic Independence in Revolutionary Virginia*. Madison, Wisc.: Madison House, 1996.

Rasmussen, William, and Robert Tilton. *Old Virginia: The Pursuit of a Pastoral Ideal*. Charlottesville: Howell Press for the Virginia Historical Society, 2003.

Rawson, David. "The Anglo-American Settlement of Virginia's Rappahannock Frontier." *Locus* 6 (1994): 93–117.

Refsell, Oliver M. "The Massies of Virginia: A Documentary History of a Planter Family in 3 Volumes." Ph.D. diss., University of Texas, 1959.

Renda, Lex. "The Advent of Agricultural Progressivism in Virginia." *Virginia Magazine of History and Biography* 96 (1998): 55–82.

Richter, Daniel, and Daniel Markewitz. *Understanding Soil Change: Soil Sustainability over Millennia, Centuries, and Decades*. Cambridge: Cambridge University Press, 2001.

Robert, Joseph Clarke. *The Tobacco Kingdom: Plantation, Market, and Factory in Virginia and North Carolina, 1800–1860*. Durham, N.C.: Duke University Press, 1938.

Roberts, Kevin. "African-Virginian Extended Kin: The Prevalence of West African Family Forms among Slaves in Virginia, 1740–1870." Master's thesis, Virginia Polytechnic Institute and State University, 1999.

Rossiter, Margaret. *The Emergence of Agricultural Science: Justus Liebig and the Americans, 1840–1880.* New Haven, Conn.: Yale University Press, 1975.

Rothenberg, Winifred. *From Market-Places to a Market Economy: The Transformation of Rural Massachusetts, 1750–1850.* Chicago; University of Chicago Press, 1992.

Rountree, Helen. *Powhatan Foreign Relations, 1500–1722.* Charlottesville: University of Virginia Press, 1993.

———. *The Powhatan Indians of Virginia: Their Traditional Culture.* Norman: University of Oklahoma Press, 1989.

Rubin, Julius. "The Limits of Agricultural Progress in the Nineteenth-Century South." *Agricultural History* 49 (1975): 362–73.

Salstrom, Paul. *Appalachia's Path to Dependency: Rethinking a Region's Economic History, 1730–1940.* Lexington: University Press of Kentucky, 1994.

Sanchez, P. A., and M. Hailu, eds. "Alternatives to Slash-and-Burn Agriculture." Special issue of *Agriculture, Ecosystems, and Environment* 58 (1996).

Santos Perez, Abelardo, and Gaston Remmers. "A Landscape in Transition: An Historical Perspective on a Spanish Latifundist Farm." *Agriculture, Ecosystems, and Environment* 63 (1997): 91–105.

Saunders, D. A., R. J. Hobbs, and C. R. Margules. "Biological Consequences of Ecosystem Fragmentation: A Review." *Conservation Biology* 5 (1991): 18–30.

Sayre, Margaret F. "Emigration from Virginia, 1820–1840." Master's thesis, University of Chicago, 1929.

Schaefer, Milner. "Some Aspects of the Dynamics of the Populations Important to the Management of Commercial Marine Fisheries." *Bulletin of the Inter-American Tropical Tuna Commission* 1 (1954): 25–56.

Scheele, Raymond. "Warfare of the Iroquois and Their Northern Neighbors." Ph.D. diss., Columbia University, 1950.

Schippes, Martin P. "Guide to the Microfilm Edition of the *Records of Antebellum Southern Plantations from the Revolution through the Civil War.* Series G, Selections from the Barker Texas History Center, University of Texas at Austin, Part 2, William Massie Collection." Bethesda, Md.: University Publications of America, 1987.

Schlotterbeck, John T. "Plantation and Farm: Social and Economic Change in Orange and Greene Counties, Virginia, 1716 to 1860." Ph.D. diss., Johns Hopkins University, 1980.

Seaman, Catherine. *Amherst County Environmental Studies.* Lynchburg, Va.: J. P. Bell, 1973.

────. "A History of Lovingston, a Courthouse Town." Sweet Briar, Va.: Sweet Briar College Printing Press, 1989.

────. *Tuckahoes and Cohees: The Settlers and Cultures of Amherst and Nelson Counties, 1607–1807.* Sweet Briar, Va.: Sweet Briar College Printing Press, 1992.

Shade, William G. *Democratizing the Old Dominion: Virginia and the Second Party System, 1824–1861.* Charlottesville: University of Virginia Press, 1996.

Shalhope, Robert E. *John Taylor of Caroline: Pastoral Republican.* Columbia: University of South Carolina Press, 1980.

Sharpe, C. F. S. "Geomorphic Aspects of Normal and Accelerated Erosion." *Transactions of the American Geophysical Union* 22, pt. 2 (1941): 237.

Sharrer, G. Terry. "Farming, Disease, and Change in the Chesapeake Ecosystem." In *Discovering the Chesapeake*, ed. Curtin, Brush, and Fisher, 304–21.

────. *A Kind of Fate: Agricultural Change in Virginia, 1861–1920.* Ames: Iowa State University Press, 2000.

Sheldon, William DuBose. *Populism in the Old Dominion: Virginia Farm Politics, 1885–1900.* Princeton, N.J.: Princeton University Press, 1935.

Sheridan, Richard. "Chemical Fertilizers in Southern Agriculture." *Agricultural History* 53 (1979): 308–18.

Shomon, Joseph J. "Vanished and Vanishing Virginia Animals." *Virginia Cavalcade* 9 (1959): 24–31.

Shore, Laurence. *Southern Capitalists: The Ideological Leadership of an Elite, 1832–1885.* Chapel Hill: University of North Carolina Press, 1986.

Siegel, Frederick. "The Paternalist Thesis: Virginia, a Test Case." *Civil War History* 25 (1979): 246–61.

────. *The Roots of Southern Distinctiveness: Tobacco and Society in Danville, Virginia, 1780–1865.* Chapel Hill: University of North Carolina Press, 1987.

Silver, Timothy. *A New Face on the Countryside: Indians, Colonists, and Slaves in South Atlantic Forests, 1500–1800.* Cambridge: Cambridge University Press, 1990.

Simms, L. Moody. "Phillip Alexander Bruce and the New South." *Mississippi Quarterly* 19 (1966): 171–83.

Skaggs, Jimmy. *The Great Guano Rush: Entrepreneurs and American Overseas Expansion.* New York: St. Martin's, 1994.

Smith, Daniel Blake. *Inside the Great House: Planter Life in Eighteenth-Century Chesapeake Society.* Ithaca, N.Y.: Cornell University Press, 1980.

Smith, Henry Nash. *Virgin Land: The American West as Symbol and Myth.* New York: Vintage Books, 1957.

Steinberg, Theodore. *Slide Mountain, or, The Folly of Owning Nature*. Berkeley: University of California Press, 1990.

Stewart, Mart. "Re-greening the South and Southernizing the Rest." *Journal of the Early Republic* 24 (2004): 242–51.

———. " 'Whether Wast, Deodand, or Stray': Cattle, Culture, and the Environment in Early Georgia." *Agricultural History* 65:3 (1991): 1–28.

Stilgoe, John R. *Common Landscape of America, 1580 to 1854*. New Haven, Conn.: Yale University Press, 1982.

Stoll, Steven. *Larding the Lean Earth: Soil and Society in Nineteenth-Century America*. New Haven, Conn.: Yale University Press, 2002.

Sutherland, Daniel. "Introduction to War: The Civilians of Culpeper County, Virginia." *Civil War History* 37 (1991): 120–37.

Sutton, Robert P. "Nostalgia, Pessimism, and Malaise: The Doomed Aristocrat in Late Jeffersonian Virginia." *Virginia Magazine of History and Biography* 76 (1968): 41–55.

Sweeney, Lenora H. *Amherst County, Virginia, in the Revolution*. Lynchburg, Va.: J. P. Bell, 1951.

Swem, Earl. "An Analysis of Ruffin's *Farmers' Register*, with a Bibliography of Edmund Ruffin." *Virginia State Library Bulletin* 11 (1918): 36–114.

Sydnor, Charles. *American Revolutionaries in the Making: Political Practices in Washington's Virginia*. New York: Free Press, 1965.

Tanner, Carol M. "Joseph C. Cabell, 1778–1856." Ph.D. diss., University of Virginia, 1948.

Tate, Thad W., and David L. Ammerman, eds. *The Chesapeake in the Seventeenth Century: Essays on Anglo-American Society*. Chapel Hill: University of North Carolina Press for the Institute of Early American History and Culture, 1979.

Taylor, Alan. *Liberty Men and Great Proprietors: The Revolutionary Settlement on the Maine Frontier, 1760–1820*. Chapel Hill: University of North Carolina Press for the Institute of Early American History and Culture, 1990.

Taylor, Rosser H. "The Sale and Application of Commercial Fertilizers in the South Atlantic States to 1900." *Agricultural History* 21 (1947): 46–52.

Taylor, R. W. "Commercial Fertilizers in South Carolina." *South Atlantic Quarterly* 29 (1930): 179–89.

Terrell, Bruce G. "The James River Bateau." *Virginia Cavalcade* 38, no. 4 (1989): 180–91.

Terry, Gail S. "Family Empires: A Frontier Elite in Virginia and Kentucky, 1740–1815." Ph.D. diss., College of William and Mary, 1992.

Thacker, Massie. "Survey Report: Pharsalia." Works Progress Administration of

Virginia Historical Inventory, 7 July 1936, Library of Virginia. http://lvaimage .lib.va.us/VHI/html/18/0603.html (accessed 18 January 2005).

———. "Survey Report: Snug Dale." Virginia Historical Inventory, 22 July 1936, Library of Virginia. http://lvaimage.lib.va.us/VHI/html/18/0643.html (accessed 19 January 2005).

———. "Survey Report: Tyro #2." Virginia Historical Inventory, 24 July 1836, Library of Virginia. http://lvaimage.lib.va.us/VHI/html/18/0681.html (accessed 18 March 2005).

Thomas, Peter. "Matthew Fontaine Maury and the Problem of Virginia's Identity, 1865–1873." *Virginia Magazine of History and Biography* 90 (1982): 213–37.

Thomas, William L., ed. *Man's Role in Changing the Face of the Earth*. Chicago: University of Chicago Press for the Wenner-Gren Foundation for Anthropological Research and the National Science Foundation, 1956.

Thompson, Edgar. "The Natural History of Agricultural Labor in the South." In *Plantation Societies, Race Relations, and the South: The Regimentation of Populations*, 213–63. Durham, N.C.: Duke University Press, 1975.

Thompson, Robert P. "The Tobacco Exports of the Upper James River Naval District, 1773–1775." *William and Mary Quarterly* 18 (1961): 393–401.

Tilley, Nannie. *The Bright-Tobacco Industry, 1860–1929*. Chapel Hill: University of North Carolina Press, 1948.

Titus, Mary. " 'Groaning Tables' and 'Spit in the Kettles': Food and Race in the Nineteenth-Century South." *Southern Quarterly* 30 (1992): 13–21.

Tivy, Joy. *Agricultural Ecology*. New York: Longman, 1990.

Townes, A. Jane. "The Effect of Emancipation on Large Landholdings, Nelson and Goochland Counties, Virginia." *Journal of Southern History* 45 (1979): 403–12.

Trimble, Stanley W. *Man-Induced Soil Erosion on the Southern Piedmont*. Ankeney, Iowa: Soil Conservation Society of America, 1974.

———. "Perspectives on the History of Soil Erosion Control in the Eastern United States." *Agricultural History* 59:2 (1985): 162–80.

Tripp, Stephen. *Yankee Town, Southern City: Race and Class Relations in Civil War Lynchburg*. New York: New York University Press, 1997.

True, Rodney H. "Early Days of the Albemarle Agricultural Society." *Annual Report of the American Historical Association for the Year 1918*, 241–59. Washington, D.C.: Government Printing Office, 1920.

Tuan, Yi-Fu. *Topophilia: A Study of Environmental Perception, Attitudes, and Values*. Englewood Cliffs, N.J.: Prentice-Hall, 1974.

Turner, Charles W. "Virginia Agricultural Reform, 1815–1860." *Agricultural History* 26 (1952): 80–89.

———. "Virginia State Agricultural Societies." *Agricultural History* 38 (1964): 167–77.

Turner, Frederick Jackson. "The Significance of the Frontier in American History." In *Rereading Frederick Jackson Turner: The Significance of the Frontier in American History and Other Essays*, 31–60. New York: Henry Holt, 1994.

Turner, Randolph E. "An Intertribal Deer Exploitation Buffer Zone for the Virginia Coastal Plain-Piedmont Region." *Quarterly Bulletin of the Archaeological Society of Virginia* 32 (1978): 42–48.

———. "A Re-examination of Powhatan Territorial Boundaries and Population, ca. A.D. 1607." *Quarterly Bulletin of the Archaeological Society of Virginia* 37 (1982): 45–64.

Tyler, Lyon G. *Encyclopedia of Virginia Biography.* 4 vols. New York: Lewis Historical Publishing, 1915.

Ucko, Peter, and G. W. Dimbleby. *The Domestication and Exploitation of Plants and Animals.* Chicago: Aldine, 1969.

U.S. Forest Service. "Kuchler Type Fire Ecology and Management." http://www.fs.fed.us/database/feis/kuchlers/k112/kuchler_type_fire_ecology_and_management.html (accessed 17 April 2006).

Virginia Cooperative Extension. "Extension History." http://www.ext.vt.edu/about.vce/miss.html#history (accessed 18 March 2005).

Walsh, Lorena. "Land, Landlord, and Leaseholder: Estate Management in Southern Maryland, 1642–1820." *Agricultural History* 59 (1985): 373–96.

———. "Plantation Management in the Chesapeake, 1620–1820." *Journal of Economic History* 49 (1989): 393–406.

———. "Provisioning Early American Towns—the Chesapeake: A Multidisciplinary Case Study." National Endowment for the Humanities Grant Report. Williamsburg, Va.: Colonial Williamsburg Foundation, 1998.

Walter P. Taylor, ed. *The Deer of North America.* Washington, D.C.: Wildlife Management Institute, 1956.

Wardle, David, Olle Zackrisson, Greger Hornberg, and Christine Gallet. "The Influence of Island Area on Ecosystem Properties." *Science* 277 (August 1997): 1296–99.

Watts, Charles. "Colonial Albemarle: The Social and Economic History of a Piedmont, Virginia, County, 1727–1775." Master's thesis, University of Virginia, 1948.

Wayland, John Walter. *The German Element in the Shenandoah Valley.* Harrisonburg, Va.: C. J. Carrier, 1978.

Weaver, Fred A. "Grain in Colonial Virginia." Master's thesis, University of California, 1945.

Weis, Marie D. "The Social Philosophy of John Taylor of Caroline." Master's thesis, University of Chicago, 1929.

Wennersten, John. "Soil Miners Redux: The Chesapeake Environment, 1680–1810." *Maryland Historical Magazine* 91 (1996): 156–79.

West, Darrell, Herman Shugart, and Daniel Botkin, eds. *Forest Succession: Concepts and Application.* New York: Springer-Verlag: 1981.

White, Lynn, Jr. "The Historic Roots of Our Ecological Crisis." *Science* 155 (1967): 1202–7.

Whitehead, Robert. "William Massie of Pharsalia." Typescript of an address, n.d., Files of the Nelson County Historical Society, Nelson County Public Library, Lovingston, Va.

Whittaker, R. H. *Communities and Ecosystems.* 2nd ed. New York: MacMillan, 1975.

Williams, G. Harold. "The Agricultural Society of Albemarle County, Virginia." Master's thesis, University of Richmond, 1965.

Williams, Michael. *Americans and Their Forests: A Historical Geography.* Cambridge: Cambridge University Press, 1989.

Wilson, Jack Hubert. "A Study of the Late Prehistoric, Protohistoric, and Historic Indians of the Carolina and Virginia Piedmont: Structure, Process, and Ecology." Ph.D. diss., University of North Carolina at Chapel Hill, 1983.

Wingo, Alfred. *Virginia's Soils and Land Use.* Richmond: Virginia State Board of Education, 1949.

Witschey, Walter R. T. "Locating Land Described in Colonial Patents by Computer Analysis." *Virginia Magazine of History and Biography* 88 (1980): 155–69.

Wood, Peter, Gregory Waselkov, and M. Thomas Hatley, eds. *Powhatan's Mantle: Indians in the Colonial Southeast.* Lincoln: University of Nebraska Press, 1989.

Worster, Donald. *Dust Bowl: The Southern Plains in the 1930s.* 1979; New York: Oxford University Press, 2004.

———, ed. *The Ends of the Earth: Perspectives on Modern Environmental History.* Cambridge: Cambridge University Press, 1988.

———. "History as Natural History: An Essay on Theory and Method." *Pacific Historical Review* 53 (1984): 1–19.

————. *The Wealth of Nature: Environmental History and the Ecological Imagination*. New York: Oxford University Press, 1993.

Wright, Gavin. *The Political Economy of the Cotton South: Households, Markets, and Wealth in the Nineteenth Century*. New York, Norton, 1978.

Yentsch, Anne, and James Reveal. "Chesapeake Gardens and Botanical Frontiers." In *Discovering the Chesapeake*, ed. Curtin, Brush, and Fisher, 249–78.

Zimdahl, R. L. *Weed-Crop Competition: A Review*. Corvallis, Ore.: International Plant Protection Program, 1980.

Zirkle, Conway. "To Plow or Not To Plow: A Comment on 'The Planter's Problems.' " *Agricultural History* 42 (1968): 69–89.

Zornow, William Frank. "Aid for the Indigent Families of Soldiers in Virginia, 1861–1865." *Virginia Magazine of History and Biography* 66 (1958): 454–58.

# INDEX

Daphne (Pharsalia slave), 188
DePriest Run. *See* Mill Dam Creek
Distilling, 143–45, 187
Double-cycle: adaptation problems
  with, 112–13; and Civil War,
  187–88; defined, 75–80, 226; at
  Pharsalia, 93–102; post–Civil War,
  210, 217; and tobacco, 114–15.
  *See also* Agricultural reform; Crop
  rotation; Taylor, John, of Caroline
Draining. *See* Stream management

Effinger, Harvey, 206
Effinger family, 191–92, 200, 216–20
  passim
Entail, 54
Environmental biography, 16–17,
  23–24, 29–30
Equipment. *See* Farm machinery
Erosion. *See* Soil erosion

Fall Line, 1
Fallowing, 57, 101–2, 107, 122, 151.
  *See also* Long fallowing
Farm machinery: and capitalism,
  160–61, 187, 209–10; end of
  purchases of, 219, 220; traditional,
  44–45
*Farmers' Register,* 70, 81. *See also*
  Ruffin, Edmund
Fences, 14–16, 182–83, 204, 230–31;
  laws regarding, 165, 182–83; live,
  165, 230; stone, 165; worm, 15,
  165
Fertility, 72, 75–77, 80
Fertilizer: commercial, 98, 101, 142,
  160, 167, 209; guano as, 151, 160,
  172–76; home, 100–101, 142, 173,

175–76; lime as, 151, 160; plaster
  of paris (gypsum) as, 101, 118, 124,
  142, 160, 209. *See also* Manure and
  manuring
Field Number Two: abandoned, 230;
  cleared for crops, 122, 123, 141;
  and old fields, 89–90, 101, 105,
  107, 115, 197
Fire, 44–45; slave arson, 178–79;
  woods-burning, 41, 184–85
Fitzgerald family, 185–86
Flat Field, 89, 167, 230
Flippin, Bill, 229
Flippin, Perkins Morton, 229
Flooding, 18, 86. *See also* Soil erosion;
  Weather
Forest: oak-hickory-chestnut, 1,
  15, 19–24 passim, 29, 33–40
  passim, 45–51 passim, 60–61;
  River-bottom, 35, 37, 87–88, 105
Free labor, 206–7
Freedpeople, 206, 218–19
Front Field, 88, 92–93, 135–36,
  150–51, 197, 230
Frontier farming. *See* Agriculture:
  extensive

Gall'd land, 58, 60, 80; defined, 18,
  46, 47; at Pharsalia, 102, 106, 116,
  134, 147. *See also* Cecil soils; Soil
  erosion
Gardens, 52–53. *See also* Pharsalia
  plantation: garden of
Gentry, Virginia: consumerism of,
  66–67, 82, 162–63, 218, 221, 227;
  debt of, 64–65, 67; home places
  of, 52–54, 91, 200–201, 253n24;
  land speculation of, 32–33; and

passim, 214, 227; transportation in,
169–70
Tyro farm, 186, 196, 197, 216, 217,
244n2

Virginia, 63–67, 69, 204–8; conservationists, 69–83; Germans, 146,
180; State Agricultural Society, 175.
*See also* Agriculture: traditional
Virginia; Gentry, Virginia
Virginia Historical Inventory (VHI),
223

Warwick, Ellen (Massie), 193, 196,
220
Warwick, Joseph, 193
Washington College, 192
Weather: at Pharsalia, 18, 86, 118,
120, 128–29; southern, 10, 80;
Virginia, 159, 214
Weeding, 132–37, 161

Weeds, 161, 168; in crop fields, 100,
113, 130–37, 141–42, 161; in old
fields, 47–49. *See also individual
species*
Westward migration, 24–25, 59,
67–69, 152, 225
Wetlands. *See* "Swamps"
Wheat, 76–77, 126–30, 135–37,
174, 215, 217; Early Purple Straw,
158–61 passim; Goose, 158; joint
worms, 161; Kloss Bluestem,
158–59, 209; Mediterranean, 138;
Mexican, 139; New York White
Flint, 139; Odessa, 209; prices
for, 92, 95, 110, 115, 171; Prince
Edward Island, 167; seed for,
138–41; White Poland, 151, 159;
Yellow Lammas, 138–40, 142, 147,
150, 156–58 passim; yields for,
126–27, 137–38, 141, 151, 210
Williams, George, 85

CPSIA information can be obtained at www.ICGtesting.com
Printed in the USA
LVOW090732050712

288750LV00004B/22/P